Happiness in Kant's Practical Philosophy

CONTEMPORARY STUDIES IN IDEALISM

Series Editor: Paolo Diego Bubbio, Western Sydney University

Editorial Board: Mark V. Alznauer (Northwestern University), Francesco Berto (University of St. Andrews), Alfredo Ferrarin (University of Pisa), Elena Ficara (University of Paderborn and City University of New York), George di Giovanni (McGill University), Douglas Hedley (Cambridge University), Stephen Houlgate (University of Warwick), Wayne Hudson (Charles Sturt University), Luca Illetterati (University of Padua), David Kolb (Bates College), Simon Lumsden (UNSW), Douglas A. Moggach (University of Ottawa), Lydia Moland (Colby College), Maurizio Pagano (University of Eastern Piedmont), Paul Redding (The University of Sydney), Julian Young (Wake Forest University)

The *Contemporary Studies in Idealism* series features cutting-edge scholarship in the field of classical German Idealism and its legacy. "Idealism" is considered both in a historical and in a theoretical sense. The series features projects that center upon Kant and the post-Kantian Idealists (including, but not limited to, early German romantic thinkers Fichte, Schelling, and Hegel) or upon other related forms of nineteenth-century philosophy—including those often considered to oppose Idealism, such as those of Kierkegaard and Nietzsche. The scholarship also seeks to critically assess the legacy of Idealism in the twentieth and twentieth-first century. The series uses the resources of classical German Idealism to engage in contemporary debates in all sub-fields of philosophy.

Happiness in Kant's Practical Philosophy: Morality, Indirect Duties, and Welfare Rights, by Alice Pinheiro Walla

Schopenhauer and the Nature of Philosophy, by Jonathan Head

Nietzsche and Adorno on Philosophical Praxis, Language, and Reconciliation: Towards an Ethics of Thinking, by Paolo A. Bolaños

Hypotyposis in Kant's Metaphysics of Judgment: Symbolizing Completeness, by Byron Ashley Clugston

Kant and Mysticism: Critique as the Experience of Baring All in Reason's Light, by Stephen R. Palmquist

Happiness in Kant's Practical Philosophy

Morality, Indirect Duties, and Welfare Rights

Alice Pinheiro Walla

LEXINGTON BOOKS
Lanham • Boulder • New York • London

Published by Lexington Books
An imprint of The Rowman & Littlefield Publishing Group, Inc.
4501 Forbes Boulevard, Suite 200, Lanham, Maryland 20706
www.rowman.com

86-90 Paul Street, London EC2A 4NE

An earlier version of chapter 6 was originally published in Jurisprudence, Volume 11, Number 1, 2020 as, "A Kantian Foundation for Welfare Rights" by Taylor & Francis Group, www.tandfonline.com.

Copyright © 2022 by The Rowman & Littlefield Publishing Group, Inc.

All rights reserved. No part of this book may be reproduced in any form or by any electronic or mechanical means, including information storage and retrieval systems, without written permission from the publisher, except by a reviewer who may quote passages in a review.

British Library Cataloguing in Publication Information Available

Library of Congress Cataloging-in-Publication Data

Names: Pinheiro Walla, Alice, author.
Title: Happiness in Kant's practical philosophy : morality, indirect duties, and welfare rights / Alice Pinheiro Walla.
Description: Lanham : Lexington Books, [2022] | Series: Contemporary studies in idealism | Includes bibliographical references and index.
Identifiers: LCCN 2022029882 (print) | LCCN 2022029883 (ebook) | ISBN 9781793633545 (cloth) | ISBN 9781793633569 (paper) | ISBN 9781793633552 (ebook)
Subjects: LCSH: Kant, Immanuel, 1724-1804. | Happiness. Classification: LCC B2799. H36 P56 2022 (print) | LCC B2799.H36 (ebook) | DDC 170--dc23/eng/20220808
LC record available at https://lccn.loc.gov/2022029882
LC ebook record available at https://lccn.loc.gov/2022029883

∞™ The paper used in this publication meets the minimum requirements of American National Standard for Information Sciences—Permanence of Paper for Printed Library Materials, ANSI/NISO Z39.48-1992.

*For my father Davi Gurgel Pinheiro (1952–2002).
May his memory always be a blessing.*

Contents

Acknowledgments	ix
Translations and Abbreviations	xi
Introduction	1
Chapter One: Happiness as a Natural Necessity	5
Chapter Two: Kant's Anti-eudaimonism in Moral Theory	31
Chapter Three: One's Own Happiness and Indirect Duty	65
Chapter Four: Happiness and the Duty of Beneficence	93
Chapter Five: Excursus: Kant's Moral Theory and Demandingness	121
Chapter Six: Happiness in Kant's Political and Legal Philosophy	139
Conclusion	173
Bibliography	177
Index	183
About the Author	189

Acknowledgments

I would like to thank Jana Hodges-Kluck for approaching me about a publication project for Rowman & Littlefield and making this publication possible; my Doktorvater Jens Timmermann for his expertise, invaluable philosophical discussions, and his good-natured tolerance of what he called my "academic parricidal tendencies." I feel very privileged to have been his student; Marcia Baron for her impressive feedback and insightful criticism on an earlier version of this manuscript. I learned a great deal from her; Sorin Baiasu, for his suggestions and very constructive comments; Ruth Böker, David Bagot, Margaux Whiskin, Jael Elisabeth Kriener, Krushil Watene, Ines de Asis, Joachim Aufderheide, Elisabeth Curzon, and Annika Firmenich for their loving help with my children and dog; Ricky Walla for proofreading an earlier version of this manuscript, Maria Eugenia Zanchet for preparing the index, and Danielle Schmitz for helping me format the final version of this book.

I am very grateful to Joseph Raz, may his memory always be a blessing, for very kindly inviting me to visit him at Oxford University when I was a graduate student at the very early stages of my research. His very helpful advice guided me for many years. I will never forget his hospitality and generosity.

Finally, my thanks to Clara and Sophie for their love and spirit of adventure in accompanying me across borders. From you, my dears, I have learned the greatest lessons about happiness.

Hamilton, December 2021
A. P. W.

Versions of chapters in this book were previously published elsewhere. I would like to thank the publishers and journal editors for allowing me to reuse that content. These articles are Pinheiro Walla, Alice (2013), "Virtue and Prudence in a Footnote of the Metaphysics of Morals (MS VI: 433n),"

Jahrbuch Für Recht Und Ethik / Annual Review of Law and Ethics, 21: 307–323; Pinheiro Walla, Alice (2015), "When the Strictest Right Is the Greatest Wrong: Kant on Fairness," *Estudos Kantianos* 3(1): 39–55; Pinheiro Walla, Alice (2015), "Local Desire Satisfaction and Long Term Wellbeing: Revisiting the Gout Sufferer of Kant's Groundwork," *Belgrade Philosophical Annual* 28: 31–44; Pinheiro Walla, Alice (2015), "Kant's Moral Theory and Demandingness," *Ethical Theory and Moral Practice*, 18(4): 731–743 and Pinheiro Walla, Alice, (2020), "A Kantian foundation for welfare rights," *Jurisprudence*, 11(1): 76–91.

Translations and Abbreviations

All references are from Kant's *gesammelte Schriften, herausgegeben von der Deutschen* (formerly *Königlichen Preussischen*) *Akademie der Wissenschaften* (Walter de Gruyter [and predecessors], 1902-). Exceptions are the *Groundwork of the Metaphysics of Morals* (German-English translation), edited and translated by Mary Gregor and Jens Timmermann, Cambridge University Press, 2011, the *Kritik der reinen Vernunft (Nach der ersten und zweiten Originalausgabe),* edited by Jens Timmermann, Felix Meiner Verlag, 1998, and the *Metaphysische Anfangsgründe der Rechtslehre (Metaphysik der Sitten, erster Teil)*, edited by Bernd Ludwig, Felix Meiner Verlag, 2009 (I use the original page and paragraph numbers of the Academy edition and not the Ludwig numeration, following his rearrangement of the *Doctrine of Right*).

Unless otherwise stated, all translations have been taken from the *Cambridge Edition of the Works of Immanuel Kant*, edited by Paul Guyer and Allen W. Wood (Cambridge University Press, 1992-).

References to Kant's works are given parenthetically in the body of the text, cited by the volume and page number, given by Roman and Arabic numbers respectively separated by a colon, according to the above cited standard edition of Kant's works (*Akademie-Ausgabe).* References are preceded by the following abbreviations of Kant's works:

Anthr Antropologie in pragmatischer Hinsicht / Anthropology from a Pragmatic Point of View (1798)
GMS Grundlegung zur Metaphysik der Sitten / The Groundwork of the Metaphysics of Morals (1785)
IAG Idee zu einer allgemeinen Geschichte in weltbürgerlicher Absicht / Idea of a Universal History in a Cosmopolitan Purpose (1784)
KpV Kritik der praktischen Vernunft / Critique of Practical Reason (1788)
KrV Kritik der reinen Vernunft / Critique of pure Reason. First edition (A) 1781, second edition (B) 1787

KU Kritik der Urteilskraft / Critique of Judgment (1790)
MA Mutmaßlicher Anfang der Menschengeschichte/ Conjectural Beginning of Human History (1786)
MS Die Metaphysik der Sitten / The Metaphysics of Morals (1797)
MS RL Metaphysische Anfangsgründe der Rechtslehre (Metaphysik der Sitten erster Teil) / The Doctrine of Right
MS TL Metaphysische Anfangsgründe der Tugendlehre (Metaphysik der Sitten zweiter Teil) / The Doctrine of Virtue
REL Die Religion innerhalb der Grenzen der blossen Vernunft / Religion within the Limits of Reason Alone (1793)
SF Streit der Fakultäten / The Conflict of the Faculties (1798)
TP Über den Gemeinspruch: Das mag in der Theorie richtig sein, taugt aber nicht für die Praxis / On the Common Saying: This May Be True in Theory but It Does Not Apply in Practice (1793)
WA Beantwortung der Frage: Was ist Aufklärung? / An Answer to the Question: "What Is Enlightenment?" (1784)
ZEF Zum ewigen Frieden / Perpetual Peace (1795)

OTHER CITED WORKS BY KANT:

Über die Buchmacherei On Turning out Books (1798), AA VIII
Über ein vermeintes Recht aus Menschenliebe zu lügen On a supposed right to lie from philanthropy (1797), AA VIII
Was heißt: Sich im Denken orientieren? What does it mean to orient oneself in thinking? (1786), AA VIII

KANT'S LECTURES:

Logik AA IX
Moral Brauer Me (after Eine *Vorlesung Kants über Ethik*" edited by Paul Menzer, Heise, 1924)
Moral Collins AA XXVII
Moral Kaehler (*Vorlesung zur Moralphilosophie*, edited by Werner Stark, De Gruyter, 2004)
Moral Mrongovius AA XXVII
Pädagogik Lectures on Pedagogy (1803), AA IX
Praktische Philosophie Herder AA XXVII

NOTES AND FRAGMENTS FROM KANT'S HANDWRITTEN REMAINS (*HANDSCHRIFLICHER NACHLASS*):

Erläuterungen Achenwall (*Erläuterungen Kants zu G. Achenwalls Iuris naturalis Pars posterior*), AA XIX
Reflexionen Reflections AA XIV-XV

Introduction

What is the place of happiness in Kant's philosophy? Anyone minimally acquainted with Kant's moral philosophy may promptly answer: *nowhere.* There seems to be no moral theory in the history of philosophy more inimical to human happiness than Immanuel Kant's. This book shows not only that this is a misconception but also that we can better understand Kant's practical philosophy (his moral, political and legal thought) once we become aware how he conceived the role of happiness in our moral lives and the reasons for thinking about happiness in that way.

Can Kant actually help us better *understand* human happiness? The thought-provoking thesis of this book is yes. Happiness is at the source of our deepest longings, motivations, and desires. It plays a significant part in the way we plan our lives and structure our everyday commitments. But what will make one happy? Kant realized that this is the greatest challenge regarding happiness: although the deep seated human need to seek happiness pervades nearly everything one chooses to do and finds worth pursuing, it is impossible to determine with certainty how to achieve happiness, or even to form a clear, concrete idea of what we take it to be. Further, what we take to constitute happiness for ourselves constantly changes in the course of our lives: what used to be happiness for your twelve-year-old self and what happiness means to you right will certainly be very different. How should one deal with something so important, and yet so elusive and unstable as one's conception of happiness, something we deeply long for and yet don't even know for sure how it looks like?

I argue that Kant offers a distinctive strategy for dealing with the indeterminacy of happiness and consequently with *uncertainty* that has not yet received due attention in philosophy. It is an *indirect* strategy, meant to offer guidance for action despite uncertainty, vagueness and constant revisions of one's personal conception of happiness over the course of one's life and life experiences. Happiness is a risky trial and error game, but here is the good news from Kant's theory: living a moral life can actually help us navigate the uncertainty of happiness and provide guidance, structure and meaning to our lives, individually and collectively. Although moral and legal principles in Kant's theory are *not about happiness,* they nevertheless presuppose the fact that we are finite creatures who want to be happy. This fact about human nature has several implications for the way we understand our duties to ourselves and others, and the way we ought to live with each other in society and in the world. This is the case even if happiness cannot be the rational principle on which these duties are based, for reasons that I will elucidate in this book.

Kant's fundamental assumptions about happiness are neither openly discussed nor treated in much detail in his works. Further, Kant not only has different definitions of happiness, but some even seem to contradict others. Consider for instance the definitions of happiness scattered in the *Groundwork*: happiness is said to be the idea of the entire well being and contentment with one's condition (GMS IV: 393); the preservation and prosperity of a being who has reason and a will (GMS IV: 395); the idea under which all inclinations unite in one sum and to which all human beings already have the most powerful and intimate inclination (GMS IV: 399); the entire satisfaction of one's needs and inclinations (GMS IV: 405). Happiness is also a "wavering idea" (GMS IV: 399), of which we cannot form a determinate idea, for it is not an ideal of reason but of imagination (GMS IV: 419).

The aim of this book is to make explicit Kant's tacit assumptions about happiness and the implications these assumptions have for his moral, legal and political theory and to offer interpretative solutions when these assumptions seem mutually incompatible. For this purpose, the book provides a "map" of the areas in which the concept of happiness or considerations about the happiness of individuals appear in Kant's practical works and analyses the way they relate to central themes of his practical theory. Each chapter of the book focuses on such a "domain" in which the concept of happiness makes a appearance.

Chapter 1 reconstructs Kant's overall conception of happiness. Since his dispersed statements about happiness are often puzzling and in need of further clarification, my starting point is to make sense of two of Kant's fundamental and yet seemingly contradictory claims about happiness: on the one hand, the idea that seeking happiness is a matter of *natural necessity* (*Naturnotwendigkeit*) for finite rational beings and, on the other, the teleological view that happiness cannot be seen as the *end of nature* for these same beings. I will show how these claims are compatible with each other by elucidating the link between the human need for happiness and the distinctive structure of the will of finite rational beings. I also identify three different meanings of the concept of happiness: as a *formal concept,* as a *material conception* and as an *ideal* of imagination. These distinctions will help us understand why, according to Kant, it is possible to act *against one's happiness* despite the fact that we *always pursue happiness*. I also clarify other puzzling claims Kant makes about happiness in regard to reason, which also brings to the fore further elements of his implicitly held understanding of happiness.

Chapter 2 examines the meta-ethical implications of Kant's rejection of happiness as a foundation for morality. For Kant, a moral theory that deserves the name should neither dismiss nor falsify our common assumptions concerning the unconditional character of moral requirements. I explain why Kant thinks that only a theory of morality as autonomy can satisfy this condition. Further, I contrast heteronomy and eudaimonism and argue that Kant provides an interesting *error theory* of eudaimonist theories: while genuine moral agents can only be motivated by duty, eudaimonist theories may lead virtuous agents to believe that the self-contentment they experience as a result from their compliance with duty is the actual motive of their conduct. I conclude that Kant's anti-eudaimonism in moral theory does not rule out human happiness as an important task imposed by practical reason on finite rational beings, but only seeks to establish its proper place when it comes to *theorizing* about morality.

Although it is ruled out as the principle of morality, the human interest in happiness nevertheless provides the *content* of certain ethical duties to oneself and others. Chapter 3 focuses on Kant's view that there is an indirect duty to secure one's own happiness. For this purpose, the chapter also elucidates the overall notions of an indirect duty and of duties to the self. I argue that the indeterminacy of happiness (chapter 1) has problematic implications for the *rationality* of one's pursuit of happiness. Given Kant's hedonistic account of non-moral ends, it would not be irrational to prefer short term pleasure over long term wellbeing when future wellbeing seems uncertain, as illustrated by the gout sufferer example in the *Groundwork*. This "hedonistic calculus" could lead rational but finite agents to neglect their future wellbeing, upon which their moral integrity and exercise of rational capacities materially depend, for the sake of pursuing immediate and more *certain* pleasures. I argue that the indirect duty to promote one's happiness can become a *direct* duty when it is necessary to counteract this hedonistic calculation under conditions of uncertainty in the pursuit of long-term satisfaction.

Chapter 4 analyzes the structure and justification of the imperfect duty to adopt the happiness of others as one's end, i.e., the duty of beneficence. I refute the view according to which Kant's duty of beneficence requires one to sacrifice one's own happiness for the happiness of others and interpret a passage in which Kant affirms that being more beneficent to ourselves and to those love is compatible with a universal maxim of beneficence. Finally, I provide an interpretation of the latitude of wide duties by analyzing Kant's reinterpretation of Horace's adage (*insani sapiens nomen habeat; aequus iniqui—ultra quam satis est virtutem si petat ipsam*, MS VI: 404n., 409 and

433) and Kant's criticism of Aristotle's doctrine of the mean. In discussing the latitude of wide duties I also discuss Kant's correspondence with Maria von Herbert, in which Kant differentiates *lying* from *reticence* and *candor*. I argue that his correspondence with Maria von Herbert can throw considerable light on the idea of the latitude characteristic of imperfect duties.

Chapter 5 is a digression into problems arising from Kant's account of beneficence as an imperfect duty. Firstly, I discuss the intuition that imperfect duties must be able to "trump" perfect duties under specific circumstances. If this intuition is correct, Kant's distinction between perfect and imperfect duties seems irrelevant, since it is not the logical structure of the duty that tells us what is to be done under the circumstances, but our judgment of the stringency of the moral call in each specific scenario. Further, one could object that beneficence may be far more demanding than Kant himself realized. I also make the case for recognizing a "tragic character" to Kant's moral theory: it does not exclude the possibility of agents having to sacrifice their happiness for the sake of moral demands, even though by Kant's own standards these agents would *deserve* happiness. Although I do not offer a solution to these problems in the chapter, I sketch a possible way to address them involving the promotion of just legal-political institutions that can alleviate the moral burden on individuals.

Finally, chapter 6 brings to the fore aspects of Kant's legal and political theory in which the welfare and needs of individuals is taken into account, in particular Kant's discussion of state policies of poverty relief and redistribution. Kant famously rejects the principle of happiness as a legitimate principle for public legislation. Since he also subsumes all considerations of welfare, including basic subsistence needs, under the heading of happiness, it seems that the Kantian *Rechtsstaat* must ignore poverty relief or redistribution. However, Kant's account of the state's right to tax the rich to maintain the poor in the *Doctrine of Right* contradicts this assumption. I put forward an interpretation of the Kantian state that offers an alternative to the traditional minimalist and more recent non-minimalist accounts of the Kantian state and argue that although the Kantian state has no *direct duty* to redistribute, Kant's conception of fairness or equity (*Billigkeit*) allows the state to apply its right to redistribute as a means to compensate systemic disadvantage and informal injustices which persist despite formal equality before the law.

Chapter One

Happiness as a Natural Necessity

What is happiness according to Immanuel Kant? He offers no unified, systematic response to this question. In his works we find several scattered statements about happiness, some of which seem incompatible with others. Consider the different definitions of happiness to be found in the *Groundwork*. Happiness is defined as the idea of the *entire wellbeing and contentment with one's condition* (GMS IV: 393); the *preservation and prosperity* of a being who has reason and a will (GMS IV: 395); the idea under which *all inclinations unite in one sum* and to which all human beings already have the most powerful and intimate inclination (GMS IV: 399) and the *entire satisfaction of one's needs and inclinations* (GMS IV: 405). Happiness is also said to be "a wavering idea" (GMS IV: 399), of which we cannot form a determinate idea, for happiness is not an ideal of reason but of *imagination* (GMS IV: 419). In the *Critique of practical Reason*, one's own happiness is the general name under which all material principles are subsumed. Material principles are practical rules based on expected feelings of pleasure or displeasure in the realization of an object (KpV V: 21–3). Happiness is thus concerned with the lower faculty of desire (KpV V: 24) and can yield no universal laws, valid for all agents (KpV V: 25). In the *Metaphysics of Morals*, happiness is not only the complete contentment with one's condition but also involves the awareness that this state will last (MS VI: 387. See also VI: 480). In another passage, happiness is identified with one's "true needs" (*wahre Bedürfnisse*), which must be left for each individual to determine according to their own sensitivities (*Empfindungsart*, MS VI: 393).

One may wonder how (and whether) these definitions of happiness fit together. How is happiness as the entire satisfaction of one's inclinations compatible, for instance, with the view that we cannot form a determinate idea of happiness? In turn, how are these two views compatible with the idea of happiness as the satisfaction of one's *true needs*, which can be determined according to the agent's own sensibilities?

The aim of this chapter is firstly to make explicit some of Kant's fundamental assumptions about happiness, which are tacitly presupposed in his claims about happiness but rarely overtly discussed in his works, and finally to provide a more or less unified picture of Kant's "overall" conception of happiness. Once we have a sufficiently clear idea of Kant's overall conception of happiness, we will also be capable of making better sense of Kant's different statements about happiness and understanding how they fit together.

I will start by focusing on two seemingly contradictory claims Kant makes about happiness whose clarification will be our guiding thread in reconstructing Kant's overall conception of happiness. Firstly, Kant says that happiness (conceived as one's self-preservation and wellbeing) cannot be the natural end of finite beings with the capacity of practical reason (GMS VI: 395). However, Kant also affirms that happiness is an end humans have *according to a natural necessity* (*nach einer Naturnothwendigkeit*, GMS IV: 415–6) and that consequently, the need to pursue happiness can be presupposed "surely and *a priori* in the case of every human being, because it belongs to his essence" (*weil sie zu seinem Wesen gehört*, IV: 416). After elucidating the claim that happiness is a natural necessity for human beings (GMS IV 415–6), I will proceed to discuss Kant's teleological argument against happiness as the end of nature for human beings in GMS IV 394–5.

I argue that Kant recognizes a fundamental link between the distinctively human ability to set oneself and pursue ends, and the "natural need" of human beings to pursue happiness. We should thus understand Kant's claim that happiness is a natural necessity as a form of *rational* necessity, although only valid for *finite* rational beings, insofar as our will presupposes subjective *material* principles (maxims) in order to be causally effective in the world. Insofar as the need for happiness arises from the specific structure of a finite human will, I call happiness as a type of rational necessity for human beings Kant's *formal concept of happiness*. However, agents must also form a *substantive* or *material conception* of happiness as a individual guide for action and choice. The material conception involves what a particular agent (consciously or subconsciously) takes to constitute happiness for her,[1] and is based on how she regards her own needs, inclinations and adopted goals, and consequently which ends have greater priority in her life. I argue that the need to form a material concept of happiness is also a necessity imposed by practical reason on finite rational beings. Paradoxically, both *the need to pursue happiness* on the one hand *and the impossibility of happiness being the highest normative standard for us*, on the other, follow from our capacity of practical reason.

1. HAPPINESS AS A NATURAL NECESSITY

There is one end that can be presupposed as actual in all rational beings (**in so far as they, namely as dependent beings, are suited to imperatives**), and thus one purpose that they not merely *can* have, but that one can safely presuppose they one and all actually do have **according to a natural necessity** (*daß sie solche insgesammt nach einer Nathurnothwendigkeit haben*), and that is the purpose of happiness (*die Absicht auf Glückseligkeit*). The hypothetical imperative that represents the practical necessity of an action as a means to the advancement of happiness is assertoric. One must present it as necessary not merely to some uncertain, merely possible purpose, but to a purpose **one can presuppose safely and a priori in every human being** because it belongs to his essence (GMS IV: 415–6, my emphasis).

According to Kant, there is a necessary (*a priori*) connection between the applicability of imperatives to the human will and the human need to pursue happiness. This necessary connection enables us to "safely presuppose" happiness as an end of all finite rational beings. However, in that same passage happiness is also said to be *a natural necessity* for human beings (nach *einer Nathurnothwendigkeit*, my emphasis). How should we understand the claim that there is a link between the pursuit of happiness and the structure of the human will, on the one hand, and the claim that happiness is a natural necessity belonging to the essence of human beings, on the other?

Imperatives apply to those rational beings whose will is not infallibly determined by laws of reason, although they are able to recognize objective rational requirements. These are purely theoretical judgments about goodness obtained by means of representations of reason (*Vorstellungen der Vernunft*) based on grounds (*Gründe*) valid for every similarly situated rational being. However, as Kant puts it, our will is *by its nature* not necessarily obedient [*dieser Wille (ist)* **seiner Natur nach** *nicht notwendig folgsam*, GMS IV: 413, my emphasis.] Actions which are *objectively* recognized as authoritative (i.e., necessary) are *subjectively contingent* (that is, from the perspective of the agent's *choice* or *interest in the action*). There is no necessary causal determination between recognizing objectively valid laws and acting accordingly, given the specific constitution of the human will. Although Kant often uses the concept of a "will" instinctively, meaning human volition in general, the relationship between subjective and objective principles of the will becomes clearer in Kant's later distinction between *Wille* and *Willkür* in the *Metaphysics of Morals*:[2]

> Laws proceed from the will (*Wille*), maxims from choice (*Willkür*). In humans the latter is a free choice; the will which is directed to nothing beyond the law itself, cannot be called either free or unfree, since it is not directed to actions but

immediately to giving laws for the maxims of actions (and is, therefore, practical reason itself). Hence the will directs with absolute necessity and is itself subject to no necessitation. Only choice can therefore be called free. (MS VI: 226)

Although our volition can be guided by objectively valid rational verdicts, it is also susceptible to influences which are not universally valid (based on the inclinations of the agent, which other agents may not share). The problem is that an objective judgment of goodness can only lead to *choice* if it is *also* made into the subjective principle of the will. *Willkür* is therefore the *vehicle* through which rational laws can become practical. *Wille*, as the source of objective laws must "give laws" to *Willkür*, which has its own subjective principles of determination (maxims). The fact that *Willkür* does not necessarily conform to the objective laws of *Wille* is why we experience the authority of reason as rational *necessitation* (*Nötigung*) and rational principles as "oughts" or *imperatives*.

But how do we know whether the will is determined by an objective or a merely subjective principle? Objective principles can be said to be the determining ground of the will (*Bestimmungsgrund*) when the agent sees to it that her volition is grounded on principles which are not *only* subjectively but *also* objectively valid. In other words, the agent must act on maxims which she recognizes to be valid not merely for herself but *also* for all other agents.[3] It is important to stress Kant's emphasis not only on the maxim's satisfaction of the universality requirement, but also on the agent's *recognition* of its universal validity (or lack thereof). This is illustrated by the use of expressions such as "als gültig erkannt wird" (is recognized as valid), "als gültig von ihm angesehen wird" (is regarded as valid by him) (KpV V: 19).[4] Maxims can be considered universally valid because they *conform* to practical laws (*praktische Gesetze*, KpV V: 19) whereas maxims considered as mere subjective principles are *Willensmeinungen des Individuums*, i.e., mere "intentions of the will of the individual" (KpV V: 66).[5] When an agent chooses to act on a maxim which she regards as merely subjectively valid, she is subordinating her will to a maxim of self-love (*Selbstliebe*), instead of to the moral law (KpV V: 73). When *all* claims of self-love are given priority over morality, that is, when we make "the dear self" into an unconditional practical principle, we speak of *self-conceit* (*Eigendünkel*) (Ibid.). Thus, the source of moral evil in human beings lies not in our sensual nature as such (in the natural inclinations), as sometimes assumed, but in the intelligible act (*intelligibler Tat*, REL VI: 31) of subordinating one's will unconditionally to the principle of self-love instead of the moral law.[6]

In *Groundwork* IV: 415–6, Kant suggests a fundamental relationship between the fact that *Willkür* presupposes subjective principles as its "material basis" and the fact that happiness is a natural necessity for us. The "natural necessity" to pursue happiness is an implication of the specific nature of the human will and not simply a need imposed on us by external laws of nature (i.e., by our inclinations, as often suggested by Kant himself).

Human action has two aspects: a formal and a material one. Although choice can be determined by a purely formal principle (as a determining ground of volition or *Bestimmungsgrund*), matter is required if the will is also to *effect* something in the world. A mere maxim of lawfulness is not yet a maxim of *action*.[7] As Mary Gregor points out, to have a maxim is none other than to adopt an end.[8] As a form of *causality*, practical reason is necessarily *purposive*: to be "practical" and to be "directed at effecting ends" is therefore one and the same. Were practical reason not ends oriented, i.e., based on maxims, it would not be practical at all.[9]

As Kant observes, "without an end there can be no will" (GTP VIII: 280, note). Particular "willings" or acts of choice (*Willkür*) presuppose ends, which are made into one's *maxim of action*. However, an end can only become the object of my volition if I can see myself as the cause of that end. This is because adopting an end analytically implies the commitment to take the means necessary for its realization (GMS IV: 417). Therefore, as a matter of definition we do not have an end unless we have committed ourselves to realize it.[10] To represent the end as being impossible turns "willing" into mere "wishing" (*wünschen*, MS VI: 213). Wishing is the representation of a state of affairs as desirable which nevertheless does not lead to action.[11]

> Whoever wills the end also wills (in so far as reason has decisive influence on his actions) the indispensably necessary means to it that **is in his control [*das in seiner Gewalt ist*]**. As far as willing is concerned, this proposition is analytic; **for in the willing of an object, as my effect, my causality is already thought as an acting cause,** i.e., the use of means, and the imperative already extracts the concept of actions necessary to this end from the concept of a willing of this end. (GMS IV: 417)

As Kant stresses, the powerful inclination we all have to happiness is because "it is just in this idea that all inclinations unite into one sum" (*weil sich gerade in dieser Idee alle Neigungen zu einer Summe vereinigen,* GMS IV: 399). Here, Kant is talking about inclinations, not yet about ends. While happiness as a system of *ends* would require that ends be more or less mutually compatible (as a condition for their realization), happiness as the sum of all our *inclinations* does not require mutual compatibility. This is because at that stage inclinations would be mere wishes and not yet *willings*. In this sense, the sum of our inclinations could be a mere chimera, including inclinations which could never be *realized* together with others, but which can nevertheless be *imagined*. We imagine all our wishes converging into a single representation and feel a powerful inclination to that representation precisely because it is the epitome (*Inbegriff*) of everything our hearts desire (or at least of what we *believe* our hearts desire). This representation does not need to be realistic in any way and this is why Kant often suggests that happiness (in its totality) is not an achievable goal, but merely an ideal of imagination.

As finite rational beings we have inclinations. But in order to satisfy these inclinations we must make their satisfaction *our* ends. Anything we want to realize in the world, as the result of our own causality (our agency) must be voluntarily adopted as an end.[12] This is because, as hypothetical imperatives illustrate, to have an end *is to be committed to its realization*. Therefore, from our many inclinations, we will also have a plurality of non-moral ends, as the inclinations we have elected for satisfaction. Some ends can be satisfied immediately (such as my drinking a sip of water now), others in the short or in the long term (i.e., my intention to publish a book); some ends require that we realize other ends first (i.e., in order to become a scholar, I must follow a certain academic path, receive academic degrees etc.). And this is when we realize that we can no longer remain attached to the fantastic ideal of a sum of one's inclinations and must seek its more realistic version: a material conception of one's own happiness.

It is impossible to satisfy all one's inclinations: when adopted as ends, some inclinations might be contingently incompatible with other ends or logically preclude their mutual realization. It is also impossible to realize all one's compatible ends at once; some ends may require more time than others or the achievement of prior ends as a condition for their realization. Because we have a plurality of ends which are incompatible with each other or must be realized at different times, agents are confronted with the task of forming a conception of the ends that constitute their happiness, in a more or less coherent hierarchy. Since the content of one's conception of happiness is the sum of one's *ends*, one's conception of happiness will require ensuring the greatest possible compatibility between our ends and coordinating their realization in the most *efficient* or *desirable* way in the eyes of the agent.[13] For instance, ensuring that short term goals do not make long term projects impossible and that particular decisions do not have a negative impact on the agent's other interests, are prudential policies that may be normative to the agent given her interest in the satisfaction of the sum (or greatest possible number) of her ends. We must also determine which ends are more important, or should be achieved first, either as a means to other ends or due to time constraints.

Since deliberation in these matters is rarely perfect, agents often make wrong judgments about their priorities, not because they do not know what matters most to them, but because they often fail to think about it clearly and thoroughly or to devote enough time to reflection. Also, one's material conception of happiness may include mutually incompatible ends, of which the agent is not aware. Not until the agent comes to experience conflict and is forced to decide between ends is she confronted with the task of reflecting upon and revising her conception of happiness. In sum: agents must form a more or less well defined conception of their happiness due to the fact that they have a plurality of ends which cannot be realized at once, but forming this conception also takes time and experience. It may also require some long term planning. Forming a conception of our own happiness is necessary as a guide not only for the adoption of new ends, but also for specifying the priority of certain ends over others (the ones we believe are more important to our happiness) and consequently which ends we must give up in case of incompatibility within the system. We must therefore distinguish between the *formal* concept of happiness as the need of finite rational agents to adopt subjective principles of action, and one's substantive or *material* conception of happiness, as the agent's specific conception of the ends her happiness must include, and of which ends are more important (or more urgent).

Kant therefore has the *formal* concept of happiness in mind when he claims that we can know *a priori* that a creature whose will is subject to imperatives *inevitably* wants to be happy. The need for happiness is therefore primarily linked to the *end-oriented* structure of the human will and only secondarily to the fact that (non-moral) ends are based on inclinations. It follows that we pursue non-moral ends for the same reason we must also adopt *moral* ends, namely, that conceiving ourselves as agents (endowed with a form of causality) requires that we adopt ends.[14] Since wanting the realization of all our ends requires forming a conception of these ends, the need to form a conception of happiness is indissolubly linked to our capacity to set ourselves ends. While the formal notion of happiness is logically prior to one's material conception of happiness, the latter is needed as an answer to the practical problem imposed by the formal concept of happiness, which is that if we are to *satisfy* some of our inclinations we must attempt to incorporate them into a system, as much as possible and desirable to the agent. As I shall explain in the next section, neither formal concept nor material conceptions of happiness are imposed on us by our inclinations (see KU V: 430), even though non-moral ends presuppose inclinations.[15]

Although it is possible for an agent to revise her personal conception of happiness, it is not possible to give up pursuing happiness altogether. This is because happiness in general provides us with the *matter* of practical deliberation. Giving up the pursuit of happiness would be to cease being an agent at all, since it would imply ceasing to have ends (non-moral and moral alike, since the justification for having ends which are also duties, equally relies on the need to counteract the influence of non-moral ends, see MS VI: 380–1 and my discussion in chapter 4).[16] Giving up happiness in a formal sense is thus impossible because in order to cease pursuing ends altogether, an agent *would have to adopt a maxim not to pursue ends*. This means to adopt the end not to adopt any ends, which is a performative self-contradiction. A performative self-contradiction obtains when the content of a proposition negates its own validity conditions, or when an action aims at undermining the conditions of its own possibility.

Presumably, even the most imprudent agent cares about some end or other, even if they are destructive or of little value. As Kant notes, a person who is tired of life and decides to kill herself is acting from self-love and *actually* has not given up happiness (GMS IV: 422). This suggests that the pursuit of happiness in the formal sense I identified earlier is not a normative concept, but a descriptive one. We cannot fail to pursue ends altogether, although we may fail to pursue the ends we find worth pursuing from the perspective of our best judgment. Whatever we do, we will end up adopting one end or another. If this interpretation is correct, the formal concept of happiness is constitutive of human agency as ends-oriented (in Kant's terminology, "of having a will").

We also need to form *some* conception of happiness as a guide for the adoption and realization of ends. However, it is hard to see how one can be *required* to form some conception of happiness and adopt it as one's end, since this is something one naturally does anyway. One cannot fail to form a conception of happiness; one can only fail to *live up* to the standards one has included in one's own conception of happiness. If one fails to live up to one's conception, there are different ways of understanding this failure: one may have formed a new conception of happiness altogether and thus not actually failed ("I didn't really want to become a ballerina after all"); lacked sufficient motivation to take what one acknowledged as the required means to one's ends (the latter would qualify as an instance of weakness of the will, which I shall not discuss here);[17] there is also the possibility of purely technical (instrumental) failure, when the agent mistakenly chooses the wrong means to the promotion of her ends while still remaining committed to her substantive conception of happiness. In contrast, the formal concept of happiness is the way the will of finite beings is constituted: finite wills presuppose subjective principles (maxims) and are subject to *imperatives*. This is why Kant says it belongs to the essence of human beings to pursue happiness. If the pursuit of happiness belongs to our essence as finite rational beings, there can be no normative *requirement* that we adopt happiness as our end.[18] If so, the only way happiness can be said to be normative is the alleged requirement that we live up to our formed conception of happiness, that is, that we give priority to the satisfaction of the sum of our adopted ends over the satisfaction of momentary desires if they are incompatible with that sum. This reading however only applies to agents who are effectively motivated by the natural inclination toward securing their overall happiness.[19] As a hypothetical imperative, prudence, or instrumental rationality at the service of one's own happiness,[20] presupposes an inclination of the agent for having normative force (GMS IV: 416, ll. 23–6);[21] in the absence of such an inclination, there is nothing binding the agent to follow the counsels of prudence[22] or to give priority to the sum of her inclinations over a particular end.

It follows that in Kant's account an agent can be criticized for instrumental failure, inconsistency or lack of judgment (given what she wants), but not for prudential irrationality if she prefers immediate desire satisfaction at the sacrifice of long term happiness, if she has no inclination for her overall happiness as well. Therefore, when we call someone imprudent, we are simply *assuming* that she has a certain end (her long term happiness). I will discuss the normativity or "bindingness" of prudential reason in chapter 3 ("One's Own Happiness and Indirect Duty").[23]

In the next section, I will analyze a further claim Kant makes about happiness in the *Groundwork* that seems to contradict the view that happiness is a matter of natural necessity for human beings. This is Kant's claim that happiness cannot be the end of nature (*Zweck der Natur*) for human beings (GMS IV: 395).

2. WHY HAPPINESS CANNOT BE THE NATURAL END (*ZWECK DER NATUR*) OF HUMAN BEINGS (GMS IV: 395)

> (. . .) In this idea of the absolute worth of a mere will, not taking into account any utility in its estimation, there is something so strange that, regardless of all the agreement with it even of common reason, a suspicion must still arise that it might perhaps covertly be founded merely in some high-flown fantastication, and that we may have misunderstood Nature's purpose in assigning Reason to our will as its ruler. (GMS IV: 394–5)

In *Groundwork* I (IV: 394–6) Kant anticipates and addresses teleological objections to his conception of unconditional morality. The good will is good in itself, independently of its fitness to achieve any ends. Usefulness or fruitlessness can neither add to this worth nor take anything away from it (GMS IV: 394). This conception of morality seems suspicious from the perspective of the teleology of Kant's time. In his discussion, Kant not only refutes possible teleological objections but also makes a *positive* teleological claim: that only a product of *reason itself for itself* (a good will) can be the "true vocation" (*Bestimmung*) of human beings (GMS IV: 390). But why does Kant need to address teleological objections in the first place? He seems to be defending the questionable view that nature has given us reason for a purpose and that this purpose is morality, as a support to his moral theory.[24]

Another interpretation explains this discussion as Kant's intention to argue at the level of "conventional wisdom," which is teleological,[25] in order to mark the transition from common to philosophical moral cognition in the first section of the *Groundwork*.[26]

Kant's controversial teleological claim has been not only strongly criticized but also considered an embarrassment even by the most orthodox proponents of Kant's moral theory.[27] However, it will become clear in the course of my discussion that these passages are particularly illuminating when it comes to understanding Kant's conception of happiness and the way he understands the relation between the human need to pursue happiness and the structure of practical reason.

In *Groundwork* (394–6), Kant adopts the perspective of teleology itself and argues that identifying happiness as the end of nature for humanity would be a *bad* teleological account. If teleology would consistently apply its own fundamental regulative principle (i.e. the principle of natural efficiency),[28] it would have to acknowledge that the good will must be the end of nature for human beings. Kant is therefore refuting a teleological claim by appealing to teleology's own internal standards. Since the ability to reason is constitutive of the animals we are, reason must also be seen as a purpose of nature.[29] Therefore, teleology must be able to account for the natural purpose of our developed ability to reason. Following the principle of natural efficiency, reason must be shown not only to be fit to promote *some* natural purpose of human beings but indeed to be the *best possible* development in the promotion of humanity's natural purpose.

Kant argues that the assumption that *happiness* is the highest end of nature for humanity does not satisfy the teleological principle of natural efficiency. This is because reason is not the fittest capacity for the furtherance of our happiness (GMS IV: 395). Instinct, Kant argues, would be a much more reliable guide to the desiderative faculty, since in matters of happiness the guidance of reason is "weak and deceptive." If we took *happiness* to be the natural purpose of human beings and accept the principle of natural efficiency, we would have to conclude that nature should have prevented reason from "break(ing) into a practical use and have the presumption, with its weak insight, to think out for itself a plan for happiness and the means for achieving it" (GMS IV: 395). Since reason often meddles with nature's purpose, nature would have had the "wise precaution" to restrict reason to a mere *theoretical* function (to contemplate the fortunate predisposition of its nature, ibid., ll. 18–19) and prevent the possibility of its *practical use*. The satisfaction of our needs in this case would be wholly delegated to instinct.

> (. . .) since reason is not sufficiently fit to guide the will reliably with regard to its objects and the satisfactions of all our needs (which in part it itself

multiplies)—an end to which an implanted natural instinct would have led much more reliably—**but reason as a practical faculty, i.e., as one that is meant to influence the *will*, has yet been imparted to us**, its true function (*wahre Bestimmung*) must be to produce a will that is good in itself—for which reason was absolutely necessary—as nature has everywhere else gone to work purposively in distributing its predispositions. (GMS IV: 396, my emphasis)

The fact that our reason is not merely contemplative but also has a practical use (i.e., is *meant to influence the will* and lead to action) is the decisive aspect ruling out the plausibility of happiness as the final end of humanity. Teleology must take into account the ability of reason to determine volition and indicate the purpose for which this natural capacity would be the best possible natural arrangement for our species. However, the function of reason, its *ergon*, to speak with Aristotle, must be an end *that only reason can promote*, or can *best promote*. This condition plays a decisive role for Kant's argument. The only end that reason can achieve "by itself" is the good will. Therefore, the promotion of a good will (and not happiness) must be seen as the final end of nature for human beings.[30]

Since nature has allowed the development of practical reason, it cannot be seen as an arbitrary arrangement, even if reason can at times undermine happiness (GMS IV: 396). However, Kant stresses that happiness is not excluded as an end of human beings: the good will is not "the entire good" but rather "the highest," that is, supreme good and the condition of everything else, even of all longing for happiness" (GMS IV: 396, ll. 24–6).[31]

Kant's teleological conclusion in the *Groundwork* relies on a number of puzzling assumptions about happiness. His central assumption is the surprising view that reason is not best fitted for promoting happiness (GMS IV: 395). Reason has often been praised as the greatest advantage human beings have over other animals. Reasoning teaches us the effects following from certain actions and allows us to extend our knowledge from past experiences to new ones through analogy (MA VIII: 111). It enables us not only to employ acquired knowledge to achieve our ends more efficiently but also to expand the choices available to us beyond the limitations of natural instinct, to which all other animals are bound (MA VIII: 112). Further, because we are able to pass on accumulated knowledge to following generations, reason has made possible an increasing technical development and control over the natural world. If this is correct, reason should make us happier animals. In the next section, I will analyze Kant's claim that reason is ill fitted for promoting happiness and bring to light further assumptions Kant makes about happiness.

3. REASON AND THE PURSUIT OF HAPPINESS

Reason not only determines the *means* conducive to happiness but also influences the way we form our conception of happiness, that is, our *beliefs* about what will make us happy. Kant expresses this idea in a negative, indirect way: "nature would have prevented Reason from striking out into practical use, and from having the impudence, with its feeble insights, to devise its own plan for happiness and for the means of achieving it" (GMS IV: 395).[32]

Although reason can, with its "feeble insights," devise its own plan for happiness and the means for achieving it, we cannot fully *derive* our conception of happiness from reason alone. All adopted non-moral ends must have some reference to the inclinations and needs of the agent; more precisely, they must be based on the agent's *beliefs* about what her inclinations and needs are. Although all elements of happiness are *empirical,* our inclinations and needs do not automatically provide us with a conception of what our happiness is. To assume that we could simply *abstract* a conception of happiness from our sensual nature would be a *naive* understanding of happiness, and I will argue that Kant rejects this view despite his hedonistic account of non-moral ends. The faculty of imagination (*Einbildungskraft*) plays a central role for the formation of an individual's conception of happiness: it is imagination which must find the *rule* under which the plurality of the agent's inclinations can be *unified* under a common concept: the concept of one's own happiness. "The concept of happiness is not one that the human being has, say, abstracted from his instincts and thus derived from the animality in himself; rather, it is a mere idea of the state to which he would make his instincts adequate under merely empirical conditions (which is impossible)" (KU V: 430).

Happiness is not an ideal of reason but of imagination (GMS IV: 418).[33] Unfortunately, Kant does not explain what precisely an ideal of imagination means; it is however possible to elucidate this concept with the help of other writings. In the third Critique, Kant also identifies an ideal of imagination, namely, the ideal of *beauty,* and provides more information about what an ideal of imagination is. While an idea is a concept of reason (*Vernunftbegriff,* KU V: 232), that is, a concept representing the absolute *totality* of conditions (KrV IV: 207), an ideal is the *representation* of an individual, object or state as being *adequate* to that idea. For instance, while wisdom (*Weisheit*) is an idea of pure reason, a *wise person* (*der Weise*) is wisdom's corresponding ideal; it is the representation of someone who is wholly congruent with the idea of wisdom but exists only in *thought* (KrV III: 384).

Ideas arise due to a natural tendency of reason to extend the application of the categories of the understanding beyond possible experience toward the unconditioned or absolute. Since no corresponding intuition (*Anschauung*) can be found for them in experience, ideas are *indeterminate* (*unbestimmt*). Because reason seeks the totality of conditions, i.e., the absolute, it impels us to form the idea of a *maximum* (see KrV III: 254, l.14). We can now make better sense of the *idea* of happiness as an absolute whole, a maximum of wellbeing in my present and future condition [*ein absolutes Ganze, ein Maximum des Wohlbefindens, in meinen gegenwärtigen und jedem zukünftigen Zustande*, GMS IV: 418] Happiness, as the idea of a *maximum* of wellbeing, may be considered from three perspectives, all having to do with the way our inclinations could be satisfied: it is the idea of the highest *extensive*, *intensive* and *protensive* satisfaction of our inclinations (*extensive* concerning their number, *intensive* with regard to their degree and *protensively* in respect to *duration*, KrV A 806/ B 834).

Darstellung is Kant's term for the presentation of the idea of an indeterminate magnitude (*Größe*) by means of imagination (KU V: 253). Therefore, imagination is also defined as the faculty of presentation (*Darstellung*, KU V: 232). Happiness, as an *ideal of imagination*, must thus be understood as the *Darstellung* or presentation of the idea of an individual's *maximum* wellbeing, extensively, intensively and uninterruptedly over time. When Kant writes in the *Groundwork* about "reason" devising its own plans for our happiness and the means to it, he must be alluding to the *indirect* role of reason for the conception of happiness, insofar as reason provides the idea (*Vernunftidee*) of a *maximum* on which basis imagination produces its ideal. If human beings did not have the capacity for conceiving *ideas of reason* in the first place, they would not be able to form a conception of happiness as an *ideal of imagination*.

> Now, it is impossible that the most insightful and at the same time singularly able, but still finite being should make for himself a determinate concept of what he actually wants there. If he wants riches, how much worry, envy and intrigue might he not by this bring down upon his shoulders! If he wants much cognition and insight, that might perhaps only sharpen his eyes all the more, to show him as all the more terrible the ills that are still concealed from him now and yet cannot be avoided, or to burden his desires, which already give him enough trouble, with more needs still. If he wants a long life, who will guarantee him that it would not be a long misery? (. . .) In short, he is not able to determine with complete certainty, according to any principle, what will make him truly happy, because omniscience would be required for this. (GMS IV: 418)

The concept of happiness is an *indeterminate* concept. Although every human being strives for happiness, no one is able to determine with certainty "and in agreement with oneself" what one actually wants. There are two reasons for the indeterminacy of happiness, both due to our cognitive limitations as finite beings. The first is that we cannot foresee all the external consequences of the achievement of an end and their impact on our happiness. Our desire for an end is based on our conception of *expected* results and not on a complete knowledge of all possible outcomes. The other is that we don't even know our own desires with certainty; we are not transparent to ourselves. We must form a conception of our own happiness by means of our *beliefs* about what we want. Our only means to define what we want is by reference to our feelings of pleasure or displeasure on the *representation* of an object or condition (see KpV V: 21 and MS VI: 211). However, pleasure and displeasure involve "what is merely subjective in the relation of our representation and contain no relation at all to an object for possible cognition of it (**or even cognition of our condition**)" (MS VI: 211, my emphasis).

Because "discovering" our wants and needs is essentially an exercise of imagination and of interpretation, our feelings of pleasure or displeasure in that imaginative process or even in our experience of achieved ends provide knowledge neither of the objects to which our representations refer nor of our own desiderative states. Feelings of pleasure and displeasure function therefore more as a touchstone in the process of belief-formation about our wants than actually providing any *cognition* about what we need and should choose at non-moral level. Failure to achieve expected satisfaction when an end is realized often signals that we misinterpreted our needs and adopted the wrong ends. Non-moral choice therefore involves not only determining ends and finding the means to the ends (prospectively), but also confirming whether or not our judgment of wants and needs was correct (retrospectively). Our urges and feelings therefore require a good deal of self-scrutiny and interpretation, and not least a certain amount of bitter life experience. This is why our conception of happiness is subject to constant corrections and revisions in the course of our lives (KU V: 430).

4. HAPPINESS AND THE OPACITY OF THE PHENOMENAL SELF

The formation of our conception of happiness "suffers" from a cognitive limitation which is similar to that of moral evaluation (the problem usually referred to as *opacity of the self*). According to Kant, "not even the most strenuous self-examination allows us to know with certainty whether an action was truly motivated by duty or by some covert impulse of self-love" (GMS IV: 404).[34] The problem is that while we can be sure to have acted on *a* maxim, we can never be absolutely sure if this maxim is the one we think we are acting on. It is a common experience that we can be mistaken or even delusional about our motives to act in a certain way ("was my action solely the expression of my commitment to justice or was I also *resentful* of the person I was so keen to criticize?").³⁵ Although *Achtung* makes us aware of the authority of the moral law and consequently of our freedom to act in accordance with laws of reason,³⁶ as a feeling it expresses no more than the effect of a representation on the subject (in this case, of the subordination of my will to the moral law). This means that also at the *phenomenal level* agents do not have direct access to their motivational states, but always need to *represent* to themselves what their intentions are. The consequence is the need of human beings to form a *conception* of their own motives as a general plan to action. This also applies to non-moral action, since one's plan of action cannot be derived from one's inclinations themselves, alone by virtue of being affected by them. However pressing our desires and needs may be, they do not per se inform us about our own condition and prescribe action.³⁷

In 'Speculative Beginning of Human History,' Kant reinterprets the biblical account of original sin in Genesis 2–6 as the discovery of our capacity to make free choices and argues that humanity's acquired ability to reason necessarily implied a "fall from paradise" as the irreparable loss of nature's guidance and providence in the form of *instinct*. Kant's interpretation of the biblical myth sheds considerable light on the way Kant conceives a subject's phenomenological relation to her own physical needs and wants as well as his conception of happiness as an ideal of the imagination.

> The discovery of a new kind of food [the apple] which was not "sanctioned" by instinct prepared the terrain for the first free choice, which had a decisive impact on the way humans were to live ever since. However insignificant that choice in itself might have been, humans became thereby aware of their ability to free themselves from the guidance of nature. The "damage" was irreparable: there was no way back into the former unreflective state of nature: humans now proceeded with eyes open. (MA VIII: 112)

The need to represent one's own needs and ultimately one's future condition emerges as a substitute for the lost "voice of nature" (i.e., natural instinct). We must now devise both the ends and the means to our own happiness. In contrast to other animals, which remained bound to instinct, humans discovered the possibility of *choosing* their own way of life. However, once under the influence of reason and imagination, humans began to long for objects for which there was no natural necessity or which even subverted their natural needs. Kant identifies three natural drives which are not based on reason: self-preservation, propagation of the species (the sexual drive) and the need to live with other human beings (the social drive). Reason distorted original natural drives into greediness and voluptuousness, as well as into the "bestial" vices of gluttony, lust and savagery towards others (REL VI: 27). The reflexivity inherent in the ability to reason ultimately *alienates* us from our animal nature: not only because it creates further needs and luxuries we may never be able to satisfy, but because our very phenomenological *access* to our needs must now be mediated by a conception of what these needs are.

Although reason might be better fitted than instinct to determine the *means* for satisfying an animal's needs (especially in a new or constantly changing natural environment), it is completely unable to identify the actual *content* of these needs with certainty. The greater fitness of instinct over happiness therefore lies in its not requiring the *representation* of the animals' needs and desiderative states in order to seek satisfaction, but in its direct determination of the animal's behavior. The influence of Rousseau's *Discours sur L'inégalité* is clear.[38]

Reason presents humans with an infinite number of objects of choice, to which instinct-bound animals have no access. By transforming original fundamental needs into sophisticated, complex desires, reason, together with imagination, also creates new sources of pleasure which are unknown to other animals. But reason does not necessarily make us happier. Life under the guidance of reason is not only toilsome but a *Sisyphean task*, since our social ambitions and the pursuit of complex cultural ends render contentment with our own condition unachievable. This bitter realization can lead cultivated persons to *hate reason*. The more cultivated, the unhappier an agent will be, if she considers happiness to be the ultimate purpose of her existence (GMS IV: 394–6).

> (. . .) We do find that the more a cultivated reason engages with the purpose of enjoying life and with happiness, so much the further does a human being stray from true contentment; and from this there arises in many, and indeed in those who are most experienced in its use, if only they are sincere enough to admit it, a certain degree of *misology*, i.e., hatred of reason (. . .). (GMS IV: 395)

Kant argues that *misology* arises from the realization that the burdens of possessing reason by far outweigh the advantages of it when it comes to attaining happiness in one's life. In the *Reflection* 2570, Kant argues that misology and misanthropy arise from expecting more from reason and from "the heart" than they can provide (*wenn man der Vernunft und dem Herzen mehr zumuthet, als beydes leisten kann, so entspringt ein Vernunfthaß und Menschenhaß*, Refl. XVI: 424) and that this affects only "the experienced" (*dieses begegnet nur die erfahrenen*, Ibid.). A certain misology is also expressed in the tendency to idealize an imaginary condition prior to the emergence of reason, where true needs are uncorrupted and satisfaction is possible, as illustrated by the myth of a Golden Age in religion and art. Reason is the angel with the fiery sword barring the way back to paradise (MA VIII: 115).

Misology is in fact unjustified, since reason is not the true cause of our failure to achieve happiness. As Kant stresses, our very nature renders the achievement of happiness impossible. Although we represent happiness to ourselves as a state of uninterrupted agreeableness, the way we experience pleasure and pain excludes the possibility of permanent satisfaction. Pain and pleasure are for Kant *complementary* feelings: one cannot experience pleasure unless there is a sufficient contrast to one's previous state (Anthr. VII: 231, see also KU V: 430). Satisfaction is therefore always a temporary state.

One question remains: why does misology affect cultivated persons?

> A reflective person feels a grief that the unreflective do not know, a grief that can well lead to moral ruination: this is discontentedness with the providence that governs the entire course of the world; and he feels it when he thinks about the evil that so greatly oppresses the human race, leaving it without (apparent) hope for something better. (MA VIII: 121)

Grief and bitterness "against providence" are based on a specific (and as we shall see, inadequate) conception of the ultimate end of our existence, which also leads to inadequate expectations from our capacity to reason. If so, the need to understand the role of reason for rational beings is not only an obsolete teleological concern, but is essential for giving meaning to our existence, a need which is the more pressing in cultivated, i.e., *reflexive* persons. This is not to say that we should be indifferent to the evils that affect humanity and that human happiness does not matter: instead, Kant's idea is that our fundamental *attitude* towards the evils that oppress humanity is deeply influenced by our underlying conception of the end of human nature, of our *vocation* as human beings. If we take our rational nature to be our highest end, we must regard these evils not merely as something that plagues humanity without hope of improvement but as something we have a *duty* to address, i.e., as presenting us with a *moral task*. This *moral vision* can help us overcome cynicism and hopelessness, and encourages us to face difficulties with determination and courage. Although we are not happier, our existence seems no longer pointless. In contrast, if we take happiness to be our whole end, what reason do we have not to despair when considering the violence of human beings and the fragility and precariousness of our human condition? Providence seems more cruel the more we focus on the natural realm and its impact on human beings. As Kant notes in the *Third Critique*, humans are no less prey to natural disasters than other species and are also victims of human domination, greed and violence, which is far worse than natural disasters. This recognition leads us to conclude that from a natural perspective, the human species is no more privileged in the realm of nature than other creatures (KU V: 430).

Assuming that reason has a function that goes *beyond* the promotion of one's own happiness opens up new prospects to us. Although it seems circular to affirm that reason requires us to *trust* the task it imposes on us, the question is whether we can do otherwise. As H. J. Paton argued,

> (. . .) although Kant may make an uncritical use of it in his moral philosophy, his doctrine of teleology is not to be interpreted in a crude way. (. . .) Perhaps the assumption that practical reason has a function or purpose and that the fulfillment of this function or purpose must be good is the root assumption of Kant's whole moral philosophy, and indeed of almost all Western moral philosophy. Perhaps, when properly understood, this is a legitimate and even necessary assumption, like the assumption that in thinking we must trust our own reason.[39]

Reason imposes on us the task of realizing rational ideals which seem impossible to achieve when we consider experience. However, as regulative practical principles, these ideals of reason nevertheless have objective reality since they play a central role in enabling moral practice (Cf. Rel. VI: 123, note 2). For instance, reason requires that we bring about a world in which the rights of all individuals are secured through juridical institutions (i.e. a perfect cosmopolitan civil constitution, MS RL VI: 354). We must therefore believe this task to be possible, even if the best we can achieve is only a constant approximation to the ideal of reason, through the cumulative efforts of many generations (MS RL VI: 354–5). However, realizing the requirements of reason requires more than blind optimism: as rational beings, we must be able to conceive the demands of pure practical reason as compatible with natural laws, and the idea of moral progress as possible despite the calamities of human history. Kant's concern with teleology arises from the need to reconcile the seemingly fantastical demands of pure practical reason with the morally indifferent world around us: it is the *practical* correlate of Kant's *theoretical* attempt to reconcile freedom and causal determination. Teleology is thus ultimately *moral* and not *natural* teleology in Kant's system.[40]

Another feature of Kant's conception of happiness is that assuming that happiness is our whole end excludes the possibility of morality (since adopting moral maxims is only possible when self-love is subordinated to the moral law), while the reverse does not exclude the possibility of happiness. Incompatibilities between commitment to duty and our happiness are merely *contingent* (KpV V: 113–4), that is, not intrinsic to morality, whereas subordinating the will to the principle of self-love *necessarily* excludes the possibility of morality.[41] Paradoxically, despite the possibility of conflict between morality and happiness "in this world," the recognition that morality is humanity's supreme good can nevertheless bring us closer to contentment than making happiness our "whole end."

> And to that extent one must admit that the judgment of those who greatly moderate and even reduce below zero the vainglorious eulogies extolling the advantages that reason was supposed to obtain for us with regard to the happiness and contentment of life, is by no means sullen, or ungrateful to the kindliness of the government of the world; but that these judgments are covertly founded on the idea of another and far worthier purpose of their existence, to which, and not to happiness, reason is quite properly destined. (GMS IV: 396)

Passages like this strongly contradict the traditional view of Kant's moral theory as an impediment to human happiness (the underlying assumption seems to be that achieving happiness would be undisputably possible if it were not for Kantian morality). For instance, Kant notes that under a maxim of happiness, the will "vacillates between its incentives as to what it should decide upon." The outcomes being highly uncertain, "a good head is required to find a way out of the crush of arguments and counterarguments without cheating oneself in the total reckoning." In contrast, when asking ourselves what is our duty, the answer is clear and certain (TP VIII: 287). While Epicureans stressed the importance of justice for a life without disturbance by appealing to prudential arguments, Kant's ethics suggests that doing the right thing can indeed eliminate much anxiety and uncertainty from the lives of agents, not for prudential reasons, but by providing clear and unequivocal guidance to action. Although a moral action may not prove the most advantageous course of action in regard to the agent's interests in a specific circumstance, acting morally is *always* valuable, irrespective of whether it furthers our non-moral interests, while an imprudent, bad decision has no value at all.[42]

In this chapter I have reconstructed Kant's overall conception of happiness, which underlies some of Kant's scattered statements about happiness. Although it receives no systematic treatment in Kant's works, Kant's conception of happiness is complex and interesting in its own right. Happiness is a necessary "end" of human beings given the ends-oriented structure of our will, although it cannot be considered the vocation (*Bestimmung*) of human beings. Further, happiness is an idea human beings make for themselves of the sum of all their inclinations and to which they feel greatly attracted. However, when it comes to deciding which inclinations the agent would like to *satisfy*, happiness must be conceived as a more or less clearly hierarchically structured system of ends. Happiness is also an indeterminate idea, not only because all its elements are empirical, that is, based on the inclinations of the agent, but mainly because happiness is based on the agent's *beliefs* about what her needs and wants are and on her *expectations* about how much satisfaction achieving the end will provide. It follows that it is never possible to know *with certainty* what will make us happy. Material conceptions of happiness will also greatly vary from individual to individual, and in different stages of a person's life. As we shall see in the coming chapters, Kant's view of happiness as indeterminate will have consequences for other domains of his practical theory. Indeterminacy is the main reason why Kant disqualifies happiness as the principle of morality and as a principle for external legislation in the domain of right (*Recht*).

I have concluded this chapter by arguing that Kant's account of morality can (indirectly) contribute to one's happiness more effectively than making happiness one's whole end in life. Morality creates meaning in a morally indifferent world. It enables us to see the suffering and injustice that plague the human race as a *task,* i.e., as something we have a duty to overcome, and not merely as something we are helplessly subjected to.

In the next chapter I shall analyze the meta-ethical implications of Kant's understanding of happiness: his anti-eudaimonism in moral theory.

NOTES

1. As Pauline Kleingeld pointed out, it is sometimes problematic to use gender sensitive language when referring to Kant. Despite his universalistic language, there were specific contexts in which he did not mean to include women and non-whites among the persons he was considering. I will use the female pronoun to refer to persons in the plural when it concerns my own application and interpretation of Kant's philosophy, and where I believe it is unproblematic to do so. See Kleingeld, Pauline (2019), "On Dealing with Kant's Sexism and Racism," SGIR Review 2 (2):3–22.

2. Although the distinction between *Wille* and *Willkür* as the legislative and the executive powers of the will is already "latent" in the *Groundwork*'s conception of the will as practical reason, as well as in the *Critique of practical Reason* and in the *Religion within the Boundaries of mere Reason,* it is only made explicit in the Introduction of the later *Metaphysics of Morals* (MS VI: 213–4 and 226). See Timmermann, *Kant's Groundwork of the Metaphysics of Morals. A Commentary*, pp. 42–3 and 115 and Henry E. Allison, *Kant's Theory of Freedom*, pp. 129–30.

3. See Paton, *The Categorical Imperative*, p. 60. Paton defines maxims as subjective principles of action arising from "the cooperation of reason and inclination" (Ibid., p. 56). He is also careful to differentiate maxims as general subjective principles from mere motives (which must be incorporated in or "generalized" into a maxim in order to determine volition (p. 60).

4. See Maria Schwartz, *Der Begriff der Maxime bei Kant. Eine Untersuchung des Maximenbegriffs in Kants praktischer Philosophie*, pp. 41.

5. *Willensmeinung* is the old German term for the expressions of the will of persons in positions of authority. The *Grimm* dictionary defines "Willensmeinung" as "offenbarung des willens, weisung, absicht (. . .); meist von herrschenden oder leitenden persönlichkeiten gebraucht, nachträglich aber auch von weniger hochgestellten." "Intentions of the will" is thus the appropriate translation as opposed

to the literal "opinions of the will." As the table of the categories of freedom in the *Critique of Practical Reason* make clear, the difference between a practical law and a maxim is not a qualitative one (as two heterogeneous, mutually exclusive principles), but a question of the *scope* of the maxim (KpV V: 66). Although reason requires that maxims be universally valid, this does not imply that we ought to act only on "impersonal" considerations. Kant's position is the very opposite: the departing point of practical reason is a consideration arising from the perspective of the finite rational agent in question (that is, her maxim). Reason must then consider whether this subjective principle can *also* be considered universally valid. The idea of mutually exclusive personal and impersonal standpoints does not capture Kant's distinction between objective and subjective practical principles. This is Bernard Williams' mistaken assumption when he asks: "how can an I that has taken on the perspective of impartiality be left with enough identity to live a life that respects its own interests? If morality is possible at all, does it leave anyone in particular for me to be?" *Ethics and the Limits of Philosophy*, Harvard University Press, 1985. pp. 64f. The question is whether Kant would have taken Williams' objection seriously, since morality in Kant's account is never meant to suspend individuality. The role of morality is mainly to impose limitations on subjective maxims of action (maxims being the proper expression of one's individuality).

6. For a discussion of Kant's distinction between self-love (*Selbstliebe*) and self-conceit (*Eigendünkel*), see Stephen Engstrom's "The Concept of the Highest Good in Kant's Moral Theory," *Philosophy and Phenomenological Research*, Vol. 52, No. 4 (Dec. 1992), pp. 759–60.

7. Mary Gregor, *Laws of Reason*, Blackwell, 1963, p. 89.

8. Mary Gregor, op. cit., p. 86. Cf. Maria Schwartz, who differentiates a mere wish from a maxim as the decision (*Entscheidung*) to act in a certain way, in order to achieve an end. *Der Begriff der Maxime bei Kant*, LIT Verlag 2006, p. 13.

9. Locating moral worth in the principle of determination of the will, instead of in its outcomes, is a way of compensating for the fact that freedom, which has its own laws, must be realized in a world which has different laws: the laws of nature. There is no necessary agreement between the laws of the pure will and the laws of nature. This means that, even though a will may be formally good, success or failure to promote moral ends is contingent, i.e., it does not follow necessarily from the determination of the will by the moral principle. Given the contingent accordance of the laws of nature with the laws of freedom, it makes sense to base moral worth only on the determination of the will. However, it does not mean that morality has no purpose and that it accomplishes nothing in the world. As Kant stresses, human action is *end oriented* (GTP VIII: 280, note, GMS IV: 427 ll.24–25) and the will itself is defined as a type of causality (GMS IV: 446). The view that moral action according to Kant "has no purpose" lies in a misunderstanding of Kant's claim that a good will is good not because of what it accomplishes, but by its willing alone (GMS IV: 394). Kant clearly distinguishes between the *object* of an action (what is supposed to be effected with the action) and the *motive* of the actions (the determining ground of the will). The object of an action is always an end, whereas the motive of the action can be either the end itself (i.e. satisfaction of an inclination for that end) or the representation of

the action as being a duty. Moral worth is thus based on an evaluation of the motive of the action, which does not preclude the action having an object to be effected in the world. See Barbara Herman, "Leaving deontology Behind" in: *The Practice of Moral Judgment*, Harvard University Press, 1993.

10. As Bernd Ludwig notes, hypothetical imperatives are actually "hypothetically necessitating imperatives": they are *descriptive* statements about what the agent *already* wills and not normative statements about what the agent *ought* to want (the latter would be a categorical imperative). This explains why Kant says that hypothetical imperatives are unproblematic: they require no transcendental philosophy to account for their normative force. They are analytic propositions describing what the agent is already motivated to pursue. Ludwig, "Kants 'hypothetische' Imperative." In: Klemme, Ludwig, Pauen and Stark (eds.) *Aufklärung und Interpretation. Studien zu Kants Philosophie und ihrem Umkreis*. Königshausen & Neumann, 1999, pp. 122 and 156.

11. "Insofar as it is joined with one's consciousness of the ability to bring about its object by one's action it is called *choice (Willkür)*; if it is not joined with this consciousness its act is called a *wish (Wunsch)*. MS VI: 213.

12. "Freedom of choice *(Willkür)* is of a wholly unique nature in that an incentive can determine the will to an action *only insofar as the individual has incorporated it into his maxim* (has made it into the general rule in accordance with which he will conduct himself." This passage in REL VI: 24 is the explicit statement of the claim Henry Allison labelled Kant's "incorporation thesis" See also MS VI: 385. As Allison notes, Kant's incorporation thesis affirms spontaneity as an essential element of rational agency. Henry E. Allison, *Kant's Theory of Freedom*, p. 5.

13. I say "the most efficient or desirable way *in the eyes of the agent*," because an agent may not be *willing* to invest effort in the realization of her ends in the objectively most efficient way. This willingness will depend on her particular conception of happiness and of what (and to what *extent)* is worth pursuing, as I shall explain soon. Although considerations of efficiency in realizing the sum of the agent's ends are certainly in the *interest* of the agent who has these ends, I do not believe the end of happiness requires us to maximize satisfaction in a way that is independent of the agent's own sensibilities and desires. Less effort may be more important for her than greatest efficiency. In other words, we cannot derive binding *objective standards of rationality* from the need to pursue happiness, independently from the agent's preferences.

14. See MS VI: 380–1: "since the sensible inclinations of human beings tempt them to ends (the matter of choice) that can be contrary to duty, lawgiving reason can in turn check their influence only by a moral end set up against the ends of inclination, an end that must therefore be given a priori, independently of inclinations" [*Denn da die sinnlichen Neigungen zu Zwecken (als die Materie der Willkür) verleiten, die der Pflicht zuwider sein können, so kann die gesetzgebende Vernunft ihrem Einfluß nicht anders wehren, als wiederum durch entgegengesetzten moralischen Zweck, der also von der Neigung unabhängig gegeben sein muss*].

15. Cf. Andrews Reath's account of the principle of happiness as a *model of choice* as opposed to a hedonistic interpretation of Kant's psychology of non-moral choice.

See his "Hedonism, Heteronomy, and Kant's Principle of Happiness," In: *Agency and Autonomy in Kant's Moral Theory*, Oxford University Press, 2006.

16. The fact that human practical reason requires ends also explains Kant's introduction of the notion of *ends which are also duties* and the definition of Ethics as a "system of the ends of pure practical reason" in the *Metaphysics of Morals*. Since sensible inclinations tempt us to adopt ends contrary to duty, lawgiving reason can only check their influence by positing a *duty* to adopt certain moral ends. Although this morally required end must be given a priori, i.e., independently of inclinations, it must have some material basis besides the formal "determining ground" of choice. Assuming the concept of an end that is in itself a duty would thus "counteract" the motivational influence of ends arising only from sensible impulses (MS VI: 380–1). If morality did not positively require us to adopt certain ends, we would only have negative juridical duties and perfect duties to the self, that is, only duties of omission (juridical and ethical prohibitions), but *no duties of commission* (i.e., positive duties). However, this is something Kant thinks we "cannot will" as finite rational beings (GMS IV: 423). This is why we are required not only to avoid treating each other as a mere means to our ends but also *positively* treat each other as ends in ourselves (and promote the morally permissible ends of others, as far as possible. GMS IV: 430). See also chapter 4.

17. For discussions on the possibility of weakness of the will (*akrasia*) in Kant's account, see Thomas E. Hill Jr., "Kant on Weakness of Will." In: *Virtue, Rules, and Justice: Kantian Aspirations*, Oxford University Press, 2012 and Lawrence Pasternack, "Can Self-Deception explain Akrasia in Kant's Theory of Moral Agency?" *Southwest Philosophy Review*, Vol. 15, No. 1, 1999, pp. 87–97.

18. I adopt John Broome's distinction between reasons for action and normative requirements. A normative requirement is a relation, where one thing requires another. According to Broome, practical rationality does not consist only in acting for good reasons, but also in following normative requirements. Having an end requires you to adopt the necessary means, even if you have no reason to adopt the end in the first place. John Broome, "Normative Requirements." *Ratio*, 12: 398–419, 1999.

19. I will argue that this natural inclination can be clouded by depression, trauma or simply by the awareness of the impossibility of pursuing happiness on the long-term, for instance, when one has a deteriorating health condition, with no hope of improvement, as in the gout sufferer example of the *Groundwork*. See my discussion in chapter 3.

20. Kant defines prudence "in the narrowest sense" as "the skill in the choice of the means to one's own greatest well-being," that is, "the choice of the means to one's own happiness" (GMS VI: 416).

21. "Giving counsel does indeed contain necessity, but it can hold only under a subjective contingent condition, if this or that human being counts this or that as belonging to his happiness" (*Die Rathgebung enthält zwar Nothwendigkeit, die aber bloß unter subjektiver zufälliger Bedingung, ob dieser oder jener Mensch dieses oder jenes zu seiner Glückseligkeit zähle, gelten kann*).

22. Kant argues that prudence (*Klugheit*) is even less authoritative than rules of skill: they are counsels (*consilia*) rather than *commands* of reason, because happiness

is an ideal of *imagination* and not of reason (GMS IV: 418, ll.31 and 36). Only reason can bind objectively and thus command categorically.

23. In chapter 3, I argue that prudence constitutes no normative standard of rationality when the agent happens to lack the natural inclination for it (due to depression or some other interference with her natural interest in happiness). Only morality can issue an authoritative command to care about our own happiness when neglecting it would amount to a violation of a duty to the self. See also my "Local Desire Satisfaction and Long Term Wellbeing: revisiting the Gout Sufferer of Kant's *Groundwork*." *Belgrade Philosophical Annual*, issue 28, pp. 31–44, 2015.

24. Paton, *Categorical Imperative, a Study in Kant's Moral Philosophy*, p. 44.

25. Jens Timmermann, *Kant's Groundwork of the Metaphysics of Morals, a Commentary*, p. 22.

26. As their titles indicate, the three sections of Kant's *Grundlegung* consist of *transitions* from a given level of moral knowledge to a higher level of moral cognition: in section one, the analysis of the moral notions implicit in common moral cognition spells out the basic elements of moral philosophy (the concept of duty and the principle of morality); in section two, accounting for the notion of duty and its principle highlight the need for a metaphysics of morals conceived as a theory of *autonomy*; in section three autonomy leads to a "critique of pure practical reason" and the "deduction" of the moral law. Timmermann, *Kant's Groundwork of the Metaphysics of Morals, a Commentary*, p. 14. Whether the position of section three is consistent with or has been abandoned in the *Critique of Practical Reason* is a matter of debate in Kant scholarship. "Deduction" is a term Kant borrowed from law; it means the proof of a legal title or *Rechtsanspruch* (*quid iuris*) as opposed to a matter of fact (*quid facti*) (KrV B 99). The task of the deduction of the categories of the understanding was to demonstrate the "title" of these pure concepts as the conditions for the possibility of experience, since they are no empirical concepts (see KrV B 116). In the *Groundwork*, the task of the deduction was to show that the moral law is objectively binding and no "phantom of the brain (*Hirngespinst*). I would like to thank Eytan Celik for pointing out to me the legal meaning of the concept of deduction in one of our discussions.

27. Jens Timmermann concedes to Kant's critics that the teleological arguments in the passage "are amongst the weakest that can *actually* be found in the body of Kant's works." *Kant's Groundwork of the Metaphysics of Morals. A Commentary*, p. 22.

28. Kant defines the principle of natural efficiency as based on the (regulative) assumption that nature "does nothing in vain." This means that no organ or faculty will be found in an organized being "that is not also the most fitting for it and the most suitable" (GMS IV: 395).

29. Kant sees our ability to reason as a specifically human development which ultimately led to an alienation from our original animal instincts. Kant clearly draws upon Rousseau's account of the emergence of reason and shares, to some extent, Rousseau's pessimist views about empirical practical reason. There are striking similarities between Rousseau's *Discours sur l'inegalite* and Kant's *Conjectural Beginnings of Human History* (*Mutmaßlicher Anfang der Menschengeschichte*, 1786) and *Idea towards a Universal History from a cosmopolitan point of view* (*Idee einer allgemeinen Geschichte in weltbürgerlichen Absicht*, 1784) in regard to the development

of reason seen as a deterioration or break of humanity's prior harmonious unity with its animal nature.

30. Cf. Aristotle's "ergon" argument in the *Nichomachean Ethics*, 1097b: "Life seems to be common even to plants, but we are seeking what is peculiar to man."

31. In the *Groundwork,* Kant uses 'highest good' in the sense of *supreme* good (the good that conditions all other goods). See KpV V: 110 for a disambiguation of the concept of the highest good.

32. [*sie würde verhütet haben, daß die Vernunft nicht in practischen Gebrauch ausschlüge, und die Vermessenheit hätte, mit ihren schwachen Einsichten **ihr selbst den Entwurf der Glückseligkeit und der Mittel dazu zu gelangen auszudenken***, my emphasis].

33. In the *Groundwork*, happiness is also called an "idea" and an "indeterminate concept" (see GMS IV: 418). I will discuss these notions in the following.

34. As Onora O'Neil observes, "the opacity of the human heart and the difficulty of self-knowledge ... constitute the fundamental context of human action ... However, the underlying intentions that guide our more specific intentions are not in principle undiscoverable. Even when not consciously formulated, they can often be inferred with some assurance, if not certainty, as the principles and policies that our more specific intentions express and implement." "Consistency in Action" In: *Constructions of Reason. Explorations of Kant's Practical Philosophy*. Cambridge University Press, 1989, p. 85.

35. It is important to note that the opacity claim at the moral level does not apply to the *end* of an action, but only to the *motive* of our actions. Although we cannot know for certain our motivational states, we can nevertheless be aware of the ends we are pursuing. Ends can play a double role: they can be both the *object* (end) and *motive* (determining ground) of the action. Although the objects of an action are always ends, the same does not apply to the motives of actions. One can either act in order to satisfy some inclination or desire (in which case the end is both object and motive of the action) or adopt an end while being motivated by respect for the moral law, that is, from the motive of duty; although my action still has an end, the motive of my action is not what I intend to *effect*, but conformity to the *rational principle* I recognize as objective. Therefore, the opacity claim should not be extended to whole maxims as such, as is often done in the secondary literature. See Maria Schwartz, *Der Begriff der Maxime bei Kant*, p. 107.

36. As Kant stresses in the *Groundwork*, *Achtung* is merely "the consciousness of the *subordination* of my will to a law, without mediation of other influences on my sense" GMS IV: 401n.

37. Kant's account of feelings in his moral theory and theory of action does not support a realist account of "moral cognition." While *Achtung* makes us aware of the authority of morality, it does not provide its content. Consequently, it plays no *cognitive* role for morality as often affirmed. For a cognitivist approach to emotions, see Nancy Sherman, *Making a Necessity of Virtue. Aristotle and Kant on Virtue*. Cambridge University Press, 1997.

38. See Jean-Jacques Rousseau, Heinrich Meier (ed.), *Discours sur l'Inégalité / Diskurs über die Ungleichheit:* kritische Ausgabe des integralen Textes. Schöningh, 1997.

39. H. J. Paton, *The Categorical Imperative. A Study in Kant's Moral Philosophy*, p. 109.

40. Cf. Lewis White Beck, *A Commentary on Kant's Critique of Practical Reason*, p. 277.

41. See Pinheiro Walla, Alice, "Kant and the Wisdom of Oedipus," *Jahrbuch Praktische Philosophie in globaler Perspektive / Yearbook Practical Philosophy in a Global Perspective*, 2019, and Pinheiro Walla, Alice, "Kant's Moral Theory and Demandingness," *Ethical Theory and Moral Practice,* vol. 18, no. 4, 2015, pp. 731–43.

42. I discuss the relationship between prudence and moral requirements in chapter 4.

Chapter Two

Kant's Anti-eudaimonism in Moral Theory

In this chapter, I analyze a meta-ethical implication of Kant's conception of happiness: his rejection of happiness as a possible foundation for moral theory. I reconstruct Kant's understanding of an adequate moral theory, that is, a theory which takes seriously the common understanding of morality as unconditionally binding and does not attempt to refute or to correct this common moral understanding.[1] I explain why Kant thinks that only a theory of morality as autonomy can be such a moral theory and analyze Kant's criticism of other types of moral theory as *heteronomous*. Further, I argue that it is helpful to highlight the distinction between heteronomy and eudaimonism in order to better understand Kant's overall moral theoretical project. Although eudaimonist theories are also heteronomous, heteronomy refers to the question of the normative source of morality (whether it originates in the will or in some other source). Eudaimonism, in turn, is a specific theory about moral motivation. As a conclusion, I argue that Kant's anti-eudaimonism in moral theory does not rule out human happiness as a task imposed on practical reason by our finite natures, but only seeks to establish its proper place when it comes to formulating an adequate moral theory. One should therefore not mistake Kant's concerns in regard to moral *theory* for a hostile attitude toward human happiness in our lives and moral practice.

In the next two sections, I will reconstruct Kant's theory of morality as autonomy of the will and his doctrine of the imperatives. This is required for understanding his criticism of eudaimonist theories and the way moral theories that fail to recognize the autonomy of the will falls short of what moral theory should accomplish, namely a theory of *moral* obligation.

1. KANT'S METHOD OF MORAL INQUIRY: WHY THE PRINCIPLE OF MORALITY MUST BE PURELY FORMAL

In the first edition of the *Critique of Pure Reason* (1781), Kant still defended the view that the existence of God and the immortality of the soul were necessary for moral motivation. As he explained in the "Canon of pure Reason,"

> (. . .) everyone also regards the moral laws as commands, which, however, they could not be if they did not connect appropriate consequences with their rule a priori, and thus carry with them promises and threats [*Verheißungen und Drohungen*]. This, however, they could not do if they did not lie in a necessary being, as the highest good, which alone can make possible such a purposive unity. (A 811–2/ B839-40)

Although in 1781 Kant recognized the need to conceive the moral law as a purely rational principle, he still believed it could not be motivating of itself, and that God had to be presupposed as a source of external incentives to moral conduct. Kant's great innovation, the doctrine of *Autonomy*, only appears from 1785 with the *Groundwork of the Metaphysics of Morals* when he realized that assigning such a practical role to the metaphysical ideas of God and immortality of the soul was inconsistent with critical philosophy and undermined the unconditional character of morality. The following passage of the *Groundwork* can thus be understood as a criticism not only of "earlier systems of moral philosophy," but as a criticism of Kant's own position prior to the doctrine of Autonomy:

> Now if we look back on all the efforts that have ever been undertaken to detect the principle of morality to this day, it is no wonder why one and all they had to fail. One saw the human being bound to laws by his duty, but it did not occur to anyone that he is subject *only to his own* and yet *universal legislation* (. . .) For if one thought of him just as subject to a law (whichever it may be), it had to carry with it some interest as stimulation or constraint because it did not as a law arise from *his* will, which instead was necessitated by *something else*, in conformity with a law, to act in a certain way. (GMS IV: 432–3)

The new doctrine of Autonomy, therefore, rendered parts of the first edition of the *Critique of Pure Reason* outdated; the ideas of God and immortality of the first edition of the *Critique of pure Reason* were then "transferred" into the "Dialectic of pure practical Reason" of the *Second Critique* and reinterpreted as practical postulates required by the idea of the *highest good* and no longer by the moral law itself. *Achtung für das Gesetz* or respect for the law is now considered the only incentive compatible with the moral principle.[2] In the *Critique of Pure Reason* Kant identifies the necessary aspects in our cognition of the world with the *a priori* structure of the mind (the pure forms of space and time and the pure categories of the understanding) and distinguished this structure from the *content* of empirical perception, as what is *contingent* or given in our experience; similarly, in his moral philosophy, Kant accounts for the necessity of moral requirements by carefully differentiating between what belongs to the formal structure of a rational will and what is empirically given or *material* in human volition: our desires, needs and inclinations. The moral principle must be conceived as a purely formal, rational principle, which *practical reason gives itself*. In order to escape heteronomy, practical reason must not rely on any external source of authority: it must be practical for itself, that is, the source of both its principle and of its motive. Unconditional (non-subordinated) goodness, Kant argues, requires autonomy of the will.

> An absolutely good will, whose principle must be a categorical imperative, will therefore, indeterminate with regard to all objects, contain merely the form of willing as such, and indeed as autonomy; i.e., the fitness of the maxim of every good will to make itself into a universal law is itself the sole law that the will of every rational being imposes upon itself, without underpinning it with any incentive or interest as its foundation. (GMS IV: 444)

The idea of morality as self-imposed rational necessity sounds an oxymoron at first. If something is "only" self-imposed, it may seem to imply that it is in our power to suspend the imposition. If so, self-imposed morality is anything but *necessary*.[3] However, this difficulty disappears if we consider that the principle Kant has in mind is meant to be constitutive of rational volition as a form of causality. The law the will gives itself is not a principle the agent arbitrarily decided to follow or which she cannot understand. While desires and inclinations are contingent (a particular agent may happen to have a certain inclination or not) the principle of morality can be presupposed for all agents, regardless of their particular differences as concrete individuals, because it *structures* rational volition (in other words, it is the principle *we must follow* if we are to will in accordance with reason).[4]

Kant's method in the first two sections of the *Groundwork* is analytical: it aims to identify the highest principle of morality through an examination of the concepts implicit in common moral understanding and popular moral philosophy, respectively. From the analysis of the concept of duty, Kant is able to spell out the conditions the moral principle must satisfy and arrives at the formulation of the moral principle (GMS IV 392 and 445). The third section of the *Groundwork* engages with the *justification* of this principle (its title or authority to oblige unconditionally), and must now proceed *synthetically*. This is because the analytic method can only explain what is already included in the concept of duty. Since the authority of morality cannot be based on an existing desire of the agent (since morality is supposed to bind us unconditionally), a moral maxim of action must be connected "a priori and necessarily" with the concept of a rational will. While the rational requirement to take the means to a desire the agent decides to satisfy (and consequently adopts as an end) can be analytically derived from the notion of having an end ("whoever wants an end must also want the necessary means," GMS IV: 417), the moral principle must be connected to the notion of a rational will independently of any desire or interest we may happen to have. This connection cannot be derived analytically from the concept of duty or from the concept of a rational will. Therefore, a *synthetic* method is needed to show that the idea of a moral principle determining volition independently of any desires is not a mere "phantom of the brain." The principle of morality is an *a priori* synthetic practical proposition, that is, "(. . .) a practical proposition that does not derive the willing of an action analytically from willing another that is already presupposed (**for we have no such perfect will**) but connects it immediately with the concept of the will of a rational being, as something that is not contained in it" (GMS IV: 420, my emphasis).

In the first section of the *Groundwork*, Kant argues that the concept of *duty* contains the notion of a *human* good will. While a holy will i.e., a will which is not tempted by the demands of empirical nature would amount to a *purely* good will, Kant notes that a human will is prey to subjective limitations and hindrances arising from the agent's needs and inclinations (GMS IV: 397, ll. 7–8). Because the will of human beings is not a pure will and is also subject to incentives from our empirical nature, morality is not the only course of action open to choice and does not infallibly determine our conduct.[5] While a holy will cannot be other than moral, the verdicts of morality are experienced by human beings as *imperatives*: they *command* that we subordinate the satisfaction of our desires to the principle of a good will. Morality for finite rational beings is therefore a matter of *duty*: an imperative implies a *rational necessitation* (*Nöthigung*) of the will (*Willkür*) of the agent (GMS IV: 413), which is however not infallible.

There are different modes of rational "necessitation," i.e., the way in which an action can be regarded as binding or required. Kant distinguishes between two main categories of imperatives: *hypothetical* and *categorical* imperatives (GMS IV: 414–17). Action based on inclination (*Neigung*) is always directed at something other than the principle of action itself: the agent desires an object outside the will. There is no reason for us to do or strive for something, unless this object or end is somehow considered good or desirable by the agent; the fact that we feel attracted to it or expect pleasure from it is usually a prima facie reason to consider an object good. Action based on inclination thus *presupposes* the representation of something regarded as good, which then determines the principle of action; but the goodness of the end in question is based on the agent's nature, her preferences, tastes and interests. For agents who do not desire to become concert pianists, the commandment to take the means to that end and, among other things, invest in a good piano teacher and practice at least eight hours a day does not apply. For this reason Kant stresses that hypothetical imperatives cannot provide the foundation of morality. If they were, agents would be justified in ignoring moral requirements whenever they lack an inclination to act as morality commands. In order to preserve the unconditional character of moral commands, we must thus posit a principle of action that can be considered unconditionally good, i.e., binding *regardless* of the inclinations of the agent.[6] It follows from the concepts of a good will and of moral obligation that the principle underlying morality can only be a *categorical* imperative (IV: 420–21). Further, the categorical imperative can only be understood as a *self-legislated principle*, i.e., a principle which not only *originates* within the agent herself, but is also *imposed* by the agent's own practical reason on herself as a phenomenal being.[7] The principle of morality is therefore identical with the principle of *autonomy* of the will. "Autonomy of the will is the characteristic of the will by which it is a law to itself (independently of any characteristic of the objects of willing). The principle of autonomy is thus: not to choose in any other way than that the maxims of one's choice are also comprised as universal law in the same willing" (GMS IV: 440).

It is possible to infer the underlying principle of the will from the specific way the object of volition relates to the faculty of willing (GMS IV: 441). If the starting point of deliberation is a desire for an object, then the law determining the will of the agent can only be a hypothetical imperative requiring the agent to take the means to satisfy an end she already has. The will in question cannot be seen as unconditionally good, since its principle is a conditional one: acting on that principle is considered good by the agent if it satisfies her inclination. Without the interest the agent has in the action, there can be no rational requirement to take the means to anything. In order to see ourselves as unconditionally bound by morality, we must conceive morality as *universally binding*. But this is only possible if each agent can regard herself as the *author* of the moral law and if the law can at the same time provide its own motive.

In the next section, I will focus on Kant's account of *respect for the law*, as his explanation of how one can be motivated to act by pure practical reason, without the "help" of existing desires of the agent. Once we understand the way Kant conceived the task of moral theory, I will proceed to discuss Kant's criticism of heteronomous and eudaimonist moral theories.

2. MORAL COGNITION AND MORAL MOTIVATION: RESPECT FOR THE LAW (*ACHTUNG FÜR DAS GESETZ*)

One can be influenced to act by different motives such as fear of punishment, the need to be admired by others or the desire to be loved. The fact these motives may determine our actions is contingent upon our having these motives in the first place. From the perspective of practical rationality, however, acting on these given empirical motives does not entail a necessary (absolute) requirement. Rational necessity is associated with the *a priori*, *formal* aspect of volition. However, as Kant himself acknowledges, human volition also involves a material aspect.

Kant assumes that it is a matter of common experience (intelligible even to children) that reason can sufficiently motivate us to act in a certain way despite the concurrence of opposite inclinations. The undeniable influence of pure practical reason on the will can be simulated by a simple thought experiment, in which we contemplate an action motivated by the moral law alone.

> (. . .) the commonest observation shows that when one represents an action of righteousness (*eine Handlung der Rechtsschaffenheit*)—as it was performed with a steadfast soul, without aiming at any advantage, in this world or another, even under the greatest temptations of need or of enticement—it leaves far behind and obscures every similar action that was even in the least affected by an alien incentive, that it elevates the soul and stirs up the wish to be able to act like that too. Even children of intermediate age feel this impression, and one should never represent duties to them in any other way. (GMS IV: 411n)

Why do we feel "elevated" when we imagine an action genuinely motivated by the moral law? Why does Kant think that this elevated feeling can be seen as a confirmation that pure practical reason is able to move us? Essential for Kant's doctrine of autonomy is his conception of moral motivation as respect for the law. Respect for the law is the emotional response to the subordination of our will to the moral law and thus inseparably connected with our awareness of the authority of the moral law (KpV V: 80). While *awareness* of the authority of the moral law (that I am under obligation) can be called the *objective* side of one's moral experience, the *feeling* of respect for the law is its subjective counterpart or the effect of that representation on our sensuous nature. The imaginative experiment Kant suggests is a device for making us aware of this psychological mechanism.

> The moral law which alone is truly objective (. . .) excludes altogether the influence of self-love on the supreme practical principle and infringes without end upon self-conceit (. . .). Now, what in our own judgment infringes upon our self-conceit humiliates (. . .). If something representing a determining ground

of our will humiliates us in our self-consciousness it also awakens respect for itself insofar as it is positive and a determining ground. Therefore the moral law is even subjectively the ground of respect. (KpV V: 74)

Since what infringes upon our inclinations must have an influence on our sensitivity, it is possible to infer *a priori* how the moral law can give rise to the feeling of respect for the moral law. Our recognition of duty has an initially *negative*, painful effect (it "humiliates" our inclinations), followed by a *positive,* elevating or inspiring effect, which is *Achtung* proper. The consciousness of duty both *mortifies* and *elevates* the agent (as a natural being and as a rational agent, respectively). This is how the moral law can be both the formal determining ground of the will and its subjective determining ground, that is, incentive (*Triebfeder*) (KpV V: 75). Unlike pathological feeling, respect for the law does not precede the determination of the will i.e., it is not what "forces" us to take the moral perspective in the first place. As Kant puts it,

> Respect for the law is not the incentive **to morality;** instead it is morality itself (*nicht Triebfeder zur Sittlichkeit sondern sie ist die Sittlichkeit selbst*) subjectively considered as an incentive inasmuch as pure practical reason, by rejecting all the claims of self-love in opposition with its own, supplies authority to the law, which now alone has influence. (KpV V: 76, my emphasis)

The moral feeling neither serves to *evaluate action* nor is it the *basis* for adopting the moral law. It is instead an incentive to make the moral law into our maxim of action (KpV V: 76). Kant's distinction between *Wille* and *Willkür*, which I discussed in chapter 1, can help us understand the motivational function of *Achtung*. Although Kant is not always consistent in his use of terminology and that *Wille* can mean three different things in his writings (the legislative part of the will, the executive part of the will and the desiderative faculty as a whole), *Wille* is *stricto sensu* the legislative faculty of the will.[8] As the *effect* of pure practical reason on our sensuous nature, respect for the law enables the transition from pure practical reason (*Wille*) to choice and action proper (*Willkür*): it mediates between *moral judgment* and the *execution* of the verdict of moral judgment.[9] Because respect is an inevitable result of our recognition of the moral law, it can be felt both in our judgment of our own conduct and of the conduct of other agents. In a moving passage of the *Second Critique*, Kant argues that human reason necessarily "bows" at the recognition of moral uprightness in the conduct or character of other people (insofar as we may infer it from what we experience of other agents), whether we like it or not. Respect "is a tribute we cannot refuse to pay to merit" regardless of cultural and social norms establishing the higher status of some individuals over others.

> Fontenelle says: "*I bow before an eminent man, but my spirit does not bow.*" I can add: before a humble common man in whom I perceive uprightness of character in a higher degree than I am aware in myself, my spirit bows, whether I want it or whether I do not and hold my head ever so high, that he may not overlook my superior position. (KpV V: 77)

Respect for the law is a *painful* and mortifying experience insofar as it makes us aware of the imperfections of our own character or lesser moral worth compared to virtuous agents. Respect thus presupposes the agent's awareness that the claims of some of her desires and inclinations to determining her conduct are *rejected* by reason. This judgment has an *impact* on our sensible nature (whose claims are "reduced to nothing" in face of the authority of the moral law). Agents who are both rational and finite (and psychologically healthy) are thus able to recognize and be motivated accordingly by the moral law.[10] This is all Kant needs to show in order to prove that there can be morally motivated action: he tells us a story about how his account of morality is psychologically plausible and draws upon our own experience as agents to confirm his account. However, although respect for the law must inevitably accompany our moral judgments, it does not infallibly *cause* us to act morally. Since respect for the law humiliates our self-love and is always a painful experience, an agent may choose to restore her hurt self-love and reject the moral incentive. Failing to act as reason commands can thus be understood as a way to compensate for the frustration imposed by morality on the "dear self."

From this reconstruction, one can now better understand Kant's assumptions about what a moral theory must achieve: moral theory must neither attempt to change our common understanding of morality nor dismiss it as being false or as an illusion. Common moral understanding clearly distinguishes between genuine moral motivation and self-interested actions; this must be taken seriously by any moral theory that deserves the name. Although we still don't know for sure whether the way we conceive morality is not a mere "phantom of the brain," our moral concepts and moral practice are evidence that we conceive morality as unconditionally authoritative, that is, as the source of *categorical* imperatives for action. Kant concludes that only the categorical imperative can be the principle underlying the reasoning of an agent who understands morality as being unconditional. I have explained why the categorical imperative must be understood as being a *self-legislated* principle and the will as *autonomous*. I have also reconstructed

Kant's conception of moral motivation and how pure respect for the law can lead us to act morally.

In the next section, I will discuss Kant's criticism of what he calls *heteronomous* theories of morality and the way this criticism relates to Kant's anti-eudaimonism in moral theory. What precisely is Kant criticizing in heteronomous theories? Kant seems to assume that all theories which do not conceive the will as autonomous and morality as self-legislated are based on hypothetical imperatives and consequently reduce morality to desire satisfaction and consequently to the pursuit of *happiness*. I will argue that Kant's criticism does not amount to the view that all heteronomous theories subordinate morality to the pursuit of happiness (a view which the proponents of non-hedonistic heteronomous theories would regard as a crude misunderstanding on Kant's part), but that subordinating morality to happiness is a necessary *implication* of the way heteronomous theories are conceived. In other words: Kant does not assume that all heteronomous theories *aim* to subordinate morality to happiness, but that this subordination nevertheless *follows* from their adopted model of the will.

3. IN SEARCH OF AN ADEQUATE MORAL THEORY

Kant's criticism of heteronomous theories is part of a central task of the *Groundwork of the Metaphysics of Morals* and the *Critique of Practical Reason*: determining what an adequate moral *theory*, that is, a theory that takes seriously the common understanding of morality as unconditional obligation, must involve. Only a moral theory which does not presuppose any material incentives for the normativity of moral requirements, that is, which relies on a purely *formal* principle, can account for the unconditional character of morality. If a given moral theory is not based on the idea of the autonomy of the will, it necessarily presupposes an empirical interest of the agent in order to be authoritative and can only generate hypothetical imperatives (*tertium non datur!*). The commands of morality in this case would be those of *instrumental* rationality.

> If it is in *anything other* than the fitness of its maxims for its own universal legislation, hence if—as it goes beyond itself—it is in a characteristic of any of its objects that the will seeks the law that is to determine it, the outcome is always *heteronomy*. Then the will does not give itself the law, but the object by its relation to the will gives the law to it. This relation, whether it rests on inclination, or on representations of reason, makes possible hypothetical imperatives only: I ought to do something because I want something else. (GMS IV: 441)

Kant claims that all previous moral theories without exception have based morality on a heteronomous conception of the will: they all conceived the relation between the will and its principle as a *conditional* one, whether they were aware of it or not. Kant calls those principles which are based on a heteronomous conception of the will *spurious* (*unächt*) principles of morality (GMS IV: 441). In the *Groundwork* he distinguishes between heteronomous theories based either on *empirical* or on *rational* principles (i.e., theories based on the principle of *happiness* and on the principle of *perfection*, respectively). In the second *Critique,* however, after having claimed in Theorem II that *all* material principles must be understood as subordinating the will under the principle of happiness or self-love (KpV V: 22), Kant replaced the distinction "empirical" *versus* "rational" principles of the *Groundwork* by the distinction "subjective" *versus* "objective" principles in his table of material determining grounds in the principle of morality (KpV V: 40).[11] The principle of happiness is no longer the specific principle of empirically based principles, but ultimately of *all* heteronomous theories.

Theorem II makes Kant's classification of heteronomous theories somewhat difficult to understand: how exactly should we understand the claim that all heteronomous (non-autonomy based) theories are subordinated to the principle of happiness? *Is Kant blatantly reducing every non-autonomy based moral theory to hedonism?* Kant's claim in Theorem II does not amount to a charge of *direct* hedonism. The principle of happiness, on which all heteronomous moral theories are said to rely, is just the general name given to a *material* principle of morality. Hedonistic *stricto sensu* are only those theories which *directly* regard feelings of pleasure and displeasure as the source of moral commands. The seeming "reductive" argument of Theorem II is that unless a moral theory bases morality on the autonomy of the will, it will be at least *indirectly* but always inevitably committed to a hedonistic conception of the *human will*. This is quite distinct from positing that the agent in these theoretical models always has a *direct* hedonistic motivation to act. Bearing this in mind, I shall focus on the differences between the heteronomous theories Kant discusses and analyze why Kant thinks it possible to bring such heterogeneous theories under a common denominator. I shall therefore adopt at times the terminology of the *Groundwork* and speak of empirical and rational theories as well as perfectionist theories in order to keep apart theories directly based on the principle of happiness (hedonistic theories proper) and those indirectly based (all other heteronomous theories).

Moral theories which *explicitly* adopt happiness as the principle of morals are the obvious examples of heteronomous theories. Less obvious are, in order of degree, moral sense theory (GMS IV: 442, ll. 22ff. and fn.) and rationalist theories basing morality either on a theological or on the ontological idea of perfection (GMS IV: 443). In the *Second Critique*, Kant associates names to heteronomous theories: theories directly based on the principle of happiness (i.e., on an *internal subjective* principle) are explicitly linked with Epicurus and Hutcheson, divine command theory (based on an *external objective* principle) with Crusius and other theological moralists and perfectionism (relying on a *internal objective* principle) with Christian Wolff and the Stoics (KpV V: 40–41). In the second *Critique* Kant also adds theories based on *external* subjective principles, which base morality on social customs and institutions, such as on education (after Montaigne)[12] and on the civil constitution (after Mandeville).[13] However, given his peculiar formulation in the original ("der Erziehung" *nach* Montaigne," "der bürgerlichen Verfassung" *nach* Mandeville" etc.) Kant's table could be interpreted as classifying broader *types* of theories. These theories would primarily stand for a theoretical model "in the manner of philosopher x," and not specifically for the theories explicitly named in the text (which merely *represent* these models). Mary Gregor's translation ("according to x") may suggest instead that Kant was targeting specific thinkers.

Kant's critics have been appalled by Kant's boldness in reducing different moral theories to a single model of the will: all these theories are heteronomous.[14] However, Kant admits that some heteronomous theories are superior than others, even if they all ultimately fail to provide an adequate account of morality. At the lowest end of the scale are theories which openly rely on the empirical interests of the agent for the normativity of morality and are thus explicitly heteronomous. *Overtly heteronomous theories* place the source of the agent's interest in morality either in something internal to the agent, i.e., her desire for happiness or her "moral sense,"[15] or in an external source such as conformity with the custom of a given society or obedience to the ruler (for prudential reasons). Since all these theories clearly presuppose empirical incentives for morality to be normative, there is no doubt that they cannot account for the source of unconditional moral requirements in Kant's perspective (see previous sections one and two of this chapter). Other theories, in contrast, are heteronomous in a less evident way. These theories put forward an *objective* conception of goodness, and therefore clearly distance themselves from overtly heteronomous theories. However, on closer inspection, these theories turn out to be *implicitly* heteronomous: although they *aim* to establish the foundations of morality on a rational idea instead of an empirical incentive, they fail to fully appreciate the *implications* of their adopted moral principles.[16] Christian Wolff, who was extremely influential in Kant's time,[17] identified morality with the requirement to increase one's perfection.[18] Human beings not only ought to strive for greater perfection (i.e., they have a duty to develop the abilities latent in human nature), but also experience satisfaction from becoming more perfect. Although increasing one's perfection comes with an increase in pleasure in one's perfection in Wolff's account, we can only perfect ourselves by increasing the clarity and distinctiveness of our thoughts, which can only be done through the study of metaphysics.[19] Wolff's perfectionism is therefore not an empirical but a *rational* moral theory and relies on an *internal* rational principle. Another rationalist theory criticized as heteronomous is the divine command theory of Christian August Crusius, which bases moral obligation on the will of God, more precisely, on God's ends and perfections.[20] We can have knowledge of God's will *a priori*, through certain innate moral ideas. Although these innate ideas have their *seat* in human reason, their *source* is in God.[21] Because Crusius' theory bases the authority of morality on a source outside the human will, it relies on an *external* rational principle.

Because Wolff and Crusius base morality on a rational idea (the idea of perfection) and not on the contingent desires of agents, they are superior to empirically based theories and seem to come closer to providing an adequate account of moral obligation. However, perfectionist ethical theories are still unsatisfactory in Kant's view. Firstly, the *ontological* concept of perfection is empty and indeterminate and consequently unfit to guide action (GMS IV: 443). As Kant explains in the second *Critique,* the theoretical concept of perfection only means the completeness of a thing (*Vollständigkeit*) either in a transcendental sense (as a thing of its kind) or in a metaphysical sense (as a thing in general), which "does not concern us here" (KpV V: 41). On the other hand, if we use the concept of perfection in a *practical* sense (which *would* concern us) perfection must be understood as the fitness or adequacy (*Tauglichkeit oder Zulänglichkeit*) of a thing for all sorts of purposes. While God is perfection in the *substance* (infinite perfection, consisting of infinite attributes), human beings' "perfections to-be" are their latent talents and skills (which presuppose ends to which these perfections are means). We are thus obliged to develop these perfections, according to Wolff. But one could wonder why developing these talents and skills is superior to other kinds of perfection (for instance, to becoming a perfect criminal mind or an accomplished egoist). Kant's criticism is that Wolff is taking for granted the very moral concepts he is supposed to explain and therefore argues in a circle (GMS IV: 443). Kant's argument is that to escape circularity, Wolff would have to posit a conception of the good that is *higher* than perfection itself. The fact that Wolff *didn't do this* emerges as an inconsistency or, worse, as an intellectual dishonesty on his part, since his theory actually *requires* it.

Crusius' *theological* concept of perfection fares even worse than Wolff's perfectionism. Since we have no direct intuition of God, we must recognize God's will through reason, more precisely, through our *moral* concepts. So whatever we cognize through our moral concepts is the will of God and authoritative for us. But we may ask ourselves why we must obey the will of

God (instead of someone else's or one's own will). The answer is that the will of God is the content of our moral concepts. But why should we heed to our moral concepts in the first place? Because our moral concepts express the will of God. Crusius' perfectionism is therefore also circular. In order to overcome this circle, Crusius would have to posit something *beyond* our moral concepts and the will of God: namely, the *fear of divine punishment*. However, positing a powerful, revengeful God would be "the foundation to a system of morals quite opposed to morality" (GMS IV: 443).[22]

Perfectionist theories merely *evade* the question of the source of moral obligation. And if they seek to overcome circularity, they will inevitably fall prey to heteronomy: they will need to subordinate morality to some material incentive. Perfectionist theories are thus heteronomous in a less obvious way; although they understand the need for a rational basis to morality, their adopted moral principle commits them to the opposite view of the human will. Kant's subtle point is that if perfectionists were to be consistent, they would *necessarily* abandon the concept of perfection and embrace Kant's own conception of morality as *self-legislated*. Only autonomy can help us escape circularity or subordinating morality to a material incentive. The reader will wonder if Kant is begging the question by assuming that there is no alternative foundation for morality other than autonomy of the will. I will discuss this question in section four ("Kant's Anti-eudaimonism as an *Error Theory* of Moral Motivation").

In the next two sections, I will draw a distinction between Kant's criticism of heteronomy and of eudaimonism. Although eudaimonist theories are also heteronomous theories, I will argue that they are primarily *theories of moral motivation*, rather than a theoretical model of the will.

4. HETERONOMY AND EUDAIMONISM

> (. . .) the moral egoist limits all ends to himself, sees no use in anything except that which is useful to himself, and as an eudaimonist puts the supreme determining ground of his will simply in utility and his own happiness, not in the thought of duty. For, since every other human being also forms his own different concept of what he counts as happiness, it is precisely egoism which drives him to have no touchstone at all of the genuine concept of duty, which absolutely must be a universally valid principle.—That is why all eudaemonists are practical egoists. (Anthr VII: 130)

Kant brings out two important, related concepts: that of a *practical egoist* and of a *eudaimonist*. In the *Anthropology*, Kant addresses three kinds of egoism: *logical*, *aesthetic* and *practical* egoism. The common feature of all three forms is the view that one's own opinions, tastes and desires ought to be made into absolute standards of evaluation without taking into account that other agents may have *different* opinions, tastes and desires. The egoist takes his own personal stance as definitive and irrefutable and does not attempt to engage in a dialogue with others which could lead her to revise and improve her own beliefs, or at least to tolerate different views. Egoism in general therefore consists in the *refusal to acknowledge the different perspectives of others* in regard to their held beliefs and opinions, their judgments of taste and their conception of happiness.

A practical egoist only recognizes her own interests as unconditional reasons for action. The practical egoist does not want to acknowledge that other people may have different interests and desires from her own. This attitude may be a strategy to preserve the primacy of her own interests over the interests of others: were the practical egoist to acknowledge that people have different desires and ends from his own, she would have to acknowledge that happiness is not an adequate basis for moral requirements after all and that neither she nor anyone else can make her own happiness the ultimate "measure of all things." As Kant puts it, egoism can only be opposed by *pluralism*, as the way of thinking (*Denkungsart*) in which one does not behave as if one comprised the *whole world* but acts instead as a mere *citizen* of the world (*Weltbürger*).[23] Acknowledging the plurality of interests, viewpoints and tastes necessarily leads to the conclusion that we can only base rational requirements on a universally binding foundation, and that happiness cannot offer that foundation.

Applied to moral theory, "eudaimonism" is Kant's technical term for theories of moral motivation based on the assumption that all agents *are practical egoists*. As I will explain, Kant regards eudaimonism merely as a theoretical model of moral motivation. In fact, he is skeptical about its applicability in real life moral practice.[24] At first sight eudaimonism seems to be a synonym for heteronomous ethical theory. However, I will explain why it is important not to conflate both terms. Although eudaimonist theories are also heteronomous theories, the specific difference between eudaimonism and heteronomy in general is that the eudaimonist makes a mistaken theoretical claim about moral *motivation* while heteronomy is a specific *model of the will*.

Schneewind observes that the main targets in Kant's criticism of "spurious principles of morality" are drawn from the moral philosophy of his time. Although Kant mentions Epicurus, this allusion was probably aimed at contemporary theorists who broadly followed what Kant identified as the pattern of Epicurean ethical theory, and not at Epicurus himself.[25] Several of Kant's contemporaries would fit this description, for instance, Johann August Eberhard, Christian Garve and Gottlob August Tittel. Eberhard identified the task of ethical theory with "the art of human happiness," i.e., with the skill in the promotion of individual happiness. As Eberhard writes, "if there is for human beings an art of happiness: so there must be also a concept of the principles of this art. The science of these principles is the doctrine of morals or morality in a broader sense."[26] In his commentary of Kant's *Groundwork*, Tittel defended the principle of happiness as the true principle of morals. Kant's theory, Tittel argues, is "mystic" in which Kant's notion of duty functions as a surrogate for the love of God.[27] Despite his appreciation of Garve's person, Kant was deeply irritated by his lack of systematicity and uncritical eudaimonist assumptions in his *Philosophical Remarks and Treatises* of 1783 [*Philosophische Anmerkungen und Abhandlungen*]. It is possible that a derogatory remark about Cicero in *The Conflict of the Faculties*, namely, that repeating Cicero's name to oneself could be used as a "stoic remedy" against insomnia (SF VII: 107), expressed Kant's opinions about *Garve's* (rather soporific) version of Cicero instead of his views of Cicero himself.[28]

Although Kant charges *all possible principles of morality* (apart from his own) with the same mistake, namely, they all presuppose an object of the will from which the principle of morality is derived, it is noteworthy that Kant does not explicitly mention Plato and Aristotle in his criticism of heteronomous theories in the published works. This may be considered as evidence that Kant's primary concern was to criticize the philosophical methods of his contemporaries: Stoicism, Epicureanism and Cicero were the main "trends" in the popular moral philosophy of Kant's time. He was eager to formulate what he perceived as the common "pattern" of moral inquiry behind these theories of moral obligation so that he could debunk them in a systematic way (see KpV V: 64 ll. 6–8).

References to Plato's and Aristotle's ethical theories can be found in Kant's lectures; for instance, Plato's idea of the highest good is described as a mystic Ideal, consisting of the union of human beings with the highest being. It is a "fanatical ideal," which has strong parallels with the Christian Ideal of Holiness (Moral Kaehler, 17–18). Aristotle's doctrine of the mean is considered next to Wolff's principle "*fac bonum et omite malum*" as a tautological principle of morals (Moral Kaehler, 60–61). The view that the doctrine of the mean does not offer appropriate guidance for practical deliberation reappears three times in the *Doctrine of Virtue*, namely, in conjunction with Kant's discussion of whether there are degrees and consequently limits to virtue.[29]

Considering Kant's scattered remarks on Plato and Aristotle in his lectures and published writings, it seems plausible to assume that Kant would or could have subsumed Plato *and* Aristotle under "objective" or "rationalist" theories, with Aristotle adopting an *internal* (empty and indeterminate) rational principle in the fashion of Wolff, while Plato would exemplify an *external* rational principle similar to Grotius. I do not see evidence for the assumption common among the critics of Kant's anti-eudaimonism that Kant would have treated Aristotle as holding an empiricist, *hedonist* theory.[30] In KpV V: 127n. Kant argues that the difference between Aristotle and Plato is only in regard to the *origin* of our moral concepts [*Aristoteles und Plato unterschieden sich nur in Ansehung des Ursprungs unserer sittlichen Begriffe*]. The emphasis on the *origin* of moral concepts corresponds to the distinction between *external and internal* principles in Kant's table of material principles of morality, and not to whether a principle is subjective (empirical) or objective (rational).

Kant was nevertheless careful to stress the merits of Ancients over the lack of method of his contemporaries. I believe that this is where Kant tries to do justice to the Ancient philosophy historically.

> The **ancients** revealed this error [heteronomy, A.P.W.] **openly** by directing their investigation entirely to the determination of the concept of the highest good, and so of an object which they intended **afterwards** to make the determining ground of the will in the moral law, an object which can much later—when the moral law has first been established by itself and justified as the immediate determining ground of the will—be represented as object to the will, now determined a priori in its form. (. . .) The **moderns**, with whom the question of the highest good seems to have gone out of use or at least have become a secondary matter, hide the above error (as in many other cases) behind indeterminate words; but one can still see it showing through their systems, since it always reveals heteronomy of practical reason, from which an a priori moral law commanding universally can never arise. (KpV V: 64)

Although the ancients erroneously presupposed the idea of the highest good to be prior to the moral principle, they did not only acknowledge their fundamental assumptions but also were consistent in their application. The moderns, in contrast, no longer used the notion of a highest good as the Ancients understood it, but continued to defend a material conception of morality in an obscure, veiled way. Therefore, although the moderns *claim* to be pursuing a different project, they are equally defending a heteronomous conception of practical reason. The only difference is that they lack the philosophical rigor of the Ancients and are thus *worse* philosophers. Kant accuses his "syncretistic age" with "dishonesty and shallowness" and with being suited to a public "satisfied with knowing something of everything and nothing as a whole." By contrast, he praises the Greek schools for their intellectual rigor, and recognizes their philosophical excellence regardless of their ultimate failure to provide an adequate basis for moral theory (KpV V: 24).

Schneewind argues that Kant anticipated the now widespread understanding of the project of modern ethics as the search for objective directives for action as opposed to the query about the ideal of the good life of ancient ethical theory. In their search for the highest good, ancient ethical theories did not explicitly formulate the question of the principle and foundations of morality. The project of the ancients consisted mainly of accounting for the relationship between happiness and virtue as elements which must be unified under the concept of the highest good. Moral theory as the search for the principle of morality is an invention of modernity. Although this distinction has traditionally been credited to Henry Sidgwick in his *Methods of Ethics*,[31] several passages of Kant's lectures and *Nachlass* indicate that Kant was well aware of this distinction,[32] which he then integrates into his criticism of eudaemonist theories. However, contra Schneewind, Kant seemed to believe that the projects were different only on the *surface*. Kant holds importantly that although the moderns sought to establish the principle of morality rather than the highest good, they still followed the method of inquiry of ancient eudaemonist theories. In Kant's view, only his own moral theory achieved a genuine rupture between ancient and modern moral theory.

5. KANT'S ANTI-EUDAIMONISM AS AN *ERROR THEORY* OF MORAL MOTIVATION

In this section, I will further elaborate the distinction between heteronomy and eudaimonism and argue that Kant provides an *error theory* of eudaimonist theories: while conscientious moral agents must regard themselves as acting from the motive of duty, eudaimonist theories lead them to form mistaken beliefs about their own motivations for acting morally, namely, that the self-contentment they experience as a result from their compliance with duty is the driving motive of their conduct. "Eudaimonism" is therefore a theory of moral motivation, while "heteronomy" refers specifically to the question of the *normative source of morality*.

The most straightforward requirement that a moral theory must observe is that it does not make the bindingness of moral requirements conditional on an pre-existing desire of the agent: in Kant's terminology, it must not make the principle of morality into a hypothetical imperative. A theory which conceives morality as a mere *means* to desire satisfaction is thus the clearest case of a dissatisfactory moral theory. *Heteronomous* moral theories derive the binding force of morality from a source *other than the agent's will*. This requires positing a *material* conception of the good from which moral requirements are derived. From the perspective of *moral motivation*, in turn, positing "the good" as an entity outside the will can only motivate us if we have an *interest* in that object. This interest however can only be a desire of the agent.

> Pleasure that must precede one's observance of the law in order for one to act in conformity with the law is pathological and one's conduct follows the *order of*

nature; but pleasure that must be *preceded* by the law in order to be felt is in the *moral order*. – If this distinction is not observed, if *eudaimonism* (the principle of happiness) is set up as the basic principle instead of *eleutheronomy* (the principle of freedom of internal lawgiving), the result is the *euthanasia* (easy death) of all morals. (MS VI: 378)

Kant believes that there is only one alternative to this inadequate kind of moral theory: autonomy or self legislation. In the above passage of the *Metaphysics of Morals*, Kant also uses the term *eleutheronomy*.[33] A moral theory which deserves the title must have two basic features: its proposed principle of morality must have unconditional authority (it must be authoritative independently of whether the agent has an inclination for the action) and be self-legislated (it must not come from an alien source other than the will itself). Insofar as Kant stresses the *purity* of the moral principle, we must distinguish between *eleutheronomy* (principle of freedom of internal lawgiving, a purely *formal* principle) and *eudaimonism* (the principle of happiness, a *material* principle). When instead the emphasis is on the *source* of the moral principle, it is helpful to think of *autonomy* (the law arises from the agent's own will) as opposed to *heteronomy* (the law is given from a source other than the agent's will). Kant's criticism of eudaimonism in moral theory is aimed at all theories which presuppose *material principles* as the basis of morality, not only those theories which are traditionally called eudaimonist (i.e., ancient ethical theories). That Kant's criticism of eudaimonism is primarily a criticism of *a conception of moral motivation* (and not of ancient eudaimonist theories themselves) can be confirmed by the passages in which the term "eudaimonism" is used.

> It is remarkable that expected advantage and honour cannot produce the strong resolution to imitate virtue, as the pure image of virtue in itself; and even if one is secretly driven by the prospect of honour, one does not act alone for the sake of that honour but only insofar as we can make ourselves believe, through a secret persuasion, that the principles of virtue had brought it about. We must hide from our own eyes the mechanism of our own self-serving drives. [*Es ist besonders, daß der vorgestellte Nutzen und Ehre nicht die so starke entschließung der Tugend nachzuahmen hervorbringen können, als das reine Bild der Tugend an sich selbst; und selbst, wenn man im Geheim durch Aussicht auf Ehre getrieben wird, thut man es doch nicht um dieser Ehre willen allein, sondern nur so ferne wir uns durch eine geheime Überredung einbilden können, die Grundsätze der Tugend hätten es hervorgebracht. Wir müssen uns vor unsern eignen Augen die mechanic unserer eigennützigen Antriebe verbergen.* Refl. 6619, *Phasen* κ-λ, around 1769-Autumn 1770, my translation]

Kant's assumption in the passage is that it is impossible to view our actions as virtuous unless we see ourselves as acting for the sake of duty. Also the simplest minds understand that there is a clear *conceptual* difference between self-interested action and genuine moral motivation, which alone has moral worth (GMS IV: 397), even if in practice it may be difficult to be certain about our true motives. Most people understand that advancing one's self-interest is a matter of prudential rationality and distinct from genuine moral conduct.[34] Actions have *moral worth* when one can assume they were done for the sake of duty (although they need not be against morality when performed for other motives).[35] As Kant stresses in the passage, even if one is driven secretly by honour or some other empirical interest, one would have to *hide* the mechanism of one's self-interested impulses from one's own eyes in order to believe that the action was moral. In other words, *awareness* of empirical motivation cannot be reconciled with the agent's own evaluation of her action as moral. This explains the self-deceit agents employ for concealing the impurity of their motives from their own eyes. However, it is not only possible to cheat ourselves about our true motivation, when it is impure: it is also possible to be deceived about the actual *purity* of our moral motives, since we can never be sure of having acted from a moral motive (GMS IV: 404).[36]

> After it has been made so clear that the principle of duty is derived from pure reason, one cannot help wondering how this principle could be reduced again to a *doctrine of happiness*, **though in such a way that a certain moral happiness not based on empirical causes**—a self contradictory absurdity—has been thought up as the end. It happens in this way. When a thoughtful man has overcome incentives to vice and is aware of having done his often bitter duty, he finds himself in a state that could well be called happiness, a state of contentment and peace of soul in which virtue is its own reward.—Now a *eudaimonist* says: this delight, this happiness is really his motive for acting virtuously. The concept of duty does not determine his will directly; he is moved to do his duty only *by means of* the happiness he anticipates.—But since he can expect this reward of virtue only from consciousness of having done his duty, it is clear that the later must have come first, that is, he must find himself under obligation to do his duty before he thinks that happiness will result from his observance of duty and without thinking of this. A eudaemonist's etiology involves him in a *circle*. (MS VI: 377–8)

Eudaimonism presupposes a specific conception of the *etiology* of moral action (which "representations" lead us to act morally). In Kant's view, eudaimonist theories mistakenly take the motivation to moral action to be something other than the thought of duty. Eudaimonist theories can thus lead the most virtuous agents to misconceive their own motivation to act. It is possible that a conscientious agent who acts for the sake of duty comes to believe her real motivation is actually the pursuit of happiness. Kant believes this misconception results from the application of a wrong moral theory to one's own moral understanding while one's moral practice could remain intact.

Kant's criticism of eudaimonist theories provides an *error theory* of moral motivation. Because the awareness of having done one's duty is connected to a feeling of satisfaction with oneself, it is possible to take this feeling to be the cause of one's action in the first place. This mistake is "sublime" insofar as it humbly diminishes the worth of one's conduct in one's own eyes and is still consistent with morality (as opposed to considering one's self-interested conduct to be an expression of virtue). Kant attributes such a mistake to the "virtuous" Epicurus (KpV V: 116). Kant assumes that Epicurus needed the principles of his theory for explanation purposes, but not for action (KpV V: 115, ll. 28–9). Epicurus rightly recognized that moral self-approval or lack thereof has a great impact on the wellbeing of virtuous agents and also that moral self-approval is itself a kind of pleasure. However, Epicurus mistakenly identified this pleasure (moral self-approval or contentment with oneself) with the *motive* of moral action.[37]

According to Kant, Epicurus presupposed a virtuous disposition in all agents, since true moral contentment can only be experienced by genuinely virtuous agents, i.e., agents who already act for the sake of duty. But Epicurus is faced with two difficulties: it doesn't make sense to recommend "peace of mind" as an incentive for action to someone who is not already virtuous (since this peace of mind can only come from virtue in the first place) nor to a virtuous agent (since the latter has no need of this incentive in order to act morally). Therefore, the *etiology* of eudaimonism (its account of the *cause* of moral action) is circular: one is motivated to do one's duty by the expectation of happiness in the form of moral contentment with oneself; however, one can only experience contentment with oneself if one does one's duty for its own sake. The circle disappears once we form a correct idea of moral motivation:

> (. . .) There is always present here the ground of an error of subreption (*vitium subreptionis*) and, as it were, of an optical illusion in the self-consciousness of what one *does* as distinguished from what one *feels*—an illusion that even the most practiced cannot altogether avoid. The moral disposition is necessarily connected with consciousness of the determination of the will *directly by the law*. Now, consciousness of a determination of the faculty of desire is always the ground of a satisfaction in the action produced by it; but this pleasure, this satisfaction with oneself is not the determining ground of the action. (KpV V: 116)

Kant has been criticized for reducing all ancient eudaimonist theories to a hedonistic, purely instrumental model of action. Since Kant seems to defend a kind of psychological hedonism for all actions which are not done for the motive of duty, he seems to have uncritically assumed that all eudaimonist theories must be hedonistic. Some commentators have argued that Kant's anti-eudaimonism in moral theory applies only to those eudaimonist theories which reduce happiness to pleasure, such as the Epicurean theory.[38] Since not all ancient eudaimonist theories equated eudaimonia with desire satisfaction, it follows that Kant did not rule out the plausibility of non-hedonistic eudaimonist theories. However, Terence Irwin objected that Kant has an incorrect understanding of Epicurus.[39] Kant's anti-eudaimonism would be flawed also in this regard. However, Kant also offers arguments against eudaimonist theories that are independent from an interpretation of eudaimonist theories as hedonistic.[40]

> But there is **also** a contradiction in this subtle reasoning (*aber es ist in dieser Vernünftelei* **auch** *ein Widerspruch*). For on the one hand [the agent] ought to **fulfill his duty** (**seine Pflicht beobachten**) without first asking what effect this will have on his happiness, and so on moral grounds; but on the other hand can **recognize that something is his duty** (**etwas für seine Pflicht anerkennen**) only by whether he can count on gaining happiness by doing it, and so in accordance with a *pathological* principle, which is the direct opposite of the moral principle. (MS VI: 377–8, my emphasis)

Besides circularity, Kant also sees a positive *contradiction* in eudaimonist theories (*aber es ist in dieser Vernünftelei* **auch** *ein Widerspruch*). Kant's point is not merely that the eudaimonist model would imply holding beliefs that are incompatible with our moral practice (although this is also the case), but that on this approach moral judgment and moral motivation must fall apart. Insofar as the real *incentive* for moral action can only be the motive of duty, a *virtuous* eudaimonist would indeed *act* from the motive of duty, even if she has a wrong conception of her motivation. The only difference between the eudaimonist and Kant's account is at the level of practical *judgment*: the eudaimonist can only recognize her duty with the reference to her happiness. In other words, motivational and justificatory reasons fall apart. The contradiction Kant calls our attention to is the puzzling idea that in eudaimonist theories the alleged objective good, that is, happiness, is not able to justify and motivate our conduct at the same time without undermining itself. If we were to take the eudaimonist justification of moral action also as an *incentive* for action, we would never have virtuous action (action for its own sake) and consequently would not be happy. This makes the claim of eudaimonia to objective goodness contradictory.

Regardless of Kant's often inaccurate interpretation of Greek ethical theories, his decisive objection against all eudaimonist theories is that we cannot have non-derivative, objective goodness unless we assume the autonomy of the will. The problem is thus not simply whether a theory views morality as a means to happiness or not, but ultimately its underlying conception of the will. This shared shortcoming is what enables Kant to treat such heterogeneous theories under the same heading with some plausibility.

One could object that Kant is presupposing his own conception of morality as autonomy in his rejection of all "spurious" ethical principles. If so, Kant's criticism of non autonomous moral theories is question begging. Although some passages suggest that Kant is begging the question in this way, Schneewind points out that Kant also gives independent arguments against individual heteronomous principles which do not rely on Kant's own conception of morality as autonomous,[41] although he concedes that Kant is for the most part simply presupposing his own account of morality.

In a passage of the *Second Critique*, Kant explicitly mentions the importance of not taking a conception of morality for granted as a way to avoid *reductionism* in moral theory; although he conceives his own method as the only possible way to escape this danger, his argument for this conclusion does not beg the question.

> Even if we did not know that the principle of morality is a pure law determining the pure will, we would at least have to leave it *undecided* in the beginning whether the will **has only empirical or also pure determining grounds a priori**, in order not to assume principles quite gratuitously (*gratis*); for, it is contrary to all basic rules of philosophic procedure to assume as already decided the foremost question to be decided. (KpV V: 63, my emphasis)[42]

That the will can be determined by empirical incentives is unproblematic and can easily be taken for granted. However, it is *also* possible for it to be determined by some non-empirical principle. We become aware of this possibility after a careful analysis of the concept of duty, which is a reality in our moral practice. The problem with moral theories which uncritically start with material principles is that they completely *exclude* the possibility of exploring this other possibility, which should at least be left open, as a methodological requirement. The key is in Kant's use of *"also,"* which I have emphasized in the quoted passage. Kant's argument is that while starting from a material principle of morals excludes purely rational determination before we may even consider it as a possibility, starting the other way around, as Kant does (from the analysis of moral concepts to the formulation of the principle of morality) enables us to maintain *both* the possibility of *pure* practical reason and of *empirical* practical reason. In other words, while in the material approach we *only* have empirical practical reason, in Kant's approach we also have the possibility of pure practical reason, even though Kant still has to show that morality is no "phantom of the brain." Note that this is not a claim about Kant's own conception of morality as autonomy, but a claim about the *method* of moral theory. "Since (. . .) an object in accordance with concepts of the good and evil had already been made the basis of all practical laws, while the former, without a law preceding it, could be thought only by empirical concepts, the possibility of even thinking of a pure practical law was already removed in advance" (KpV V: 63–4).

The "paradox" of the method of the *Critique of Practical Reason* is that in order to define the moral categories of good (*Gut*) and bad (*Böse*) as opposed to weal (*Wohl*) and woe (*Übel*), as categories relating to our wellbeing, we must start with the formal principle and not with an independent, material conception of goodness. We are then able to accommodate both categories of goodness (moral and empirical), whereas starting with a material conception of goodness undermines the possibility of pure practical reason before it has been investigated. This argument regarding the method of moral inquiry "explains at once the occasioning ground of all the errors of philosophers with respect to the supreme principle of morals" (KpV V: 64). The mistake Kant attributes to all his predecessors is thus not simply that they failed to adopt a conception of morality as autonomy (although this is also the case), but rather that their method of philosophical inquiry itself *precludes* the possibility of regarding morality from a different perspective other than empirical reason. Kant's criticism of spurious principles is thus not based on a presupposition that his own moral theory is the only appropriate one, but on a consideration of the *method* we should adopt in moral inquiry.

Interestingly, all rejected heteronomous principles are reintegrated into Kant's system after the purity of the moral principle has been established. External subjective grounds reappear as the duty of decorum and obedience to authority (Anthr. §14 VII: 151–3), there is an indirect duty to cultivate moral feeling (MS VI: 399–400, KpV V: 38 ll. 33–8) and one's own happiness (GMS IV: 399, KpV V: 93 ll. 15–9), as well as a duty to the self to develop one's own perfection (MS TL VI: 385). The will of God also reappears as an ideal of the holiness of the will (KpV V: 158 ll. 25–6).[43] Here Kant shows again that instead of excluding possibilities, his moral theory can make space for different aspects of the ethical life, including the insights and views advocated by non-autonomous moral theories. Kant's moral theory therefore aims to be more inclusive than its alternatives.

6. REDEFINING THE HIGHEST GOOD: KANT'S NON-REDUCTIVE ACCOUNT OF THE VALUE OF HUMAN HAPPINESS

> The human being is a being with needs, insofar as he belongs to the sensible world, and to this extent his reason certainly has a commission from the side of his sensibility which it cannot refuse, to attend to its interest and to form practical maxims with a view to happiness in this life and, where possible, in a future life as well. But he is nevertheless not so completely an animal as to be indifferent to all that reason says on its own and to use reason merely as a tool for the satisfaction of his needs as a sensible being. (KpV V: 51)

Kant did not dismiss the Ancient idea of the highest good, which he posits as the object of the will once the moral principle has been established independently of it. However, in order to reflect the priority of the formal principle of morals over material conceptions of the good, Kant had to *redefine* the relationship between the constitutive elements of the highest good, i.e., the relation between morality and happiness.

Despite Kant's emphasis on the unconditional value of morality and consequently on the subordination of considerations of happiness to the moral law, he does not attempt to reduce human happiness to satisfaction arising from one's moral conduct. The relation between morality and happiness in Kant is one of *subordination* and not a reductive one. The non-reductive character of Kant's doctrine of the highest good becomes clear in Kant's criticism of the Stoic and Epicurean conception of the highest good. Kant argues that both schools failed to understand virtue and happiness as heterogeneous elements and sought to reduce one element to the other "in accordance with the rule of identity" (KpV 5:111). In Kant's view both Stoics and Epicureans are *reductionists* about the human good: they failed to recognize a proper place either for morality or for human happiness in the idea of the highest good. While Epicureans reduced morality to happiness, the Stoics reduced happiness to morality. The difference between Stoics and Epicureans lies only in which concept each school took to be the fundamental one.

> Of the ancient Greek schools there were, strictly speaking, only two, which in determining the concept of the highest good followed one and the same method insofar as they did not let virtue and happiness hold as two different elements of the highest good and consequently sought the unity of the principle in accordance with a rule of identity; but they differed, in turn, in their choice of which of the two was to be the fundamental concept. The Epicurean said: to be conscious of one's maxim leading to happiness is virtue; the Stoic said: to be conscious of one's virtue is happiness. For the first, *prudence* was equivalent

to morality; for the second, who chose a higher designation for virtue, *morality* alone was true wisdom. (KpV V: 111)

The ancients were unanimous that the *summum bonum* was a simple concept and their disagreement was only about which element ought to be regarded as the *analysandum*. In contrast, Kant rejects an identity relation between virtue and happiness. The highest good must be understood instead as a synthetic connection between two heterogeneous, irreducible components. Although the Stoics were closer to Kant's position, in which they at least correctly accounted for morality as unconditional, Kant argues that the feeling of self-approval we derive from the consciousness of our moral conduct cannot replace the human need for happiness (KpV V: 88). Thus, Kant has two specific objections to the ancients: one is their philosophical method which posits a conception of the highest good as a starting point for moral theory; the other is their wrong conception of the relationship between morality and happiness for finite rational beings.

Terence Irwin was puzzled by Kant's criticism of the Stoics. On the one hand, Kant argued that the Stoics failed to account correctly for the status of the moral law since they presuppose a *material* conception of the good; on the other hand, Kant also claimed that the Stoics were *correct* in the way they account for morality. Kant seemed to be holding two contradictory views about the Stoics.[44] While acknowledging that the Stoics correctly recognized the unconditional value of morality, Kant's objection is that the Stoics reached a correct result for the wrong reasons. In the same way as other ancient eudaimonists, the Stoics departed from a material conception of the good, which poses a methodological problem. Although the possibility of pure moral motivation is not excluded in the Stoic account, the Stoic conception of the highest good nevertheless seems contingent and thus arbitrary: since the concept of the good is posited *before* we can know the moral principle, it is no more *compelling* than the Epicurean conception of the good, despite the Stoic's correct conclusions about the priority of virtue over human happiness. Further, the Stoic also has a wrong conception of human nature. The human need for happiness cannot be satisfied by moral self-approval alone. The Stoic is thus a reductionist about human happiness.

While in the *Analytic* of the *Critique of Practical Reason* Kant dealt only with the object of *pure* practical reason (the moral law), in the *Dialectic* section he analyzes the so-called whole object of practical reason (the morally determined will and its material ends). However, in contrast to the *Dialectic* of the *Critique of Pure Reason*, which dealt with theoretical *illusions* arising from reason's own tendency to seek the absolute, the Dialectic of the *Critique of Practical Reason* deals with an idea which has "practical reality." Although the highest good cannot be the determining ground of moral volition (it would undermine the pure character of morality if it were), the highest good must be thought as a necessary object for the *moral disposition* of human beings, given their finite, sensible nature.[45] It is the idea of a second-order end that unifies all other human ends into *a system* and so must reflect not only the formal principle of a rational will, but also the *material* interests of finite rational beings.

Kant redefines the function of the highest good in moral theory by making this notion the object of pure practical reason although he rules out its role as a *determining ground of the will*.[46] This is only possible because he does not start with a conception of the highest good, but derives the highest good from his conception of the moral law. The inclusion of happiness in the notion of the complete good follows from the requirement to regard persons as ends in themselves, i.e., to take into account *all* the permissible ends of rational agents, not only her moral ends. Insofar as we are *finite* rational beings, happiness also matters to us and is morally relevant.

The possibility of integrating happiness and moral worth constitutes the highest good for human beings, as creatures who are both needy and rational. Connecting moral worth and happiness in a relation of *cause and effect* is not only something a partial spectator would think desirable, but something that even an impartial spectator would regard as necessary. A rational finite creature who needs happiness and *has made herself worthy of happiness* should, it seems, be made happy in accordance to her moral worth. This is because if the agent is an end in herself, *all* her ends must be taken into account, not only her moral ends. To treat someone as an end in itself in Kant's conception implies not only respecting the person in a negative sense (not harming or impairing her) but also in a positive sense, as adopting her morally permissible ends as our own. If a person has a good will, all her ends will be good in principle. There might be ends which are *contingently* impermissible, say, because they externally hinder another person's rights, but the point is that from the perspective of her moral attitude (her *Gesinnung*), all her non-moral ends are morally apt to be realized. Although one might be worthy of happiness, moral worth alone does not also guarantee that one's permissible ends will be realized.

The relation between moral worth and happiness in this world is purely *contingent*. It obeys two different kinds of laws: while moral worth is determined by laws of freedom, happiness depends on natural laws being favorable to our ends. Since virtue and happiness are heterogeneous concepts, being in possession of the one is not *ipso facto* being in possession of the other (KpV 5:113). Although the antinomy of practical reason is that the moral law *commands us to realize the highest good in the world,* since there is no such thing as a causal connection between moral worth and happiness, all we can do is to make ourselves worthy of happiness.[47]

In this chapter, I have clarified Kant's reasons for excluding happiness as a foundation of morality. I have also argued that one should not confuse Kant's claims about moral theory with a hostile attitude toward human happiness in general and an attempt to eradicate happiness from the moral life. In the next chapter, I shall analyze the relationship between the legitimate pursuit of one's own happiness and duty, namely, indirect duties and perfect duties to the self.

NOTES

1. One could question whether common human understanding indeed regards morality as unconditionally binding, as Kant believes. I shall set this problem aside and will take Kant's assumption for granted for the purposes of the chapter.

2. The doctrine of Autonomy still required deeper changes in Kant's theory than he was initially aware of in the *Grundlegung*. Bernd Ludwig argues that in the first *Critique* Kant still understood the problem of human freedom as a task of theoretical or speculative reason and that this view is taken for granted in *Groundwork* III (see for instance GMS IV: 461). Speculative reason shows that freedom is *possible* (*möglich*), i.e., that it is not incompatible with causal determination in the phenomenal world. But freedom is also *necessary* (*notwendig*) from a practical perspective, since we cannot consider ourselves responsible for our actions without at the same time viewing ourselves as belonging to an intellectual world (IV: 452). Ludwig argues that the "two-worlds" doctrine of the *Groundwork* presupposes Kant's conception of *apperception* defended in the first Paralogism of the first edition of the *Critique of pure Reason* (Substantiality). According to this conception, since the "I" (*das Ich*) is the subject on which all thoughts are inherent as predicates, one must necessarily *see oneself* as a substance and one's thoughts as predicates of that substance (KrV A: 394). That "the soul is a substance" is thus a valid proposition. However, since we can have no *intuition* (*Anschauung*) of the "I," we should refrain from claiming that the soul is immortal (A 350). A similar idea is present in *Groundwork III*: from the consciousness of one's freedom, Kant tries to derive one's "membership" in an intellectual world, a world we nevertheless "cannot know" (GMS IV: 452). It was Pistorius, Kant's "forgotten reviewer" (to use the title of B. Gesang's book *Kants vergessener Rezensent*) who made Kant aware that his doctrine of freedom of 1781/5 implicitly committed him to dogmatic Rationalism and consequently to an *uncritical* theory of the subject. It is only with the "fact of reason" of the *Second Critique* that Kant succeeded in consistently living up to the standards of his own critical philosophy. There, it is no longer our awareness of ourselves as rational beings, but the consciousness of the fact that we are *necessitated by the moral law,* in other words, *that we are under obligation,* that opens up an intelligible dimension to human beings. The awareness that we *ought* to do something is what enables the insight that *we can do otherwise*, that is, that we can do other than what inclination and self-interest dictate (see Kant's famous gallows example in KpV V: 30). This is how in Kant's moral theory "ought

implies can." This famous expression has been rightly associated with Kant's moral theory but often misunderstood. It does not mean that duty can only command actions we are *able* to perform (as a matter of fact) but that our *freedom* is revealed to us once we are aware of moral obligation. The possibility of freedom is now wholly based on pure *practical* reason. See Bernd Ludwig, "Was weiß ich vom Ich? Kants Lehre vom Faktum der reinen praktischen Vernunft, seine Neufassung der Paralogismen und die verborgenen Fortschritte der Kritischen Metaphysik im Jahre 1786." in: Mario Brandhorst, Andree Hahmann, Bernd Ludwig (eds) Sind wir Bürger zweier Welten? Freiheit und moralische Verantwortung im transzendentalen Idealismus. Felix Meiner Verlag, Hamburg 2012, S. 155–194.

3. Kant's idea of autonomy has been misunderstood in many ways. See for instance Anscombe's famous criticism that Kant's law centered conception of morality is unintelligible without a divine legislator or supreme power. G. E. M. Anscombe, "Modern Moral Philosophy," *Philosophical Review*, 33, 1958 and Iris Murdoch's identification of autonomy with an ideal of satanic self-assertion, impersonated a century before Kant by Milton's Lucifer. Murdoch also sees a continuous development from Kant's ideal of the autonomous agent to Nietzsche and to existentialism. Iris Murdoch, *The Sovereignty of the Good*, Routledge, 1970, p. 80. For discussions of these readings, see Onora O'Neill, "Action, Anthropology and Autonomy," In: *Constructions of Reason. Explorations of Kant's Practical Philosophy*. Cambridge University Press, 1989, pp. 75–7 and Wood, *Kant's Ethical Thought*, Cambridge University Press, 1999, chapter 5, notes 1 and 2, p. 373.

4. As Onora O'Neill puts it, "the Categorical Imperative is the supreme principle of reasoning not because it is an algorithm either for thought or for actions, but because it is an indispensable strategy for disciplining thinking or action in ways that are not contingent upon specific and variable circumstances (. . .) The supreme principle of reason both emerges from and disciplines human thought, action and communication. There is no gap between reason and autonomy because the authority of reason is grounded in autonomy." "Reason and Autonomy in Grundlegung III," In: *Constructions of Reason. Explorations of Kant's Practical Philosophy*. Cambridge University Press, 1989, p. 59.

5. Timmermann notes that from a moral perspective, having more options than what morality commands is a *shortcoming* rather than an advantage of human beings over a holy will, which cannot do other than follow pure practical reason. *Kant's Groundwork of the Metaphysics of Morals. A Commentary*, p. 177.

6. This assumption prompts the question whether there is such a thing as an "unconditional good," and if there is, whether it can *motivate* us to act regardless of the fact that we may have no inclination for it. This type of scepticism (scepticism about the motivational power of *pure* practical reason) is addressed in *Groundwork III*, where Kant explains *how reason can determine the will* (the so-called "deduction" or demonstration of the authority of moral law to bind unconditionally). However, the question of how we can take an *interest* in morality in the absence of inclinations remains unanswered. The later *Faktumslehre* of the second *Critique* makes both the "deduction" the moral law and the latter question about the possibility of moral interest redundant.

7. See Timmermann, *Kant's Groundwork of the Metaphysics of Morals. A Commentary*, p. 114.

8. Jens Timmermann, *Sittengesetz und Freiheit. Untersuchungen zu Immanuel Kants Theorie des freien Willens*, Walter de Gruyter 2003, pp.196–198.

9. Cf. Paul Guyer, "Moral Feelings in the Metaphysics of Morals." In: Lara Denis (ed.), *Kant's Metaphysics of Morals, A Critical Guide*, Cambridge University Press, 2010, p. 134. While Kant treats respect for the law in the Groundwork as a mere epiphenomenon (GMS IV: 401n), his more extensive discussion of this concept in the second Critique emphasizes its *causal role* for moral action. It is however only in the *Metaphysics of Morals* that Kant presents a sophisticated version of the moral feeling as an "aesthetic precondition" for the receptivity of duty.

10. I offer a detailed discussion of Kant's account of the moral feeling in the *Doctrine of Virtue* in chapter 3.

11. See Lewis White Beck, *A Commentary on Kant's Critique of Practical Reason*. University of Chicago Press, 1960, pp. 103–4.

12. The reason for the identification of Montaigne's theory with a principle of education is not obvious. Kant seems to interpret Montaigne as defending the variability of human customs and ultimately of morality in different environments. As White Beck stresses, there is "only a short step from 'custom' to 'education' especially when education is fallible and variable (because not guided by an ideal of universal validity) as Montaigne regarded it." Montaigne however, not only stressed but also provided a *criticism* of the variability of customs. See Essays, Book II, chap. XII and L. White Beck, *A Commentary on Kant's Critique of Practical Reason*, pp. 104–5, including footnote 31.

13. White Beck argues that Kant's attribution of this view to Mandeville can be explained with reference to Mandeville's famous aphorism: "moral virtues are the political offspring which flattery begot upon pride" (*An Inquiry into the Origin of Moral Virtue*, 1723, In: Selby-Bigge, *British Moralists*, vol. II, p. 352). L. White Beck, *A Commentary on Kant's Critique of Practical Reason*, p. 104, footnote 29.

14. As Allison notes, a similar reduction can be found in the First Critique: "Kant's procedure here constitutes a precise parallel to his procedure in the *Critique of Pure Reason*. Just as he there subsumed all noncritical positions under the generic label "transcendental realism" to which he juxtaposed his own "transcendental idealism," so now in the *Groundwork* and in the *Critique of Pure Reason*, he subsumes all opposing moral theories under the label "heteronomy" and contrasts them with his own conception of "autonomy." Henry Allison, *Kant's Theory of Freedom*, p. 99.

15. Even Lewis White Beck strongly criticizes Kant for reducing moral sense theory to the desire for one's own happiness. He argues that the British moralists took care to distinguish between gaining pleasure (hedonistically) and the disinterested pleasure we feel when doing or contemplating a morally good action. He thinks that Kant's objection that "one must already value the importance of what we call duty" in order to be susceptible to the moral feeling begs the question and that pleasure in this case could be considered "a mark of ethical value." L. White Beck, *A Commentary on Kant's Critique of Practical Reason*, pp. 105–6. I think White Beck misunderstands Kant's point here.

16. I owe the distinction between overtly and implicitly heteronomous theories to discussions with Jens Timmermann.

17. Wolff's practical philosophy (*philosophia practica universalis*) was compressed into a textbook by his student Alexander Baumgarten, which Kant used in his lectures.

18. "I need the notion of perfection for dealing with morals. For, when I see that some actions tend toward our perfection and that of others, while others tend toward our imperfection and that of others, the sensation of perfection excites a certain pleasure [*voluptas*] and the sensation of imperfection a certain displeasure [*nausea*]. And the emotions [*affectus*], by virtue of which the mind is, in the end, inclined or disinclined, are modifications of this pleasure and displeasure; I explain the origin of natural obligation in this way . . . From this also comes the general rule or law of nature that our actions ought to be directed toward the highest perfection of ourselves and others." Wolff's Letter to Leibniz, dated 4 May 1715. In: *G.W. Leibniz: Philosophical Essays*, translated by Roger Ariew and Daniel Garber, Hackett Publishing Company, 1989, pp. 231–32.

19. Wolff's perfectionism is based on an intellectualist view of the mind, which takes all its contents to be cognitions (sensations and feelings included). By increasing the mind's cognitive ability, we are also increasing our ability to realize the good. Since pleasure results from perfection, perfecting ourselves amounts to an increase in happiness. See Henry Allison, *Kants Groundwork of the Metaphysics of Morals, A Commentary*. Oxford University Press, 2011, pp. 42–3.

20. Christian August Crusius, *Anweisungen vernünftig zu leben: darinnen nach Erklärung der Natur des menschlichen Willens die natürlichen Pflichten und allgemeinen Klugheitslehren im richtigen Zusammenhange vorgetragen werden* (1744), Gleditsch, 1767, §174.

21. Following Allison, I apply Rüdiger Bittner's distinction between *Sitz* and *Ursprung* of moral concepts. As Bittner argues, it is not enough for a moral theory to be based on *a priori* concepts; non-heteronomous moral theory requires that moral concepts have not only their *seat* but also their *origin* in reason. Crusius falls short of this requirement. Rüdiger Bittner, "Das Unternehmen einer Grundlegung zur Metaphysik der Sitten," In: Otfried Höffe (ed.), *Grundlegung zur Metaphysik der Sitten. Ein kooperativer Kommentar*. Vittorio Klostermann, 1989, pp. 17–8. See also Allison, *Kant's Groundwork to the Metaphysics of Morals. A Commentary*. Oxford University Press, 2011, p. 26 for a criticism of Bittner's objections to Kant's reading of Crusius.

22. See J. B. Schneewind's reconstruction of Kant's objection to rationalist theories in his "Kant against the 'spurious principles of morality'" In: Jens Timmermann (ed.), Kant's *Groundwork of the Metaphysics of Morals. A Critical Guide*. Cambridge University Press, 2009, pp. 151–2.

23. "*Dem Egoism kann nur der Pluralism entgegengesetzt werden, d. i. die Denkungsart: sich nicht als die ganze Welt in seinem Selbst befassend, sondern als einen bloßen Weltbürger zu betrachten und zu verhalten.*" Anthr. VII: 130.

24. I draw here on White Beck, who argues that practical reason as such is never dialectical, and that all illusions relating to practical reason are those of moral *theory*,

not of morality itself. L. White Beck, *A Commentary on Kant's Critique of practical Reason*, The University of Chicago Press, 1960, p. 241.

25. As Kant stresses in a lecture, the pathological principle of morality, consisting in the satisfaction of all one's desires would be "beastly" Epicureanism (*der Viehische Epicureanismus*). "True" Epicureanism, however, consists of a *pragmatic* principle, which only seems to be intellectual (*Dieses Schein intellectuale principium*). This consists of using the understanding as a means to the satisfaction of one's inclinations. Although still based on inclination, "true" Epicureanism seems to be more rational than the undiscerning desire satisfaction of beastly Epicureanism (see Moral Kaehler). Kant does not bring this distinction into the published works, which may be taken as a sign that his target was not the historical Epicurus after all.

26. *Wenn es für den Menschen eine Kunst der Glückseligkeit gibt: so muss es auch einen Inbegriff von Regeln dieser Kunst geben. Die Wissenschaft dieser Regeln ist die Sittenlehre oder die Moral in weiterer Bedeutung.* Eberhard, *Sittenlehre der Vernunft*, Nicolai, 1781, p. 1, my translation.

27. G. A. Tittel, *Über Herrn Kants Moralreform*, Aetas Kantiana 285, Pfähler, 1786, "An den Leser," p.6.

28. Garve translated and commented Cicero's *De officiis* in 1783. As Kant explains in the *Conflict of the Faculties*, the soporific effect of repeating Cicero's name is due to the representations associated with it (*Nebenvorstellungen*). The speculation that this is an allusion to Garve is made by Timmermann, *Kant's Groundwork of the Metaphysics of Morals*, Introduction, xxvii.

29. I discuss these passages in detail in chapter 4. See also Pinheiro Walla, Alice, "Virtue and Prudence in a Footnote of the Metaphysics of Morals" (MS VI: 433n), *Jahrbuch für Recht und Ethik / Annual review of law and ethics*, vol. 21 (2013), pp. 307–23.

30. According to Terence Irwin, Kant was claiming that Greek eudaimonists openly subordinate practical reason to pleasure and consequently are openly committed to hedonism. Irwin argues that Kant's objections to eudaimonism rest on his general psychological hedonism and on a crude misunderstanding of Greek conceptions of eudaimonia. Irwin, "Kant's Criticism of Eudaimonism," In: Stephen Engstrom and Jennifer Whiting, *Aristotle, Kant and the Stoics. Rethinking Happiness and Duty*. Cambridge University Press, 1996, especially section III.

31. "It is, however, possible, to take a view of virtuous action in which, though the validity of moral institutions is not disputed, this notion of rule or dictate is at any rate only latent or implicit, the moral ideal being presented as attractive rather than imperative. Such a view seems to be taken when the action to which we are morally prompted, or the quality of character manifested in it, is judged to be good in itself (and not merely as a means to some ulterior Good). This, as was before noticed, was the fundamental ethical conception in the Greek schools of Moral Philosophy generally; including even the Stoics, though their system, from the prominence that it gives to the conception of natural law, forms a transitional link between ancient and modern ethics." H. Sidgwick, *The Method of Ethics*, p. 105. See also Gisela Striker, "Greek Ethics and Moral Theory," The Tanner Lectures on Human Values, p. 184–5. J. and B. Schneewind, "Kant against the 'spurious principles of morality,'" pp.143–4.

32. See also Moral Collins, XXIX: 599 and Nachlass XIX: 104 (6601).

33. MS VI: 378 (which I quote below). See also Über die Buchmacherei VIII: 434n.

34. Cf. GMS IV: 397: "It certainly conforms with duty that a shopkeeper not overcharge his inexperienced customer, and where there is much commerce, a prudent merchant actually does not do this, but keeps a fixed price for everyone, so that a child may buy from him just as well as everyone else. Thus one is served honestly, but this is not nearly enough for us to believe that the merchant proceeded in this way from duty and principles of honesty; his advantage required it."

35. Actions not done from the motive of duty are not *ipso facto* immoral. Consider permissible actions done from inclination: if the agent acts on a non-moral maxim (say, she chooses to satisfy a desire) with the consciousness of doing something that is morally permissible (that is, she is aware her maxim does not contradict the moral law), her action has a *moral dimension* although it is not done from duty in a strong, *positive* sense. After all, the categorical imperative does not command us to act from the motive of duty, but merely that we only adopt maxims that we can *will* to become universal laws. Acting directly from the awareness of duty is necessary in the presence of opposed inclinations; the action in this case is not only permissible but *morally required*. Were we required to act from the motive of duty at all times, we would indeed end up with the absurd scenario suggested by Schiller (that I must hate my friends in order to help them as virtue requires). See Schiller's "Gewissensskrupel" and Timmermann's discussion of this short poem in his Kant's Groundwork to the Metaphysiics of Morals. A Commentary, Appendix A.

36. It's important to note that this poses a problem for moral *evaluation* but not for moral *action*.

37. Kant is clearly skeptical about the possibility of being a true moral hedonist in *practice*. Virtue without the thought of duty is simply impossible and yet Kant took Epicurus to be a virtuous man; he *must* have acted from duty even though he *thought* he was a hedonist. The same view is held by Mill, who is convinced that Epicurus was actually a utilitarian. *Utilitarianism*, Roger Crisp (ed.), Oxford University Press, 1998, Ch. 2, pp 54–6. I owe Timmermann for making me aware of this parallel between Kant and Mill.

38. See for instance Maximilian Forschner, „Guter Wille und Haß der Vernunft" in: Otfried Höffe, *Grundlegung zur Metaphysik der Sitten. Ein kooperativer Kommentar*, p. 72 and Hermann Weidemann, „Kants Kritik am Eudämonismus und die Platonische Ethik," *Kant Studien* 92, p. 32

39. Irwin, "Kant's criticism of Eudaimonism" In: Stephen Engstrom and Jennifer Whiting, *Aristotle, Kant and the Stoics. Rethinking Happiness and Duty*. Cambridge University Press, 1996.

40. Irwin himself acknowledges this (op. cit. p.68.)

41. J. B. Schneewind, "Kant against spurious principles of Morality." In: Jens Timmermann, *Kant's Groundwork to the Metaphysics of Morals. A Critical Guide*, Cambridge, 2009.

42. *Wenn wir nämlich auch nicht wüßten, daß das Prinzip der Sittlichkeit ein reines,* a priori *den Willen bestimmendes Gesetz sei, so müßten wir doch, um nicht*

ganz umsonst (gratis) Grundsätze anzunehmen, es anfänglich wenigstens unausgemacht *lassen, ob der Wille bloß empirische oder auch reine Bestimmungsgründe a priori habe; denn es ist wider alle Grundregeln des philosophischen Verfahrens, das, worüber man allererst entscheiden soll, schon zum voraus als entschieden anzunehmen.*

43. Lewis White Beck, *A Commentary on Kant's Critique of Practical Reason.* *University of Chicago Press*, 1960, p. 107.

44. Irwin, "Kant's Criticism of Eudaimonism," In: Stephen Engstrom and Jennifer Whitting, *Aristotle, Kant and the Stoics: Rethinking Happiness and Duty.* Cambridge University Press, Cambridge, New York, 1996. pp. 83–4.

45. White Beck, op. cit. p. 243

46. "It is, however, evident that if the moral law is already included as supreme condition in the concept of the highest good, the highest good is then not merely object: the concept of it and the representation of its existence as possible by our practical reason are at the same time the *determining ground* of the pure will because in that case the moral law, already included and thought in this concept, and no other object, in fact determines the will in accordance with the principle of autonomy." (KpV V: 110)

47. Making ourselves worthy of happiness also includes adopting the permissible ends of others as our own. Therefore, making other people happy is also a way of becoming worthy of happiness.

Chapter Three

One's Own Happiness and Indirect Duty

This chapter explores Kant's claim that there is an indirect duty to promote one's own happiness (GMS IV: 399). Since the rationale of the duty is to avoid dissatisfaction with one's own condition insofar as it may create a strong temptation to violate duty, the object of indirect duty seems to be the agent's *overall, long term wellbeing,* as opposed to mere desire satisfaction. However, Kant's view that happiness is indeterminate brings in some complications. Although in some circumstances it seems *likely* that the permissible pursuit of happiness will make us more satisfied and consequently less inclined to violate duty, in other cases caring about our overall wellbeing may seem less promising. This is illustrated by the gout sufferer example of the *Groundwork*. For the gout sufferer, pursuing some immediate short term pleasure such as enjoying food and drink is a more certain pleasure than investing in a long term, uncertain goal like health (GMS IV: 399). Since the sick man is prepared to suffer what he must to enjoy what he fancies, it seems that Kant would have no objections against the gout sufferer's choice of short term over long term satisfaction.

Surprisingly, Kant argues that the gout sufferer *has a duty* to promote his health instead of indulging in unhealthy pleasure. I argue that in the absence of a natural inclination to do so, we have a *direct duty* to promote our overall wellbeing, although the rationale of the duty is never happiness *per se* but our moral personality. Given Kant's conception of happiness as indeterminate, only moral constraints can ensure the normative priority of our overall wellbeing over the satisfaction of isolated desires by providing a minimally objective conception of happiness. I shall thus reject the view that prudential reason for Kant constitutes a standard of rationality which is normative independently of the agent's inclinations.

In section one, I will reconstruct Kant's account of indirect duties on the basis of relevant passages. I will engage not only with the idea that there is an indirect duty to cultivate some natural dispositions and feelings such as sympathy for the suffering of others but also differentiate indirect duties from the notion of an *indirectly ethical duty*, as this distinction will help us understand what is distinctive about indirect duties. In section two, I discuss Kant's idea that we may have a *direct* duty to promote our long term happiness when tempted by incompatible, short term inclinations.

1. INDIRECT DUTIES IN KANT'S MORAL THEORY

I shall start by analyzing the notion of an *indirect duty* in Kant's moral theory. Although Kant talks about indirect duties in several passages of his ethical works, he does not provide an explicit definition of what indirect duties are.[1] As we shall see, this lack of clarification is also reflected in the secondary literature: the notion of indirect duty has often been conflated either with the duty of moral self-perfection or with the demands of instrumental rationality. I offer an alternative understanding of indirect duties as policies of "moral prudence," which bring indirect duties closer to prudential reasoning than to rules of skill.[2]

Kant recognizes the following objects of indirect duties:

1. Natural predispositions to be *emotionally affected* by the moral law (conscience or "moral sense");
2. Natural feelings and inclinations of human beings, which can *facilitate* and *support* moral agency (natural sympathy or love of humanity; sensitivity to the pain of animals and beauty in nature);
3. Natural needs of human beings whose neglect or non-fulfilment can render agents more vulnerable to violate duties and to vices (happiness in the sense of "contentment with one's condition" or *overall wellbeing*). I will also argue that when neglecting overall wellbeing is *not morally required*, when the agent would be neglecting her overall wellbeing to satisfy an inclination, she is violating a duty to the self in Kant's account.

A. Indirect Duty and Moral Predispositions of Human Beings

Kant associates our ability to be responsive to pure rational requirements with certain natural moral endowments (*moralische Beschaffenheiten*) of human beings. These are the *moral feeling*, as in our ability to feel pleasure and displeasure when aware of the conformity or contrariness of our actions to the moral law; our ability to hear the voice of *conscience* as our "internal judge" (MS VI: 400–1), our natural inclination to general benevolence (*Menschenliebe*, MS VI: 401–2) and our ability to feel respect (*Achtung*) for law within ourselves (MS VI: 402–3). Because these are natural features of human beings which enable morality in the first place, "anyone lacking them could have no duty to acquire them" (MS VI: 399).

Although Kant's account of these moral endowments in the *Doctrine of Virtue* is primarily concerned with dispelling a wrong conception of the role of feelings in moral judgment and motivation, feelings are nevertheless shown to play a greater role in Kant's moral theory than traditionally acknowledged. In the passages I shall analyze, Kant explicitly acknowledges that our ability to respond *emotionally* to the recognition of duty is a necessary condition for moral accountability: it is in virtue of these "natural predispositions of the mind (*natürliche Gemüthsanlagen, praedispositio*, MS VI: 399, l. 11), that a human being can be put under obligation (*kraft deren er verpflichtet werden kann*, Ibid., ll. 13–14). These moral endowments therefore make the transition from practical judgment (about what one should do) to actual choice or action possible. I will defend the view that natural dispositions either mediate or support morally determined volition[3] but play no cognitive role, contrary to what has been defended by some Kant scholars.[4] Although the idea of an additional motivational support may seem inconsistent with Kant's requirement that moral motivation be pure, I shall explain in the course of this chapter why this is no contradiction in Kant's account and how one should understand the claim that feelings may "support" moral agency.

Conscience (*Gewissen*) is "practical reason holding the human being's duty before him for his acquittal or condemnation in every case that comes under a law." Thus, conscience is our ability to compare our *actual* conduct with what we recognize to be our duty at the level of practical judgment or deliberation. Therefore, conscience presupposes the ability to recognize duties in the first place. Further, conscience is directed "merely at the subject, to affect the moral feeling by its act" (*das moralische Gefühl durch ihren Act zu afficieren*, MS VI: 400, l. 30). This means that there is a causal relation between the verdicts of one's conscience and the agent's experience of the so-called "moral feeling." This causal relation is made possible by the fact that rational judgments are naturally accompanied by emotional responses by the agent (as epiphenomena).

Just as our ability to recognize duties is inevitable, it cannot be a (direct) duty to *acquire* conscience (MS VI: 400). We can nevertheless deliberately improve or numb our *attentiveness* to the voice of conscience. When we say that some persons "have no conscience," Kant thinks that they have *chosen* to ignore the voice of the internal judge and have done it for so long as to have become insensitive to it.[5] Since it is in our power "to sharpen one's *attentiveness* to the voice of the inner judge," there is an *indirect* duty to *cultivate* one's conscience (MS VI: 401).

Similarly, we cannot have a duty to have *moral feeling* (*moralisches Gefühl*), since this is our natural emotional response to the awareness of the conformity or lack of conformity of our actions to duty (the so-called "voice of conscience"). As Kant stresses, without the moral feeling we would be "morally dead" and humanity would dissolve into mere animality (MS VI: 400, ll.11–14). It is possible nevertheless to *cultivate* and strengthen this capacity "through wonder at its inscrutable source" (MS VI: 399–400) and cultivating this feeling is what our obligation actually consists of (*die Verbindlichkeit kann nur darauf gehen, es zu cultivieren*, MS VI: 399 ll. 32–3).

Kant distinguishes between benevolence (*Wohlwollen, amor benevolentia*) and pathological love of others (*Liebe des Wohlgefallens, amor complatentiae*) (MS VI: 402). Since *feeling* love cannot be commanded, the love required by morality is the free adoption of certain maxims in regard to other fellow humans: it is not passive, but an active, *practical* love.[6] Duties of *love* are imprecisely named, since they require not that we feel love for one another but that we adopt a maxim of beneficence. As opposed to duties *of respect*, duties of love do not imply a corresponding right of the person helped. Duties of love cannot be externally coerced and the benefactor's compliance with the duty must be regarded as *meritorious* (MS TL §23 at MS VI: 448).

However, by adopting a maxim of practical love, that is, of active benevolence toward others, we may indeed be able to *feel love* for the persons we help as a consequence of one's benevolent attitude. Kant's interpretation of the golden rule is thus "*do good* to your fellow human beings, and your beneficence will *produce* the love of them in you (as an aptitude [*Fertigkeit*] of the inclination to beneficence in general)" (MS VI: 402, my emphasis). This resulting feeling of love is possible given an existing natural inclination to beneficence in general. Although this inclination is not the determining ground of the will in a moral agent, this inclination will nevertheless be "stimulated" or "activated" by a benevolent attitude toward others. Kant's view seems to be that a maxim of beneficence alone could not *cause* pathological love if we did not also have the *capacity* for this emotional response. Love may thus follow as a natural consequence from "doing good," simply because we have the natural aptitude to feel love as a result of an adopted maxim of beneficence. Therefore, pathological love for others is consistent with a maxim of beneficence toward others when it is a consequence and not the determining ground of the agent's volition.[7]

In the *Doctrine of Virtue*, Kant also discusses the feeling of *respect* or *reverence* (*Achtung, reverentia*), which unavoidably arises from our recognition of duty. Although Kant seems to be repeating his views on *Achtung fürs*

Gesetz in the *Groundwork* and second *Critique*, he also seeks to differentiate this concept from that of self-respect (*Selbstachtung*). Respect is not a judgment about an object, but a subjective, distinctive feeling (*ein Gefühl eigener Art*, MS TL VI: 402 ll. 29–30). It is an ambiguous feeling: at the same time as we feel *awe* for the purity and authority of the moral law, we also feel *humiliated* by it from the perspective of our own finitude (our desires and inclinations, in sum, our self-love is "reduced to nothing" at the recognition of unconditional value). However, Kant stresses that there is no need to posit an additional duty to *value* oneself (*Selbstschätzung*, MS VI: 402, ll. 34–35), since the respect for the moral law within ourselves already requires us to respect our person as the bearer of humanity (MS VI: 403). The term "duty to the self" is therefore misleading because the object of the duty of respect is not the agent herself, but the humanity in her person. Nevertheless, the humanity in us imposes a duty to respect our person in a holistic sense, i.e., not only as a *moral*, but also as an *animal* being.

Although Kant strictly separates pure reason from human nature for methodological purposes, he never denies that both animal and rational natures are constitutive of the creatures we are. Although moral worth is derived from our rational nature, the sense of *dignity* it instills in us extends to our *whole* person, including our animal nature. The awareness of having moral *personality* (being subject to the moral law) is thus the source of our feeling of self-worth or self-esteem and consequently of the idea that being a *person* implies possessing dignity (*Würde*). As the awareness of our capacity to be determined by the moral law, dignity places us beyond everything that has a *price* (i.e., that is not capable of freedom).

True humility follows unavoidably from our sincere and exact comparison of ourselves with the moral law (*its holiness and strictness*). But from our capacity for internal lawgiving and from the (*natural*) human being's feeling himself compelled to revere the (*moral*) human being within his own person, at the same time there comes exaltation of the highest self-esteem, the feeling of his inner worth (*valor*), in terms of which he is above any price (*pretium*) and possesses an inalienable dignity (*dignitas interna*) which instills in him respect for himself. (MS VI: 436).[8]

As bearers of Humanity, we have a perfect duty to avoid actions which denigrate our moral personality in favor of mere inclinations. The vices of servility and flattery are examples of an immoral use of our own person (MS VI: 434–37). Moral self-esteem, conceived as the *negative* duty not to let the interests of our animal nature infringe upon our moral dignity, is a perfect duty of the human being to herself (MS VI: 435). However, having a perfect duty to maintain one's dignity is different from a duty to *feel* self-esteem. This cannot be commanded, as it is the inevitable result of our recognition of the moral law. In the casuistic question at MS VI: 437, Kant suggests that we can also *cultivate* the feeling of self-esteem (analogously to conscience and moral feeling). But since the line between self-esteem and self-conceit is a very subtle one (MS VI: 437), the question is whether it is not wiser to cultivate *humility* instead of self-esteem (MS VI: 437). Although humility can be problematic since it tends to turn into self-abnegation (*Selbstverläugnung*, ll. 10) and leads to a violation of a duty to the self, the passage suggests a *possible* object of indirect duty (the cultivation of a feeling). Kant leaves open whether this feeling is self-esteem or humility (or both). Presumably, deciding between cultivating humility or self-esteem would be a matter of personal discernment according to whether one is prone to self-conceit or self-denial.

B. Natural Features of Human Beings as Support to Moral Agency

Human beings have natural feelings and inclinations which can greatly facilitate moral agency when *subordinated* to moral motivation. These feelings or natural capacities are not meant to *replace* genuine moral motivation, but merely to *counteract* or *eliminate* obstructive inclinations, given the specific way humans are motivated to act (Cf. KU V: 273). The "support" in question is thus not *toward* the moral action (a function that *Achtung fürs Gesetz* alone must be sufficient to accomplish) but is directed at possible obstacles or interferences to the morally determined volition. These are our ability to empathize with other human beings (MS §35 at VI: 457), sensitivity to the pain of living creatures and the capacity to appreciate beauty in nature (MS §17 at VI: 443). Because these are natural features of human beings, it cannot be a direct duty to acquire them. However, we have a duty to *cultivate* them insofar as they can facilitate moral agency in the way described above.

Although Kant recognizes that the agent's degree of effort in overcoming internal and external obstacles to duty "proves the sublimity and inner dignity (*Erhabenheit und innere Würde*) of duty's command (GMS IV: 425), his conception of indirect duties to cultivate sympathetic feelings shows that we are nevertheless not required to *struggle* as much as possible when doing what duty commands. When inner conflict is predictable and we can do something to reduce it, we *ought* to do so. As Ulysses providently tied himself to his ship's mast in order to escape a known irresistible threat, Kant's conception of indirect duties is also based on knowledge of the limitations of human nature. Indirect duties are policies of "moral prudence": they aim at ensuring or at least improving our responsiveness to rational requirements. It is morally "provident" to avoid poverty, not simply because it brings discomfort and pain, but because discomfort and pain make us vulnerable to temptations against duty (see MS TL VI: 388 for the indirect duty to secure one's wealth and health). It is also morally "provident" to actively cultivate those feelings which can facilitate the compliance with our duty because we know that the motive of duty alone may not lead us to act the way we ought to in the end (MS TL VI: 456–7).

This controversial passage seems to suggest that Kant viewed the support provided by feelings as *additional* incentives, operating side by side to respect for the law. However, the interpretation of feelings as additional motives is incompatible with the *Groundwork*'s view according to which there can be no genuine moral motivation if the incentive for the action is not *pure* (GMS IV: 398). Interpreting the role of feelings as counteracting *interferences* to moral determination avoids this difficulty. Therefore, when Kant says that "the motive of duty alone may not lead us to act the way we ought," he does not mean that respect for the law is not able to motivate without the concurring support from inclination, but rather that moral motivation alone is not always capable of eradicating *opposing* inclinations, which may be stronger on balance and lead us to disregard duty. Cultivating certain feelings would thus "prepare the dispositional terrain" to the advantage of moral determination.

Kant is therefore not recommending that agents should struggle as much as possible (the greater the struggle, the higher the moral worth) but concerned with ensuring that the verdicts of reason lead us to *act* by eliminating or counteracting the interferences of inclination as much as possible. By actively shaping ourselves into agents who comply with moral verdicts more easily, reason becomes more able to influence our conduct. Besides the main concern with the determination of the will by the *correct* principle (the moral law), Kant is concerned that reason also effectively leads us to act on its basis.

Humans also have the natural ability to *sympathize* i.e., to share in other people's joys and pains (MS VI: 456). Because sympathy can greatly facilitate compliance with the duty of beneficence, we have an indirect duty to cultivate our ability to sympathize with other people's fate (provided we do not pathologically lack the ability to empathize with others altogether). "Active sympathy" means to endorse and cultivate the natural feeling of sympathy, as an active support to the agent's adopted maxim of beneficence (in the way described above). Sympathy in this sense must be based on *practical reason* and not merely on the passive feelings or receptivity of the subject.

Kant calls the duty to actively empathize with the fate of others "duty of humanity" since it considers other agents not *only* as rational beings, but as *animals* who also have the ability to reason, that is, as *human beings* (MS §34 at VI: 456). The duty of humanity is thus the requirement to regard our finitude and specific vulnerabilities as human beings as something we have in common and to attempt to adopt the perspective of the other agent in her particular situation (an exercise which also requires a degree of *imagination*). Cultivating sympathy would also counteract the tendency to malice (*Schadenfreude*), which is the direct opposite of sympathy (MS TL VI: 459).

Kant does not restrict the natural ability to empathize to suffering, but also extends it to the *joy* of others. Although he does not say much about sympathetic joy, it is plausible to conclude that we also have an indirect duty to cultivate our ability to rejoice at another person's success and happiness, as long as these have been achieved through permissible means,[9] since this attitude can help us counteract our natural tendencies to envy and jealousy (*Neid, Mißgunst,* MS TL VI: 458–9).[10]

Kant stresses the *conditional* character of the duty to cultivate natural sympathy for others (MS TL VI: 456). When helping a person in distress is not possible, suffering with the person (feeling *pity* for her) not only increases overall suffering unnecessarily, but may also hurt the pitied person's self-esteem, since pity is usually displayed at the sight of "unworthy persons" (VI: 457). There can be no indirect duty to actively share in another's suffering in that case. Although it is the awareness of our shared animal nature which provides the basis for sympathy with others, we should always bear in mind that persons are not only *needy* creatures, but also persons with *dignity*. Perceiving oneself as an object of pity to others is a humiliating experience. The requirement to *respect* the dignity of other persons thus *limits* the extent to which indulging in feelings of sympathy for them is morally permissible. Even when feeling sorry for persons in distressing situations is inevitable, we have a duty to treat them in a way that is compatible with their dignity and self-worth and does not debase them to an object of pity. Therefore, sympathy must be always subordinated to *respect for persons.*

According to Kant, we can only have duties to other human beings, as the only creatures known to us to be capable of moral obligation and whose actions can be imputed to them (*dessen Handlungen einer Zurechnung fähig sind* MS VI: 223). Nevertheless, we tend to believe that we also have obligations to non-human animals. Kant argues that the *direct* duty is in fact to ourselves, namely, not to undermine those natural dispositions necessary for compliance with our duty to others, in this case, sensitivity to the pain of living creatures (MS VI: 442). We therefore have an indirect duty *in regard to non-human animals* to avoid treating them cruelly and even of showing *gratitude* to domestic animals such as an old dog or horse for their services (MS VI: 443).[11]

Wantonly destroying nature also weakens a natural disposition which, although not itself moral, greatly promotes morality or paves the way to it. This is the capacity to contemplate *beauty* as the ability to love something disinterestedly, i.e., "apart from the interest of using it for any specific purpose"

(MS VI: 443). Our capacity to experience aesthetic pleasure in nature is akin to morality in that it is non-instrumental. Although having the sensibility to appreciate beauty in nature is not itself a virtue, cultivating this sensibility enables us to abstract from our inclinations and adopt the *disinterested*, universalistic perspective required for morality.[12] The cultivation of our sensitivity to natural beauty can be thus seen as a *preparation* to morality.[13] Cruel treatment of animals is, however, "far more intimately opposed to a human being's duty to himself" because it dampens our sensitivity to the suffering of living creatures and consequently undermines this natural disposition also in regard to human beings (*weil dadurch das Mitgefühl an ihrem Leiden im Menschen abgestumpft und dadurch eine der Moralität im Verhältnisse zu anderen Menschen sehr diensame natürliche Anlage geschwächt und nach und nach ausgetilgt wird.* MS VI: 443, ll. 13–16).

Kant's position concerning animals brings to the fore a psychological feature of human beings, which is that a moral character presupposes unified attitudes and coherent emotional responses, which pervade all areas of our lives. As Kant stresses in his lectures, animals are *analoga* of humanity (*Moral Brauer* Me 302–3, *Moral Collins* XXVII: 458–551, *Moral Mrongovius* XXVII: 1572–4). Although animals lack the capacity to have obligations and the condition for having rights (what Kant calls *moral personality*), animals are similar to us in everything else: in needs, vulnerability and finitude. Some of their characteristics also remind us of human virtues: their devotion in caring for their young, the loyalty and friendship of a dog, the patience and endurance of a work horse may inspire admiration and gratitude in humans. Even when this must be ultimately attributed to our tendency to project our moral ideas on nature, we nevertheless have an indirect duty to treat animals as *analoga* of humanity.[14]

Moral commitment requires responsiveness to suffering; but this sensitivity per se is not discriminating: since suffering is a concern of finite rational beings derived from their *animal* nature, which we share with other sentient creatures, our responsiveness to suffering naturally extends to the suffering of non-rational creatures; we are naturally able to empathize with their suffering. Kant's claim is that it is not possible to be cruel to animals, to destroy nature and to be a moral agent at the same time. This is because restricting sensitive and respectful treatment to those we can clearly identify as rational agents, while permitting ourselves anything else regarding other living beings, would inevitably undermine the coherency of attitudes and emotional responses required for moral agency. While the commitment to moral principles shapes our emotions into more or less consistent and stable patterns of responses, giving free way to cruel dispositions to animals breaks the continuity of these responses and ultimately leads to an analogous inclination to cruelty in regard to human beings. As Kant himself stresses in his lectures, from cruelty to animals to cruelty to other human beings is just a small step.[15] Our relation to animals is thus a further domain in which our dispositions and feelings can be cultivated in a specific way. It has an indirect impact on the kind of *person* we are to be, i.e., on *character formation*.

One could object along the lines of Schopenhauer that animals for Kant are merely the opportunity to "rehearse" moral conduct toward humans and that the animals themselves count for nothing. It is important to stress that Kant is concerned with the *justification* (*Begründung*) of our obligation to animals. Although *all* obligations in Kant's framework can only be justified on the basis of a capacity of moral accountability (*Zurechnungsfähigkeit*, MS VI: 223) which non-human animals lack, from the first-person perspective, our *attitude* towards animals will be just the same as if we were to take animals to be the *direct* object of these duties: we must develop certain feelings to *them*, avoid treating *them* cruelly and so on. The worry seems to be that Kant's account of our duties to animals implies *devaluing* them (animals are considered mere means to the integrity of persons and have "no moral standing of their own"). I do not think this is an implication of Kant's view. As a matter of fact, we cannot hold animals responsible in the same way we can hold ourselves in regard to them (although we tend to *reflect* our moral categories on them). We need to justify our duties in regard to them in another way. Kant's account does not rule out the development of genuine attachment between humans and household animals and *encourages* humans to care about animals, if they do not already do so. Cruelty to animals and indifference to their suffering denotes *lack of humanity* on our side. But it is not possible to be humane and to devalue a creature as "a mere means to my integrity," at the same time. Our attitudes must be coherent in this aspect as well.

In the *Metaphysics of Morals*, Kant also writes about duties which are *indirectly ethical*. Although indirect duties and indirectly ethical duties have little in common, stressing the way they are "indirect" will help us understand what is distinctive about indirect duties. Kant explains how juridical duties can be regarded as indirectly ethical in the introduction of the *Metaphysics of Morals* (MS Section III at VI: 218). Duties are based either on juridical legislation (on the principle of right) or on ethical legislation (on the first principle of ethics). The difference between ethical and juridical legislation lies primarily not in the content of the duties they generate (which can be the same for both domains), but in the kind of *legislation* and consequently on the type of *incentive* required by each. As Kant observes, all legislation (*Gesetzgebung*) has two elements: *a law* (*ein Gesetz*) representing some action as objectively necessary and *an incentive* (*Triebfeder*) which subjectively connects the representation of the law with the power of choice (*Willkür*). The incentive is what makes the recognition of a duty (which is initially merely theoretical) properly *practical*. While the principle of right allows *both* external and internal legislation, the principle of ethics allows *only* internal legislation. Juridical legislation can therefore be external or internal, whereas ethical legislation can only be internal. If my duty can be imposed on me from outside, it is a case of external lawgiving. If duty can *only* be self-imposed, then we have internal, i.e., ethical lawgiving. Because juridical legislation also allows internal lawgiving, complying with juridical duties is *indirectly* an ethical duty. While there are many direct ethical duties (*direct-ethische Pflichten*), the possibility of internal lawgiving makes all other duties (that is, juridical duties) indirectly ethical (*indirect-ethische Pflichten*, MS VI: 221 ll. 1–3). It follows that all duties, just by being duties, already belong to Ethics (MS VI: 219 ll. 31–34).

The crucial difference between a duty which is *indirectly ethical* and *indirect duty* proper is that in the first case we can be *directly* motivated by duty. The notion of indirect duty, in contrast, involves some natural feature of human beings that we can neither create nor manipulate at will, although they might allow cultivation (as I shall explain, this does not apply to the indirect duty to secure one's happiness). Although complying with indirect duties expresses a commitment to practical principles (*moralische Gründsätze*), it is distinctive of indirect duties that all we can do is to consciously let ourselves be moved by natural feelings, which are themselves naturally given. What this precisely means will be clarified in the next section.

2. WHAT IS AN INDIRECT DUTY?

How are indirect duties generated? Nancy Sherman argues that the indirect duties to cultivate certain feelings belong to "an underlying project of natural perfection that supports our moral perfection and its application to both self and others."[16] According to Sherman, emotions are "modes of attention that help us track what is morally salient in our circumstances." For instance, sympathy "draws us to occasions of distress and need."[17] Our ability to feel grief "primes us to notice human mourning and loss," whereas compassion enables us "to notice that others suffer in ways that often seem undeserving."[18] Central in this interpretation is the idea that feelings play a *cognitive* role in moral judgment. The rationale for cultivating them is that we will become more apt moral agents (more aware to the "call of duty," when the occasion presents itself).

Sherman's interpretation overlooks the fact that moral self-perfection (*moralische Vollkommenheit*) in Kant's account is neither greater *emotional* responsiveness to moral commands nor *causal efficiency*. Moral self-perfection has to do with the *purity* of moral motivation (*be holy!* MS TL VI: 446). As Kant stresses, perfection entails that *subjectively* the moral law *alone* be the incentive of a moral action. Therefore, the more perfect one is, the *less* one will need the additional support of empirical incentives for compliance with duty.[19] Interpreting Kant as identifying the indirect duty to cultivate natural dispositions and feelings with the duty of self-perfection is thus incorrect. In Kant's account, having to rely on empirical incentives, even if only as a support to moral agency, is a mark of the *imperfection* of our nature. Rendering our emotional responses less accidental by conscious habituation and purposive channelling of motivational states in favor of moral action does not make us more perfect either. It only makes us more reliable agents, who struggle less to comply with duty.

At first glance, not having to struggle to do our duty seems to brings us closer to a holy will, which cannot will other than what the moral law commands and for whom there are no imperatives. But it only seems to be that way: our will is not holy and *we can will otherwise*. The lack of struggle seems to point instead to a greater degree of *human* virtue. This also seems to be confirmed by Kant's view that a holy will would *gladly* follow the moral law (MS VI: 405 ll. 14–5). But this conclusion is misleading. Kant defines virtue as *fortitude*, as strength in resisting obstacles to the moral disposition within us (MS VI: 308) or as the moral strength of a human being's will in fulfilling her duty (MS VI: 405). Although cultivating feelings and dispositions, as well as securing a certain degree of contentment with one's life as a support to moral agency is an *expression* of commitment to moral ends (I will do everything in my power to realize my moral ends), virtue lies not in the absence of struggle itself, but in the strength of one's commitment to moral principles. In other words, one is not virtuous because it is "easy" for her to do what duty to commands, but because of her resolve to act as the moral law commands. As Kant puts it, habit or facility in action is at most a *subjective* perfection of the faculty of choice (*Willkür*). Only internal freedom is a moral perfection (MS VI: 407).[20] The "ideal" state for morality would be *moral apathy* understood as the greater power of the moral incentive (pure respect for the law) over the influence of inclinations (MS VI: 408).

Since moral apathy is not a realistic option for finite rational beings with needs, a suitable strategy would be to work on those inclinations which could interfere with our compliance with duty, either by *cultivating* inclinations favorable to moral conduct which would counteract or replace unfavorable ones or by simply *satisfying* pressing, permissible inclinations and needs which could tempt us against duty (i.e., by promoting one's overall well-being). This does not amount to doing duty "from inclination," but "with inclination" since respect for the law remains the sole determining ground of choice.[21]

It is important to stress that Kant mentions neither feelings nor dispositions in his account of the duty of perfection, only *natural powers* (MS TL VI: 444–5). Sherman argues that Kant would have nothing against including feelings under the duty of self-perfection. Sherman looks for support in Guyer, who also tries to make the case for including the cultivation of feelings under the duty of self-perfection and speculates that Kant must be following Wolff's conception of perfection when referring only to those natural capacities which can be used as means to various ends (talents and skills).[22] The problem with this interpretation is that it fails to capture what is distinctive about indirect duties, namely why they are *indirect*, as opposed to the *direct* duty to cultivate our natural and intellectual powers.

Another interpretation explains indirect duties as not being duties proper, i.e., as not binding "in their own right," as opposed to the categories of perfect and imperfect duties.[23] Although it is a matter of duty to do what is commanded, the injunction of indirect duties is only accidental, as *means* to the realization of a directly commanded moral end. Indirect duties are not generated by the categorical imperative alone, but also require instrumental reasoning. It follows that complying with indirect duty does not have any moral worth "as such," only as a means to a direct duty. As Timmermann rightly observes, indirect duties express our concern with the effectiveness of moral agency, which is that we be able to bring about what the motive of duty alone may not be able to effect, given the limitations and "frailty" of human nature (MS TL VI: 456–7). Kant's notion of indirect duties is therefore evidence that his moral theory is not indifferent to the consequences of moral endeavors.[24] However, the problem with this interpretation is that it creates more indirect duties than Kant himself acknowledges. To identify whatever is a necessary means to moral ends with indirect duties as Timmermann suggests would imply that all hypothetical imperatives we need to follow in order to realize our duty in the world would have to be considered indirect duties: for example, if my helping you out of a pond requires taking off my shoes, I would have an indirect duty to take off my shoes. However, this is not only incorrect but also unnecessary, since according to Kant, to have an end analytically implies the commitment to take the necessary means to that end (GMS IV: 417). Since the requirement to take the means is analytically implicit in the notion of willing an end, there is no need to posit further duties to take the necessary means to fulfil one's duty.

Misunderstanding indirect duties for means to direct duties overshadows the real function of indirect duties and why Kant saw fit to posit them. They are *indirect* because it is not possible to feel or love or have a natural disposition on command (KpV V: 83). The feelings or dispositions in question can only be naturally *given*.²⁵ As Kant stresses, an imperative is a rule the representation of which makes necessary an action that is *subjectively contingent*; the subject must therefore be constrained (necessitated) to conform to the rule (MS VI: 222). But we cannot be constrained to something we already want or are naturally disposed to. When the object in question is morally relevant (when it can reduce possible obstacles to moral agency), is a naturally given disposition or feeling and *cannot be activated on command*, we have an indirect duty to cultivate, develop or realize it, as far as possible.

But are indirect duties *real* duties? If their function is to *support* moral agency, it seems correct to conclude that they are mere hypothetical imperatives. The categorical imperative "is one that represents an action as objectively necessary **and makes it necessary not indirectly**, through the representation of some *end* that can be attained by the action, but through the mere representation of this action itself (its form), **and hence directly**" (MS VI: 222, my emphasis). However, it does not follow from this definition that indirect duties must be means to one's duties; there are other examples of duties which are *also* means to more fundamental ones in Kant's system of moral ends and which are nevertheless *direct* duties.²⁶ An example is the duty to develop our talents: we cannot will a maxim of neglecting our talents for as rational beings, we necessarily will all our capacities to be developed, so they can serve us and be used to all sorts of purposes (GMS IV: 423). Although the development of our talents can *also* be regarded as means to agency in general, it does not disqualify it from being a direct duty and a duty proper.

If indirect duties could be directly commanded, for instance, if it were possible to evoke feelings of sympathy or to silence the voice of conscience at will, *having these feelings or capacities would be direct duties*, just as the duty to cultivate our talents and natural powers are direct duties.²⁷ Although indirect duties are means to more fundamental moral ends, they are not *direct* means to any particular moral action, but enable moral action *generally* and in the long run. Indirect duties are thus closer to the precepts of *prudence* than to rules of skill. After all, it is not my sympathetic feelings which will save you from drowning (how can mere sympathy help you actually?) but rather my ability and willingness to jump in the pool and bring you back to the surface. Perhaps I feel suddenly afraid of jumping in the water, although I know I can swim well enough to rescue you. But I see you suffering and struggling in the water, and the empathy with your suffering, the horrendous thought of you dying will help me overcome my fears more easily and do what I ought to do. In other words, indirect duties are about making sure that no obstructive inclinations impede reason in determining action; they are not themselves means to the end. If indirect duties can be correctly said to be means, then they are the necessary means for *human beings* to shape themselves into more efficient and reliable moral agents (when it comes to taking the means to their moral ends).[28] But they make us neither more perfect from a moral perspective nor improve moral cognition (which they *presuppose* in order to be correctly employed). The role of indirect duties is thus to counteract the impediments arising from our finite human will via our own natural resources.[29]

The interpretation of indirect duties I have put forward regards the objects of indirect duties as those dispositional or emotional states which exclude the possibility of direct moral motivation, because the disposition or emotion in question can only be naturally given. If a non-moral disposition happens to coincide with what duty commands, indirect duty does not command that it be suppressed or replaced by the moral motive. Its presence is desirable insofar as it excludes the presence of inclinations contrary to duty, which could tempt us to act otherwise as reason commands.

When I *pursue* happiness, I do not act out of duty, even if I am aware that I have an indirect duty to *secure* my own happiness.[30] When I choose to indulge myself with a generous slice of cake and an *espresso*, my motivation is my actual desire for the treats and for relaxation, even though I might also be aware that enjoying myself now and then within the limits of morality will make it easier for me to forego pleasures, when it is impermissible to satisfy them. Similarly, I may give way to my natural feelings of sympathy when I know that duty requires me to help a person in need and that my feelings will make this task easier. We can thus allow some greater latitude to inclinations in influencing us once we are aware of their beneficial "side effects" to our integrity or to our efficiency as agents. However, it may be more appropriate to *suppress* inclinations and focus on acting from principle alone, for instance, when an agent has a personal tendency to act impulsively and without careful consideration, however beautiful and appropriate this may happen to be under certain circumstances. *Governing oneself* (*Herrschaft über sich selbst*, MS VI: 407) makes virtue possible in the first place and is the condition for the making use of emotions and natural dispositions as supports to moral agency.[31]

The following claims about indirect duties have been made: (i) indirect duties concern capacities and inclinations which are *naturally given* in human beings and therefore cannot be *directly* commanded; (ii) it is nevertheless possible to *cultivate* these natural capacities and inclinations in a way which can provide support to our capacity of moral agency. Indirect duties are therefore an important component of Kant's *moral anthropology*. As the necessary counterpart to a metaphysics of morals, moral anthropology deals with the subjective conditions in human nature that hinder or help agents in fulfilling the laws of a metaphysics of morals (MS VI: 217), that is, with the principles of *application* of pure morality to human beings (MS VI: 216–7).

But just as there must be principles in a metaphysics of nature for applying those highest universal principles of a nature in general to objects of experience, a metaphysics of morals cannot dispense with principles of application, and we shall often have to take as our object the particular *nature* of human beings, which is cognized only by experience, in order to *show* in it what can be inferred from universal moral principles. But this will in no way detract from the purity of these principles or cast doubt on their a priori source (MS VI: 216–7).

3. HUMAN NEEDS AND INDIRECT DUTIES

> To secure one's own happiness is one's duty (at least indirectly) [*wenigstens indirect*]; for lack of contentment with one's condition, in the trouble of many worries and amidst unsatisfied needs, could easily become a great temptation to transgress one's duties. But, even without taking note of duty [*auch ohne hier auf Pflicht zu sehen*], all human beings have already of their own the most powerful and intimate inclination to happiness, as it is just in this idea that all inclinations unite into one sum. (IV: 399)

What does Kant mean by "securing one's happiness" (*seine eigene Glückseligkeit sichern*)? As Kant notes in the above passage of the *Groundwork*, "lack of contentment with one's condition, in the trouble of many worries and amidst unsatisfied needs, could easily become a great temptation to transgress one's duties." The rationale of the duty is thus to make us less susceptible to temptations arising from unsatisfied needs and general discontentment with one's life. In other words, the indirect duty is about taking into account and avoiding possible impediments to morality arising from human nature. We can therefore assume that Kant is thinking of happiness in the sense of one's *overall, long term wellbeing*, as opposed to the satisfaction of isolated desires. Although happiness in this sense is far from being an uninterrupted state of satisfaction, where all needs and inclinations of the agent are satisfied (GMS IV: 405), Kant clearly thinks that humans can achieve a certain level of satisfaction, sufficient to enable them to comply with moral commands. Were pain and discontentment a constant state, one's whole life would become unbearable and morality would be impossible. Happiness as overall, long term wellbeing will include a certain level of health, wealth and agreeableness in one's life (KpV V: 93, MS VI 388 and 432).[32] How much wellbeing is necessary is presumably an individual question which cannot be settled in advance for all agents.[33]

Securing one's happiness is one's duty *at least* indirectly (*wenigstens indirect*). This formulation suggests that securing one's happiness can become the object of a *direct* duty, presumably when the agent feels no inclination to pursue her own happiness and the neglect of her wellbeing *has moral relevance*, i.e., has an indirect or direct impact on moral agency or the agent's integrity. The agent is thus required to secure her happiness *out of duty*. If so, the indirect duty to promote one's happiness differs from the other indirect duties we have analyzed so far, for it also qualifies as a direct duty under specific circumstances. Should we lack the natural inclination to do so, we then have a *direct* duty to secure our welfare insofar as failing to do so would imply a violation of a *duty to the self*.[34]

In the *Second Critique*, Kant identifies both local desire satisfaction and our interest in prudence with the principle of one's own happiness or self-love (KpV V: 22), suggesting that there is no relevant difference between the two. As Kant notes, "the principle of one's happiness, however much understanding and reason may be used in it, still contains no determining ground of the will other than such as is suitable to the *lower* faculty of desire" (KpV V: 24). However, in the *Groundwork* Kant draws an explicit contrast between the gout sufferer's desire to overeat and the "general inclination to happiness" (*allgemeine Neigung nach Glückseligkeit*), in this case, the gout sufferer's general wellbeing in the form of *health*.

The gout sufferer does not know for sure if health will make him happy. Having adopted for a long time an excessive, unhealthy lifestyle, restoring his health would involve drastically changing his eating and drinking habits and sacrificing many pleasures. What could motivate the gout sufferer to make such a change? If he is not morally required to promote his health, the only motive the gout sufferer could have would be expectation of pleasure or the desire to avoid pain (KpV V: 23, 25–6).[35] However, he is aware that restoring his health will be extremely toilsome. From the perspective of expected satisfaction, restoring his health is perhaps not worth the effort. If all he wants is pleasure, then it might be better just to eat and drink what he can and to suffer afterwards. From the perspective of happiness it is thus *not irrational* for the gout sufferer to sacrifice his health for his immediate desire for food and drink. This is because when it comes to expected satisfaction, satisfying a single actual desire can be, under the circumstances, more likely to bring satisfaction than the "wavering" promise of long term happiness. While happiness as long term satisfaction is uncertain for the gout sufferer, immediate desire satisfaction seems less uncertain to him. Whether this is in fact the case is something no one can know for sure, since this would require omniscience (GMS IV: 418).

Even if we assume that it is often the case that satisfying as many ends as possible will make us happier than satisfying some short-term desires which are incompatible with the whole, the indeterminacy of happiness may *undermine* the rationality of these prudential policies. Under the circumstances, what we would call prudent behavior may appear to the agent as a "gamble" with promises of satisfaction, whereas short term pleasure may be less risky in terms of expected satisfaction.

> . . . the prescription of happiness is predominantly such, **that it greatly infringes on some inclinations** and yet human beings can form no determinate and reliable concept of the sum of the satisfaction of all under the name of happiness; which is why it is not surprising that **a single inclination—if determinate in regard to what it promises, and to the time its satisfaction can be obtained—can outweigh a wavering idea,** and that a human being, e.g., someone suffering from gout of the foot, can choose to enjoy what he fancies and to suffer what he can, since, according to his calculation, at least then he has not denied himself the enjoyment of the present moment because of possibly groundless expectations of some good fortune that is meant (?) to lie in health. (GMS IV: 399, my emphasis)

Because most agents are naturally inclined to promote their overall well-being or happiness, Kant argues that it is needless to posit a duty to pursue one's own happiness. However, as the gout sufferer shows, it is possible that agents come to *lack* the healthy self-regard most people naturally have.[36] Surprisingly, Kant argues that the gout sufferer has *a duty* to promote his health. When promoting his health in the absence of an inclination to it, the conduct of the gout sufferer acquires *moral worth*. Is Kant confusing a maxim of *prudence* with a moral duty?

My view is that Kant implicitly distinguished between an *objective* and a merely *subjective* conception of happiness. While the objective conception includes the basic ends of our animal nature which have an impact on our moral integrity and which can thus be commanded in case of neglect, the subjective conception of happiness is arbitrary: while it may coincide with the objective conception of happiness, this coincidence is merely contingent. Even though we usually adopt these basic ends from inclination and not duty (what Kant calls our general inclination for happiness, *allgemeine Neigung nach Glückseligkeit*), we cannot arbitrarily *reject* these ends without violating a duty to the self:

> But also in this case, **if the universal inclination to happiness [*allgemeine Neigung nach Glückseligkeit*] did not determine [the gout sufferer's] will**, if health, at least for him, did not enter his calculation so necessarily, then here, as in all other cases, there still remains a law, namely to **advance one's happiness, not from inclination, but from duty**, and it is not until then that **his conduct has its actual moral worth.** (GMS IV: 399, my emphasis)[37]

As Kant surprisingly remarks in the *Critique of Judgment*, our species is in thoroughgoing consensus (*durchgängig mit sich übereinstimmt*) in regard to genuine natural needs of human beings (*wahrhafte Naturbedürfniß*, KU V: 430). However, there can be no categorical imperative commanding us to include these natural needs in one's subjective conception of happiness, since most people are already naturally inclined to adopt these ends (in which case it cannot be a duty to adopt them). From the perspective of happiness there can be no *prudential imperative* to adopt these ends either, since there is no guarantee that these ends will make us happy. Telling someone that it would be prudent for her to adopt a certain end (say, that she should save money) is thus merely *giving counsel* (*Rathgebung*) in the assumption that the person has included certain things in their conception of happiness and would thus have a reason to follow our counsels. Therefore, a counsel of prudence contains necessity (*Nothwendigkeit*) or normative force only for those agents who *already want* the end in question, given their conception of happiness (GMS IV: 416), but not for those who have a different conception of happiness.

In his account of the vice of intemperance in the *Metaphysics of Morals*, Kant stresses that "the reason for considering this kind of excess a vice is not the harm or bodily pain (diseases) that a human being brings on himself by it; for then the principle by which it is would be one of well-being and comfort (and so of happiness), and such a principle can establish only a rule of prudence (*Klugheitsregel*), never a duty—**at least not a direct duty**" (MS VI:427, my emphasis). Although rules of prudence do not give rise to duties, the object of rules of prudence can nevertheless *coincide* with the object of certain duties. In this case, the ends recommended by prudence may either be the object of an *indirect duty* (when we have an inclination for the end anyway and consequently cannot be necessitated to act by an imperative of duty) or the object of a *direct duty* (when we lack the inclination for the end and the end can be directly commanded, as in the case of happiness).

One may eat healthily and exercise regularly not out of duty, but because one is afraid of having a stroke or a heart attack, or simply is afraid of pain or death. However, good health also belongs to those genuine natural ends all finite rational beings ought to care about for moral reasons. If, similarly to the gout sufferer, one no longer cares to maintain her health because some short term pleasure seems more likely to bring satisfaction, morality can command directly that one secures one's health instead of indulging in short-term pleasure. The agent would be then securing her health out of respect for the moral law and her conduct would have moral worth.

Kant thinks that there are ends it is rational for all finite rational agents to adopt insofar as rational agents cannot want the animal basis of their rational nature to be destroyed. Kant's moral theory can thus provide a *minimally objective conception of happiness,* as those ends indispensable not merely for self-preservation and general wellbeing, but mainly for maintaining our moral integrity as finite rational beings.[38] While morality can legitimately command the sacrifice of our true needs (KpV V: 160), willfully neglecting these needs for the sake of one's inclinations is a violation of duty. This means that if not strictly morally required, voluntary neglect of one's basic needs implies an arbitrary, impermissible use of one's own person. I shall say more about duties to respect one's natural needs in the next and final section of this chapter.

4. KANT'S CONCEPTION OF DUTIES TO THE SELF

While *Ius* has to do with the *right* of humanity in our person and in the person of others, Ethics enjoins us to respect the *end* of humanity in our own person (MS VI: 240). Duties to the self are derived from two possible ways of viewing the subject of the duty: either as *an animal and moral being* or merely as a *moral being*.

Perfect duties to the self as a mere *moral being* consist in the formal compatibility (*im Formalen der Übereinstimmung*) of one's maxims with the dignity (*Würde*) of Humanity in one's person. This is the requirement not to deprive oneself of the prerogatives of a rational being, i.e., the capacity to act in accordance with principles and the preservation of one's internal freedom (*innere Freiheit*) as opposed to making oneself a mere toy of one's inclinations. One has a perfect duty to the self "not to throw oneself away "and to cultivate instead love of honour (*Ehrliebe, honestas interna, iustum sui aestimium*) (MS VI: 420).[39]

The end of humanity in our person includes two kinds of ends: firstly, the ends we are required to adopt by ethical laws (moral ends or ends which are also duties) and the ends of our nature as animal and moral beings (HN XXIII: 398).[40] While moral ends give rise to duties of *commission* (to adopt certain ends), our natural ends are the object of ethical prohibitions and give rise to duties of *omission*. Perfect duties to the self *as an animal and moral being* "forbid a human being to act contrary to the 'end of his nature' (*Zweck seiner Natur*) and so have to do merely with his moral self-preservation" (MS VI: 419).

Kant identifies the principle of the duties to oneself as an animal and moral being with the stoic principle *naturae convenienter vivere*, which he interprets as a command to *preserve* oneself in the perfection of one's natural condition (MS VI: 419). Imperfect duties to the self command us to *perfect* our nature, as far as possible:

> Negative duties forbid a human being to act contrary to the **end** of his nature and so have to do merely with his moral *self-preservation*; positive duties, which *command* him to make a certain object of choice his end, concern his *perfecting* of himself. (. . .) The first belong to the moral **health** (*ad esse*) of a human being as object of both his outer senses and his inner sense, to the *preservation* of his nature in its perfection (as *receptivity*). The second belong to his moral *prosperity* (*ad melius esse, opulentia moralis*) which consists in possessing a *capacity* sufficient for all his ends, insofar as this can be acquired; they belong to his *cultivation* (active perfecting) of himself. The first principle of duty to oneself lies in the dictum "live with conformity with nature" (*naturae convenienter vive*), that is *preserve* yourself in the perfection of your nature; the second, in the saying "*make yourself more perfect* than mere nature has made you" (*perfice te ut finem, perfice te ut medium*). (MS VI: 419)[41]

Kant assumes that nature has implanted some instincts in us for a *purpose*. These are the original instincts of self-preservation, preservation of the species and the capacity to enjoy life at the mere animal level (MS VI: 420). The corresponding vices are "murdering oneself," the "unnatural" use of one's sexual inclinations and excessive consumption of food and drink (under which Kant also includes the consumption of alcohol and drugs). Controversially, Kant argues that these vices are distortions of human beings' natural instincts inasmuch as they go against a purposive use of our natural powers. The idea of an "unnatural" use of instincts is especially prominent in Kant's discussion of sexuality, for instance, in his condemnation of masturbation:

> Lust is called *unnatural* if one is aroused to it not by a real object but by his imagining it, so that he himself creates one, contrapurposively [*zweckwidrig*]; for in this way imagination brings forth a desire contrary to nature's end, and indeed to an end even more important than love of life itself, since it aims at the preservation of the whole species and not only of the individual. (MS VI: 424–5)

As Kant stresses, sexual lust means not merely *debasing* the humanity in one's own person, but *defiling* oneself [*eine Schändung (nicht blos Abwürdigung) der Menschheit in seiner eigenen Person*, MS VI: 424, l.28]. In contrast to suicide, sexual lust is a vice "indecent to call by its own name" (425, ll. 10–12) and even an allusion to sex within marriage requires "much delicacy" when mentioned in polite society (Ibid., ll.16–19). Sexual lust is a more serious violation of a duty to the self than suicide itself (Ibid., ll. 28–29). However, it is not clear why the vice of gluttony is not as bad or a worse vice than sexual lust by Kant's own standards, since it not only denigrates our personality to purely bestial pleasure, but to *passive* bestial pleasure. As Kant notes, although drinking is also low animal pleasure, it at least stimulates our faculty of Imagination (MS VI: 427, ll. 29ff.). Kant however, thinks that the involvement of imagination in sexual lust makes it a *worse* vice.

Kant argues that procreation furthers the end of the *species* which is higher than the end of the individual itself. This seems at first to be the reason why he takes "perverting" the natural purpose of the sexual instinct to be a more serious violation of a duty to the self than frustrating other natural instincts, for instance, the instinct of self-preservation. However, as Mary Gregor rightly observes, it is not clear why frustrating a natural instinct amounts to *perverting* the instinct. Morality itself often requires us to frustrate our instincts, *especially* the sexual instinct.[42] The frustration of a natural purpose per se therefore cannot be the reason why a certain use of our person violates a duty to the self. Kant's idea seems to be that *only morality* can command the frustration of a natural instinct, not inclination. When inclination determines the frustration of a natural instinct, this is taken to be a sign of perversion of our animal nature (by empirical practical reason). But for moral reasons, practical reason may nevertheless permit sexual intercourse without view to procreation "in order to prevent a still greater violation" (MS TL VI: 426).

Kant offers two distinct arguments for perfect duties to oneself as an animal being: a *rational* and a *teleological* one. While the teleological argument associates impermissible actions with violations of natural ends, the rational argument is based on the idea of preserving the agent's *moral health* and *moral integrity*. Certain uses of our natural instincts impose not only a danger to the animal creature who is also a rational being, but imply degrading our moral personality to a mere means to our inclinations. As Mary Gregor observes, although both arguments are at least implicitly present in all vices analyzed in the *Doctrine of Virtue*, the emphasis on a specific argument varies.[43] For instance, while the rational argument plays a major role in Kant's discussion of suicide (MS VI: 422–23), the teleological argument is the prominent one in his discussion of sexuality. However, as Kant observes in the *Metaphysics of Morals* itself, " . . . for any one duty only *one* ground of obligation can be found; and if someone produces one or more proofs for a duty, this is a sure sign either that he has not yet found a valid proof or that he has mistaken two or more different duties for one" (MS VI: 403).

Is Kant proposing two different grounds of obligation for perfect duties to the self and contradicting himself? If not, what is the role of the teleological argument? Gregor argues that although Kant's original intention is to use nature merely as a *medium* for expounding an independent moral argument, the coincidence of natural purposes with rational ends, as well as Kant's belief in purposiveness in nature, seem to have led him to assign some independent importance to the teleological argument.⁴⁴ However, as Gregor plausibly argues, it is possible to set aside Kant's teleological arguments without damage to the rational arguments he gives for perfect duties to the self. Duties to oneself as a *moral being* seem more plausible as they are more explicitly grounded on the notion of human agency itself, despite the persistence of a reference to a natural end of human beings. Duties to the self as moral beings are prohibitions against depriving oneself of the "prerogative of a moral being, namely, that of acting in accordance with principles." Lying, miserly avarice and servility are vices which deprive oneself of inner freedom in which they transform the agent into a mere toy of one's own inclinations, thus making "a mere thing" of herself (MS VI: 420).

The line drawn between duties to oneself and rules of prudence is a very subtle one. Kant stresses that violations of duties to the self often seem at first glance a matter of imprudence rather than proper vices. Kant makes this worry explicit in the case of the vice of stupefying oneself by excessive drink and food (MS VI: 426) and the maxims of prodigality and miserliness (MS VI: 434). However, the rationale of the duty is not primarily the harm or bodily pain caused by such vices. There are two ways in which actions can be regarded as violations of duties to the self. I shall therefore distinguish between an *instrumental* and a *constitutive* argument for perfect duties to the self as an animal and moral being.

In the case of gluttony, drunkenness and drug addiction, it is usually the impairment of our ability to use our capacity for enjoyment *intelligently* which makes these actions vices. This is why the enjoyment of alcohol to the extent that it stimulates conviviality and conversation should not be regarded as a vice (VI: 428). The idea is that, since an enjoyment is just one subjective end among others, it should neither hinder the pursuit of the other ends of the agent nor impair the use of her rational capacities. The agent's capacity to set herself ends is what enables the pursuit of particular ends; choosing ends that undermine this capacity is self-contradictory and a perversion of one's ability of non-moral choice in general. This is morally relevant insofar as the way we dispose of our ability to choose in non-moral matters also has an impact on our ability to act morally. In other words, these vices ultimately impair us as moral agents, temporarily or permanently.

Surprisingly, Kant argues that drunkenness may be considered morally objectionable even if the agent does not harm herself physically (for instance, when she is very strongly constituted). This is a case Kant considers in his lectures (Moral Collins, XXVII: 341). If a drunkard does not harm others and cannot harm herself, is drunkenness still a vice? Since Kant grounds duties to the self independently of the agent's relations to others, it is possible to violate a duty to the self even when no one is affected (not even the agent herself in her ability to comply with duties to others). Timmermann thus calls duties to the self "desert-island duties."⁴⁵ In this case, it is our *moral personality* alone which prohibits drunkenness as a use of our person. Since certain uses of our person imply reducing ourselves to mere impulses and inclinations, they are incompatible with the agent's self-esteem (MS VI: 435). No instrumental connection between the omission of an action and our capacity for moral agency is required: omitting certain actions can be *identical* to the preservation of the agent's dignity or self-esteem. I conclude that the rationale of duties to self is ultimately the humanity in the person of the agent, and not merely the preservation of her capacity of rational agency.

In this chapter, I have analyzed Kant's idea that we have an indirect duty to secure our own happiness. As the notion of an indirect duty is a puzzling one, I have provided a general account of what indirect duties are and which concept of happiness Kant has in mind when he says that we have an indirect duty to secure our happiness. I have argued that Kant did not conceive prudence as an independent standard of rationality, which is normative regardless of the inclinations of agents. Although most agents have a natural inclination to adopt certain prudential measures (maintaining one's health, securing a certain degree of financial security, acquiring certain useful skills), one may nevertheless come to *exclude* these things from one's conception of happiness. This is because, in the agent's calculations, under specific circumstances, satisfying some incompatible, short term inclination may be more likely to bring satisfaction than promoting uncertain, long term ends such as health. However, Kant also recognizes ends of our animal nature that we ought to adopt independently of whether we feel inclined to them or not. These ends of our animal nature often have the same *content* as the counsels of prudence. Therefore, we might be *directly required* to promote one's health or to secure a certain level when we lack the natural, healthy interest in them. To illustrate this claim, I have used Kant's gout sufferer example of the *Groundwork*.

In the next chapter, I will focus on happiness as the content of duties to others. I will analyze Kant's justification of the duty to adopt the happiness of others as our own end, i.e., the duty of beneficence.

NOTES

1. Kant offers no systematic account of indirect duties. For a very useful summary of Kant's scattered remarks on indirect duties, see Alix Cohen, *Kant and the Human Sciences. Biology, Anthropology and History.* Palgrave Macmillan, 2009, p. 92.

2. Although I deny that prudential reason is normative independently of an agent's existing desire for her long-term wellbeing, this does not undermine the interpretation of indirect duties I am putting forward. Indirect duties are only *analogous* to the

counsels of prudence; in fact they are *duties*. They are *indirect*, I shall argue, because in the case of feelings and natural dispositions *direct* moral motivation is not possible. However, securing our happiness is an exception: here direct moral motivation is possible, although it is not the *usual* motive we adopt when pursuing our happiness.

3. Feelings are subjective sensations which tell us nothing about the object inciting the feeling, not even about our own condition; feelings are the subjective relation of an object to the subject and provide no cognition of object or internal states (MS VI: 212, see also KU V: 206).

4. See for instance, Nancy Sherman, *Making a Necessity of Virtue. Aristotle and Kant on Virtue*. Cambridge University Press, 1997, p. 145 and Marcia W. Baron, *Kantian Ethics without Apology*, Cornell University Press, 1995, p. 220. Baron's account however is restricted to sympathetic feelings.

5. It follows from Kant's claim that "anyone lacking [the moral endowments] could have no duty to acquire them" (MS VI: 399) that persons who for pathological reasons lack the capacity to respond emotionally to the verdicts of conscience would not be considered morally accountable. In contrast, Kant clearly takes the *active* numbing of the voice of conscience as a more usual phenomenon, making the agent morally responsible for a lack of moral responsiveness.

6. As Kant stresses, only the love that is delight in another person (*amor complacentiae*) is direct love (MS VI: 402). If any feelings of love arise from adopting a maxim of benevolence, it is thus always *indirect*.

7. It does not mean that it is impermissible to feel pathological love for others when it does not follow from adopting a maxim of beneficence. Kant's point in the passage is to stress the proper place of pathological love concerning the duty of beneficence: morality concerns the agent's adopted *principles* and not her feelings.

8. See also GMS IV: 426, 434.

9. It goes without saying that there can be no indirect duty to rejoice at the happiness of others when it is achieved by immoral means or when the agent is a bad person. Kant suggests that if one is impartial and aware of an agent's badness, it will be impossible to feel glad for that person's happiness (although one ought not to feel envy or *Schadenfreude* either). As he observes in the opening paragraph of the *Groundwork*, "a impartial spectator can nevermore take any delight in the sight of the uninterrupted prosperity of a being adorned with no feature of a pure and good will" (GMS IV: 393).

10. Jealousy (*Eifersucht*) is a vice based on the tendency of human beings to derive self-worth from comparison with others; when jealousy is made into a stable principle of conduct, it becomes envy proper (*Neid*). For an account of envy and jealousy as social vices, see A. Wood, *Kant's Ethical Theory*, pp. 264–5.

11. I take Kant to mean not that we have an indirect duty to *feel* gratitude but to treat old domestic animals as the virtue of gratitude (toward another human being) would recommend. This implies not to abandon them to their own fate once they are no longer useful but to provide for them in old age. The ingratitude of humans toward old domestic animals is a theme of the Grimm brothers' well known tale *Die Bremer Stadtmusikanten*.

12. Henry Allison, *Kant's Theory of Freedom*, Cambridge University Press, 1990, p. 167.

13. "Wo Menschen singen, da lass dich ruhig nieder. Böse Menschen haben keine Lieder" (where people sing, there should you stay, bad people have no songs) is a German proverb, but similar ones are to be found in other parts of the world. However, Kant is right to stress that aesthetic cultivation can be a *preparation* but not education to morality itself. Aesthetic cultivation does not guarantee morality and can also happen *in opposition* to morality.

14. *Wenn z.E. ein Hund seinem Herrn sehr lange treu gedient hat, so ist das ein Analogon des Verdienstes, deswegen muß ich es belohnen und den Hund, wenn er nicht mehr dienen kann, bis an sein Ende erhalten. Denn dadurch befördere ich meine Pflicht gegen die Menschheit, wo ich solches zu tun schuldig bin.* [If for instance a dog has faithfully served his master for a long time, this is an analogon of merit, this is why I must reward it and provide for the dog when it can no longer be of service. This is because I promote in this way my duty to humanity, where I am obliged to do so], *Moral Brauer* Me 302, my translation.

15. *Man kann das menschliche Herz schon kennen auch in Ansehung der Tiere. So zeigt Hogarth in seinen Kupferstücken auf einen Anfang der Grausamkeit, wo schon die Kinder gegen die Tiere solche ausüben, z.E. wenn sie dem Hund oder der Katze den Schwanz klemmen, auf einem anderen Stücke den Fortgang der Grausamkeit, wo er ein Kind überfährt und denn das Ende der Grausamkeit durch einen Mord, worauf dann der Lohn der Grausamkeit schrecklich erscheint. Dieses gibt gute Lehren für Kinder.* [One can already know a human heart also in regard to animals. Hogarth shows in his etchings a beginning of cruelty, where already children practise this against animals, for instance, when they pinch the tail of a dog or cat, in another piece the continuation of cruelty, where he runs over a child and then the end of cruelty with a murder, after which the reward for cruelty appears terrible]. *Moral Brauer* Me 302–3, my translation.

16. Nancy Sherman, *Making a Necessity of Virtue. Aristotle and Kant on Virtue*. Cambridge University Press, 1997, p. 143.

17. Ibid., p. 145.

18. Ibid., p. 146.

19. Kant also talks about the duty of self-perfection from an *objective* perspective as concerning the complete *realization* of the moral end in regard to oneself (*be perfect!* Ibid.), an ideal which is to be continually approximated, but can never be fully achieved by finite rational beings. However, there is no textual evidence for the claim that cultivating our feelings is a condition for the constant progress toward perfection in this sense either.

20. I agree with Alix Cohen's interpretation of indirect duties as belonging to a "culture of discipline" or self-mastery as a strategy for *human beings*, who may be not strong enough to tame all inclinations. As Cohen correctly stresses, it "is not a matter of becoming free from the determination of desires when one is not already free, or becoming freer than one already is, but rather a matter of developing control over one's inclinations, thereby indirectly consolidating moral resolve, determination and strength of character." *Kant and the Human Sciences*, p. 93.

21. I agree with Timmerman's understanding of overdetermination in moral action as moral action "with" but not "from" inclination. Since inclination and morality correspond to two heterogeneous interests, there can be, strictly speaking, "no real inclination to duty or feeling attuned to morality." Jens Timmermann, *Kant's Groundwork of the Metaphysics of Morals. A Commentary*, p. 152.

22. Paul Guyer, *Kant and the experience of freedom*. Cambridge University Press, 1993, p. 376. Sherman, *Making a Necessity of Virtue. Aristotle and Kant on Virtue*. Cambridge University Press, 1997, p. 142 n.53.

23. Jens Timmermann, *Kant's Groundwork of the Metaphysics of Morals. A Commentary*. Cambridge University Press, 2007, p. 36. See also Timmermann, 'Kant on *Conscience*, Indirect Duty and Moral Error,' *International Philosophical Quarterly*, vol. 46, no. 3 Issue 183, September 2006.

24. It is important to stress that indirect duties do not guarantee successful actions, only a successful determination of the will by the moral law (given the lack or reduction of temptations against duty). The *consequences* of the agent's successful determination of the will are thus secondary.

25. As I shall explain, this does not always apply to the duty to promote one's happiness.

26. See also the duty to develop our natural powers in MS TL VI: 392.

27. The duty to cultivate our talents and natural powers are direct duties which are also means to our moral integrity, insofar as they enable us to raise ourselves from mere animality to humanity, MS TL VI: 392.

28. As Allison points out, cultivated feelings function as "weapons against the propensity to evil rather than as direct motivating factors." Henry Allison, *Kant's Theory of Freedom, Cambridge University Press*, 1990, p. 167.

29. Kant assumes that dispositions and feelings which can coincide with the commands of morality have been implanted by nature in us for a purpose. As he notes in Moral Collins, XXVII: 415–6, we seem to have received feelings of compassion from nature as compensation for our lack of principles.

30. I owe the distinction between pursuing and securing one's own happiness to Timmermann, *Kant's Groundwork of the Metaphysics of Morals. A Commentary*, p. 36.

31. Paul Guyer observes that while we are not allowed to let ourselves be governed by inclination, we are not forbidden to let reason use one set of inclinations to govern another. *Kant and the experience of Reason*, Cambridge University Press, 1993, p. 379. I think this is how we arrive at indirect duties.

32. In MS VI: 432, Kant criticizes the miser for restricting her enjoyment of the means to good living to the point of leaving her true needs unsatisfied. As Kant stresses, the miser would be violating a duty to the self. Cf. also MS VI: 420, where preserving one's natural capacity for enjoying life is said to be an end of nature human beings must not violate for arbitrary reasons.

33. Cf. MS VI: 395, where Kant identifies happiness with one's true needs and argues that one must decide for oneself "in view of one's sensibilities" how much to contribute to the happiness of others.

34. As we shall see, this is not the duty to secure one's wellbeing *per se*, but in fact the duty to protect the conditions of moral integrity and agency.

35. "In the desire for happiness, it is not the form of lawfulness that counts but simply the matter, namely whether I am to expect satisfaction from following the law, and how much" (KpV V: 25–6).

36. A similar example is the miser in the *Doctrine of Virtue* (MS TL VI: 432–3) which I discuss below.

37. "Aber auch in diesem Falle, wenn die allgemeine Neigung zur Glückseligkeit seinen Willen nicht bestimmte, wenn Gesundheit für ihn wenigstens nicht so nothwendig in diesen Überschlag gehörte, so bleibt noch hier wie in allen andern Fällen ein Gesetz übrig, nämlich seine Glückseligkeit zu befördern, nicht aus Neigung, sondern aus Pflicht, und da hat sein Verhalten allererst den eigentlichen moralischen Werth" (GMS IV: 399).

38. One may wonder whether one should call the minimally objective conception a conception of happiness *at all*. This is correct insofar as there can be no duty to promote one's happiness *per se* (KpV: V: 93). The duty is in fact to respect the humanity in one's own person. However, one may nevertheless call those ends to which we all usually have a natural inclination *and* have a duty not to neglect *a conception of happiness* in so far as the *content* of duties to the self *coincide* with the content of "typical" counsels of prudence (health, moderation, securing a certain degree of wealth, etc.). It is *objective* because it has to do with natural needs which all human beings have and *minimal* because it does not *exhaust* what one may conceive as one's happiness (subjectively). The denomination is thus imprecise and I hope it is not too confusing to the reader. I thank Sorin Baiasu for making me aware of this problem.

39. There is a clear parallel between duties to the self as a mere moral being and Kant's use of the Ulpian first principle of natural right in the *Doctrine of Right* (*Honeste vive,* MS VI: 236). Bernd Ludwig argued that despite being included in the *Doctrine of Virtue*, *honeste vive* or the duty of being an honorable human being is in fact an *internal juridical* duty, or a *juridical duty to the self*. It is subsumed under duties of virtue because it lacks the relation to the rights of other agents. See Bernd Ludwig, "Die Einteilung der Metaphysik der Sitten im Allgemeinen und die der Metaphysischen Anfangsgründen der Tugendlehre im Besonderen." Forthcoming in: Andreas Trampota, Oliver Sensen and Jens Timmermann (eds.), *Kant's Tugendlehre. A Comprehensive Commentary*, De Gruyter. I shall come back to perfect duties to the self as a moral being in chapter 4.

40. See Gregor, *Laws of Freedom*, p. 125.

41. While the first class constitutes *perfect* duties to the self (not to undermine one's natural perfection), the second class includes *imperfect* duties to the self (to cultivate oneself, to become more perfect than one naturally is). For the purposes of this chapter, I shall concentrate on perfect duties to the self.

42. Mary Gregor, Laws of Freedom, p. 132.

43. Mary Gregor, *Laws of Freedom*, p. 135.

44. Mary Gregor, Laws of Freedom, p. 134.

45. Timmermann, "Kantian Duties to the Self, Explained and Defended," *Philosophy*, 81, p. 508.

Chapter Four

Happiness and the Duty of Beneficence

In this chapter, I analyze Kant's justification of the duty to "adopt the happiness of others as our end," as well as the relation of this duty to duties of respect or indebtedness. I explain why morality according to Kant imposes a duty of *commission* on us (to further the ends of others) in addition to the requirement to omit certain actions. I argue that duties of love and respect are *complementary* duties (section two), following from the requirement not only to refrain from treating *finite* rational beings as mere means but to treat them positively as *ends in themselves*. Further, I briefly discuss the mistaken view that Kant's duty of beneficence requires impersonal treatment regardless of the agent's personal relations and interests and then discuss a passage which clearly contradicts this view (MS VI: 451–2). Finally, I analyze the concept of *latitude* (*Spielraum*) characteristic of imperfect duties implicit in Kant's discussion of Horace's adage in the *Metaphysics of Morals* "insani sapiens nomen habeat; aequus iniqui—**ultra quam satis est** virtutem si petat ipsam" ("The wise man has the name of being a fool, the just man of being iniquitous, if he seeks virtue *beyond what is sufficient*" (MS VI: 404n, VI: 409 and VI: 433, note). As we shall see, latitude does not apply to one's commitment to the moral principle. But since there is no upper limit to the extent we may realize moral ends, depending on the circumstances prudence is morally permitted to shape the degree to which an agent may choose to comply with wide duties.[1]

1. BENEFICENCE IN THE *GROUNDWORK* AND *DOCTRINE OF VIRTUE*

I shall start by analyzing the taxonomy of duties in the *Groundwork,* in which the distinction between perfect and imperfect duties is based on the way a maxim fails to satisfy the universalization requirement expressed by the categorical imperative. As Kant announces, a division of duties (*Eintheilung der Pflichten*) is reserved entirely for a future *Metaphysics of Morals*, the present division being "only discretionary" (*beliebig*), to order his examples (GMS IV: 421, note). As Timmermann notes, Kant does not mean that the classification of the Groundwork is "arbitrary" but that it is one possible but incomplete way to classify duties. This preliminary classification however is sufficient for the purposes of the *Groundwork*.[2]

There are two ways in which a maxim can fail the universalization test and generate a contradiction: either a contradiction in *conception* or a contradiction in the *will*. A contradiction in conception implies that the maxim in question could not be made into a law of nature without undermining its own aim. Underlying this contradiction is the idea that one must be able to imagine one's maxim as a law of nature. Would my maxim be able to exist without undermining itself if adopted by all other rational agents? With this model, Kant offers his own version of the Stoic principle *naturae convenienter vivere*.[3] Permissible maxims are conceived in analogy with the laws enabling a self-sustaining, well-functioning system of nature. A contradiction in the will, by contrast, implies a substantive impossibility: although the maxim could be made into a law of nature without undermining itself, a rational agent could not possibly *will* this to be the case. When universalized, the maxim would not make impossible its own end, but would undermine a constitutive end of *finite* rational agents.[4]

An example of the first kind (contradiction in conception) is a maxim of false promising. If adopted by *all* agents, a maxim of false promising would render false promises ultimately impossible: in a world in which false promising is the rule, no one would ever take each other's promises seriously. False promising is therefore only possible because most people take the institution of promise making seriously. Agents who make false promises take advantage of the general practice of promise making and must therefore hide their intention from others. Another consequence is thus that a maxim of false promise is unfit to be made public without undermining its aim.[5] Since the condition for the successful realization of the agent's aim depends on the existence of the institution of promise making, it follows that false promising must be understood by the agent as an *exception* she makes to herself (GMS IV: 422. Cf. IV: 424, ll. 15–17). However, because we are morally required to act only on those maxims that are fit to become universal laws, a requirement arises to refrain from making a false promise. In other words, we have a *perfect duty* to reject a maxim of false promising.

Other maxims, however, can be conceived as laws of nature without rendering action on their basis impossible in such a hypothetical world. This is the case of a maxim of indifference regarding the fate of others.

[An agent] who is prospering while he sees that others have to struggle with great hardships (whom he could just as well help), thinks: what's it to me? May everyone be as happy as heaven wills, or as he can make himself, I shall take nothing away from him, not even envy him; I just do not feel like contributing anything to his wellbeing, or his assistance in need! (GMS IV: 423)

It is important to note that the maxim of indifference Kant has in mind has an important limiting condition: the agent sees herself as entitled or at least allowed to ignore the needs of others because she neither harms others nor takes away what belongs to them. Not being the *cause* of their distress, the indifferent agent believes herself free from having to do anything positive to alleviate other people's condition.[6] The indifferent agent tells herself "I have nothing to do with this."[7] She does not infringe upon anyone's rights and consequently does not see why she is required to help those she hasn't harmed. If made into a universal law of nature, a maxim of indifference in regard to the happiness of others would not render universal indifference impossible. It is conceivable that a considerable amount of people would perish as the result of a universal indifference to each other's welfare, but on the other hand, it is plausible to expect that the implied universal commitment to avoid harming others (as a condition for non-beneficence) would also spare a considerable number of lives. It is therefore plausible to think that there would still be enough agents in the world to act on a maxim of indifference in a world in which indifference is a universal law of nature. This conclusion depends however on the limitation of indifference to the needs and wellbeing of other agents and not to their *rights*.

A maxim of indifference nevertheless fails to fully satisfy the universalization requirement because it cannot be *willed* by a rational agent without a certain kind of contradiction: given the reciprocity of the duty of beneficence, freeing oneself from the duty to help others would entail the willingness to give up any claim to the help of others when the agent is in need. But giving up any claim to the help of others would amount to deliberately *wanting* that our needs be ignored by others when we need their help. Kant argues that this is something finite rational agents cannot rationally want. Deliberately giving up the possibility of being helped by others as the condition for freeing oneself from the duty of beneficence would undermine the very rationale of such a "deal," namely, our interest in our own happiness. This is where the "contradiction in willing" actually lies.

Insofar as we necessarily have our own happiness as an end, it is not possible to free ourselves from the requirement to adopt the happiness of others as our own end. In the course of this section, I shall explain in more detail why this is the case in Kant's account. For the moment, it is enough to stress that Kant is not offering a *prudential* or even *egoistic* argument for beneficence ("because we want to be helped, we must also help others in turn").[8] On the contrary, we are obliged to be beneficent even to those who might never help us in return or help anyone else,[9]

Wolfgang Kersting has argued that the way Kant attempts to derive duties in the *Groundwork* only succeeds in accounting for obligations which require the cooperation of other agents for the success of one's action (such as in the false promise example), that is, in the case of perfect duties against others. This is because the logical contradiction revealed by the categorical imperative consists of the impossibility of *realizing* one's intent if the maxim is universalized. In contrast, the universalization of maxims having to do with the needs of others (imperfect duties to others) or with the agent's own person (duties to the self) has no adverse implications for the realization of these maxims. In this shortcoming of the *Groundwork*, Kersting sees the reason for a change in the derivation of duties in the *Metaphysics of Morals*. In the later work, Kant derives imperfect duties from a material principle commanding the adoption of certain ends, the so-called *principle of ethics*, as opposed to applying the categorical imperative *directly* to maxims of action, as he does in the *Groundwork*.[10]

Contra Kersting, I argue that the prohibition of a maxim of indifference in the *Groundwork* is also a requirement of logical consistency, in this case not in *thinking* but in *willing*. It is important to understand how exactly this contradiction works. Kant's argument for the duty of non-indifference in the *Groundwork* presupposes the view that we necessarily have happiness as our end (GMS IV: 415). Kant's point is that the promotion of our own happiness is only morally permissible if it can be made into a universal law and this requires including the happiness of all other agents among my ends. It follows that anyone who has happiness as her end (any finite rational being) must regard herself as being under a duty of beneficence to others as a matter of rational consistency.[11] Therefore, the duty to help others is also an implication of the requirement to act only on morally permissible actions, i.e., maxims we can *will* to become universal laws. Since the categorical imperative can only command the opposite of what it forbids, we have a duty to adopt the ends of others as our own, as opposed to being indifferent to their needs. This point is made clearer in Kant's account of beneficence in the *Metaphysics of Morals*:

> Every morally practical relation to human beings is a relation among them represented by pure reason, that is, a relation of free actions in accordance with maxims that qualify for universal legislation [*allgemeinen Gesetzgebung*] and so cannot be selfish (*ex solipsism prodeuntes*). I want everyone else to be benevolent toward me (*benevolentiam*); hence I ought also to be benevolent toward everyone else. But since all *others* with the exception of myself would not be *all* [. . .] lawgiving reason, which includes the whole species (and so myself as well)

in its idea of humanity as such, includes me as giving universal law along with all others in the duty of mutual benevolence, in accordance with the principle of equality, and *permits* you to be benevolent to yourself [*erlaubt es dir dir selbst wohlzuwollen*] on the condition of your being benevolent to every other as well; for it is only in this way that your maxim (of beneficence) qualifies for universal legislation. (MS VI: 451)[12]

It becomes clear from Kant's justification of the duty of beneficence that this duty should not be confused with a maxim of *self-sacrifice* for the ends of others. The reason why we should attend to the needs of others is ultimately the agent's own happiness (not as a *means* to this happiness, but as the *condition of its permissibility*). Since under normal circumstances every agent has a natural inclination to her own happiness, there is no need to posit an *obligation* to be beneficent to oneself (MS VI: 451, ll. 10–12).[13] The only moral requirement agents must satisfy is that the promotion of their own happiness be permissible, that is, that their maxim be fit to be made a universal law: it must not be an egoistic maxim, but a maxim we can reconcile with the ends of other agents. The promotion of the happiness of others, in contrast, is not an end we naturally want; the adoption of this end must therefore be rationally required.

But to what extent is it permissible to attend to one's own happiness and how much should we do to promote the happiness of others? Since the duty of beneficence is a duty of *commission*, it requires not only imposing constraints on the choice of our non-moral ends (as with duties of omission), but also positively investing time, energy and material resources in helping others, which could be otherwise used to further our own happiness. We must therefore ask ourselves how to understand the relationship between the adoption of the happiness of others as our end and the permission to be beneficent to ourselves.

Kant's position has often been characterized in contemporary ethical theory as requiring a strictly impartial equal treatment of all persons, regardless of personal relations. A classic statement of this position can be found in Bernard Williams' criticism of impartial moralities, in which Kantian moral theory is put on the same level as utilitarianism in allegedly requiring agents to treat others impartially regardless of their character, projects and personal attachments.[14] According to this view, one would be required to be impartial in choosing which of two drowning people to save, even if one of them is the agent's wife. Impartial morality would require one to flip a coin instead of simply giving preference to one's wife. Further, since I am not allowed to be more partial to the wellbeing of those closer to me than to strangers, the same seems to apply to one's own wellbeing: impartial treatment would require the agent to invest no more in her own happiness than she would invest in the happiness of others. This seems to be the reason for the view that impartial morality is self-alienating and allows no space for the pursuit of personal projects and human flourishing.

Kant's own views on personal relations are very different from the impartiality view sketched above. This becomes clear when taking into account Kant's distinction between the duties of benevolence (*Wohlwollen*) and of beneficence (*Wohltun*) in the *Doctrine of Virtue*.[15] Benevolence is defined as a feeling of satisfaction in the wellbeing of others. It is a disposition we have an indirect duty to develop (MS VI: 450–1). Beneficence, in contrast, is the maxim of making other people's happiness (their permissible ends) into one's own end (MS VI: 452). While benevolence requires no more than wishing others well (a benevolent attitude), beneficence requires concrete actions (MS VI: 393).

Although a maxim of benevolence can lead to beneficent actions (MS VI: 449) and this is why we have an indirect duty to cultivate a benevolent disposition, insofar as benevolence remains a mere *wish,* it is possible to extend one's benevolence to all human beings without limitation. Conceived as general love of humanity (*allgemeine Menschenliebe*), the duty of benevolence is thus the widest in *scope* while being the smallest in *degree*. Benevolence demands only that agents be "not indifferent" to the situation of others (MS VI: 451, l. 21ff.). It requires a *minimal* concern for other people, without necessarily leading to any concrete action. Sincerely "wishing others well" would be enough. Beneficence, in contrast, is a requirement to positively further the ends of others, as long as these ends are permissible and the beneficent agent does not violate any perfect duties by offering help.[16] It is a willing (*Wollen*) and not a mere wish (*Wünschen,* Cf. GMS IV: 394 ll. 23–4).

Consider the following passage of the *Doctrine of Virtue*:

> Yet one human being is closer to me than another, and in benevolence I am closest to myself. How does this fit in with the precept "love your neighbour" (your fellow human being) as yourself? If one is closer to me than another (in the duty of benevolence) **and I am therefore under obligation to greater benevolence to one than to the other** but am admittedly closer to myself (even with accordance with duty) than to any other, then it would seem that I cannot, without contradicting myself, say that I ought to love every human being as myself, since the measure of self-love would allow for no difference in degree. –But it is quite obvious that what is meant here is not benevolence in *wishes* (. . .); what is meant is, rather, active, practical benevolence (beneficence) (. . .). **For in wishing I can be *equally* benevolent to everyone, whereas in acting I can, without violating the universality of the maxim, vary the degree greatly in accordance with the different objects of my love (one of whom concerns me more closely than another).** (MS VI: 451–2, my emphasis)[17]

The above passage contains some puzzling claims, which might surprise those readers acquainted with the traditional picture of Kant's moral theory. Kant says that varying the degree of beneficence "in accordance with the different objects of my love (one of whom concerns me more closely than another)" would not violate the universality of the maxim of beneficence. Since I am "closer to myself" in matters of self-love, I am presumably allowed to be more beneficent to my own person than anyone else; the persons I love are the next objects of my beneficence. How can giving priority to oneself and those we love be consistent with a universal maxim of beneficence?

While it is possible to be equally *benevolent* to everyone (to wish them well), when it comes to *action* it is impossible to treat all persons equally (unless we do not benefit anyone at all). One could argue that since it is impossible to help everyone, it must be permissible to benefit some persons more than others, including myself. Although this is undeniably correct, this is not the point Kant is making in the passage.

It is important to note that Kant is not claiming that we are allowed to make an *exception* (*Erlaubnis zu Ausnahmen*) to the universal principle when we favor ourselves and those we love, but that *special obligations* arise from the fact that I am directly responsible for my own wellbeing and for the wellbeing of those closer to me.[18] Closeness creates responsibility: by caring for those close to us, we are not merely benefiting the "objects of our love" as the objects of our inclination, but those we are directly or indirectly responsible for, given our personal relations with them. The possibility of limiting our duty to humanity at large by another maxim of imperfect duty, arising from the special personal relations of the agent (including her responsibility to provide for herself in the first place) enables us "to expand the domain of the practice of virtue" by introducing different contexts in which virtue can be exercised, although to a limited number of persons and to the inevitable exclusion of others. Kant's example is the limitation of the general love of one's neighbor (*allgemeine Nächstenliebe*) by the love of one's parents (*Elternliebe,* MS VI: 390). The idea behind this claim is Kant's recognition that our specific relations to certain persons generate special duties and that, being imperfect duties (the duty to adopt an end, i.e., the happiness of some particular persons), action on their basis will limit our broader duty of love to humanity in general. Interestingly, Kant sees the "limitation" (*Einschränkung*) of one imperfect duty by another as an *expansion* of the field (*Feld*) for the practice of virtue (MS VI: 390, ll. 9–14).

Although they are just as universal in character as our general duty of love to humanity, duties to particular persons are "special" because they arise from the contingent relations between individuals. They do not yield different kinds of obligation (*Arten der ethischen Verpflichtung*), since there is only *one* obligation of virtue, but are only different *corollaries* or *applications* of the universal principle to particular situations (cf. MS §45 at VI: 468–9). There is clear textual evidence confirming that Kant did recognize special duties arising from the specific relations between individuals as well as from the special condition or social status of particular persons; In MS VI: 168 9, Kant acknowledges that sex, rank, poverty, etc., may require different treatment (not primarily for the sake of complying with social conventions, but in order to maintain *respect* for persons, due to their specific social circumstances). In MS VI: 422, when Kant speaks about the prohibition of suicide, he explicitly acknowledges special duties of spouses to each other, parents to their children and subjects to their superiors and fellow citizens, which he deliberately sets aside, in order to consider suicide solely as a violation of a duty to the self. Further, in the *Doctrine of Right*, the duty of parents not to abandon their offspring, as well as the duty to ensure that they are satisfied with their condition, is based on the fact that they have, by their own initiative, brought a child, a being endowed with freedom, into the world without its consent (MS VI: 280) thus creating a special responsibility to their offspring. Kant also recognizes a duty of friendship (MS VI: 469–73), which can only be carried out in regard to few, particular persons.[19] These duties, however, need no extra chapter in the *Metaphysics of Morals,* since special treatment does not imply special moral principles, only the application of the universal principle to particular circumstances (MS VI: 468–9).

By claiming that it is permissible to be more beneficent to loved ones, Kant seems to be following Cicero in his interpretation of the stoic *oikeiosis* doctrine. While the stoic ideal is to expand the attachment we have from those close to us to humanity at large, Cicero takes our duties to our close social circles to be weightier than our duty to the further circles of human society.[20] The further away we get from those close to us, the weaker the obligation. By defending closeness to oneself, Kant would be drawing a further implication from Cicero's view, which is that if we have a stronger duty to those closer to us, then we must have a stronger obligation to ourselves.[21] However, Kant does not argue for a single "direction" for dealing with the latitude of wide duty; he also allows the possibility of enlarging the scope of beneficence in a Stoic fashion to encompass humanity at large, which would imply drastically reducing the number of other moral ends imposing limits on the general love to humanity.

The wider the duty, Kant argues, the more imperfect the subject's obligation to act; this means that she may "expand the domain for the practice of virtue," not by making exceptions, but by adopting several maxims of imperfect duties, which are applications of the same universal principle to her particular circumstances. She may fulfil her duty of beneficence by devoting time and energy to her elderly parents, nuclear family, friends or community. However, it is also possible to do the reverse and to treat the wider obligation to humanity in the manner of *narrow duty*: the agent may choose to spend more time and energy helping distant strangers than most people, who are too busy with their families and close relations.

By treating wide duty as a narrow one, the agent will not allow different maxims of imperfect duty to limit her duty of beneficence. Because this person treats wide duty as a strict one, Kant argues that her action will be the more perfect (MS VI: 390). Paradoxically, Kant seems to be suggesting that the less we "extend the domain for the practice of virtue" the closer we get to an ideal of moral perfection. If this is correct, the difference between a saint and the average moral agent would be not merely the *degree* of effort invested in wide duty, but also the *scope* of her duty of love. A saint is not someone who devotes herself to a particular person or a group of persons, however ardently: she is an ideal of love to *humanity in general*. The most loving, caring mother is not a saint, although someone who extends motherly care to humanity as a whole, as much as she can, may be considered one. This agent would willfully bring a degree of "impartiality" to the practice of love which is not strictly required by wide duty itself; as we have seen, we do not violate the universality of the maxim of beneficence by giving priority to those close to us. Although strict impartiality is not required by duties of good will or benevolence (*Pflichten des Wohlwollens, Gütigkeit*), but only by duties of indebtedness (*Pflichten der Schuldigkeit, der Gerechtigkeit*, Moral Collins, XXVII: 413), duties of love can be treated in the manner of strict duty, if the agent chooses to. Latitude thus works both ways: one may make use of its wideness by adopting several particular moral ends, or "narrow down" compliance in the manner of strict duty. Merit, Kant suggests, would be greater in the last case.

2. RESPECTING RIGHTS AND DOING GOOD

Although widely discussed in Kant's lectures, the relation between moral merit and indebtedness is only explicitly discussed in the published works in the late *Metaphysics of Morals*.[22] Indebtedness and merit correspond to separate domains of Morals (*Sitten*), namely, to the domain of Right (*Recht, Jus*) and to the domain of ethics or virtue (*Tugend*), respectively.

Jus is the domain of duties which not only involves corresponding rights, but whose compliance can also be externally coerced. *Ethics*, in contrast, requires per definition that duties be self imposed: since ethics commands the free, i.e., *voluntary* adoption of certain ends, ethical duties cannot be externally coerced (MS VI: 383). If a duty can be externally coerced without losing its meaningfulness as a duty, this implies that the motive from which the agent acts is *secondary* and that *external* compliance is enough to satisfy the requirement. We are therefore dealing with a juridical duty.[23] In this case, the prudential interest in avoiding coercion and sanctions is *permitted* as an incentive for compliance with right although the possibility of *ethical motivation* in our compliance with juridical duty is not excluded. In contrast, ethics strictly requires a *moral* motive as the incentive for the action. As a matter of definition, moral motivation cannot be imposed from outside, but is something that only the agent herself can bring about by her own choice. This is why right is said to give laws to *actions*, while ethics gives laws to *maxims of actions* (MS VI: 368–9).

Because ethics has to do with duties to adopt certain ends, ethics is strictly speaking the domain of *wide* obligation and of *imperfect duties*. Right, in contrast, has to do with *narrow* obligations (requirements to do or refrain from doing specific actions, i.e., *perfect duties*, MS VI: 390). However, the dividing line between right and ethics is not always clear. Kant also subsumes perfect duties to oneself and others under the *Doctrine of Virtue* and acknowledges that there are also non-coercive juridical duties in the *Doctrine of Right* (the domain of *equity* or *Billigkeit*, which I shall discuss in chapter six).

The perfect duties of the *Doctrine of Virtue* have to do with the *respect* we owe to ourselves and to others, as a consequence of the humanity in our persons.[24] Perfect duties to oneself considered as an *animal being* involve prohibitions of suicide, defiling oneself by lust and stupefying oneself by food or drink (MS VI: 421–8); considered *as a moral being,* we are required to refrain from lying and from the vices of avarice and servility (MS VI: 428–37), since these vices are incompatible with the dignity of humanity in one's own person (see chapter 3, section A). Perfect duties to others involve prohibitions against arrogance, defamation and exposing others to ridicule (MS VI: 462–8). These duties seem to share characteristics of both right and ethics. While as perfect duties they involve corresponding rights (even in the case of a duty to the self), they preclude the possibility of external coercion. Since they must be self-imposed by the agent, they are similar to the paradigmatic (imperfect) duties of virtue.

In the *Groundwork*, the priority of perfect over imperfect duties is established on the basis of the universalization requirement imposed on maxims by the categorical imperative, more precisely, on the specific *level* of universalization a maxim fails to satisfy. While duties of indebtedness correspond to those maxims which would generate a contradiction in conception, meritorious duty arises from those maxims which could be conceived as laws of nature without contradiction, but could not be *willed* by rational agents.

> Now, certainly, if such a way of thinking [a maxim of indifference] were to become a universal law of nature, the human race could very well subsist,

and no doubt still better than when everyone chatters about compassion and benevolence, even develops the zeal to perform such actions occasionally, but also cheats wherever he can, sells out the right of human beings, or infringes it in some other way. (GMS IV; 423, II 23-28)

Perfect duty implies something we *owe* to other persons or to ourselves (*schuldige Pflicht, officium debiti,* MS VI: 390). In contrast, a meritorious duty (*verdienstliche Pflicht, officia honestatis,* MS VI: 395) is regarded as a positive moral achievement of the agent, for compliance with it goes beyond what is strictly morally required, i.e., strictly due to others (see *Anmerkung*, MS VI: 384). Duties of indebtedness therefore impose normative constraints on our compliance with meritorious duty. Kant often stresses this priority relation in his sharp criticism of the practice of beneficence as a mere means to camouflage or compensate violations of rights (Moral Collins XXVII: 433) and of the view that all duties toward others are meritorious and consequently that nothing is owed to others as a matter of right. As Kant stresses, it is preferable to be strict about respecting other people's rights and less beneficent than to be greatly beneficent while infringing upon others' rights: "one cannot wipe out injustice by doing beneficent acts" (Moral Collins, XXVII: 433).

Kant viewed respect for rights not only as having *priority* over beneficence, but indeed as being incommensurable moral values. As Kant stresses, if a person wrongs another in her rights, a lifetime of kind and beneficent acts to her will count for less than the injustice done to her (Moral Collins, XXVII: 416). Kant is deeply suspicious about the discourse of compassion and benevolence: firstly because it is better to be beneficent anonymously, in order to avoid self-glorification and humiliation for the person helped (MS VI: 453),[25] secondly because the rhetoric of beneficence has often been used to divert attention from or justify serious violations of rights (see for instance Kant's criticism of "Jesuitism" in MS VI: 266).[26] Kant argues that if we would only observe what is *owed* to others, even we did nothing beyond that to help other people, humanity would already be in a better condition than if we concentrated only on benevolence. Further, Kant makes clear that the notion of meritorious duties is problematic in a world in which dependence on the beneficence of others is often a result of injustice in the first place.

> If we have taken something away from a person and do him a kindness when in need, that is not generosity but a poor recompense for what has been taken from him. Even the civil order is so arranged that we participate in public and general oppressions, and thus we have to regard an act we perform for another, not as an act of kindness and generosity, but as a small return of what we have taken from him in virtue of the general arrangement. All acts and duties, moreover, arising from the right of others, are the greatest of our duties to others. (Moral Collins, XXVII: 432)[27]

It is not always possible to draw a clear line between what is owed and what is meritorious in our compliance with duty.[28] This is why Kant recommends that we regard meritorious duty as much as possible as a matter of justice and not of kindness (Moral Collins XXVII: 417). The implication is that we should not dismiss beneficence as a less important duty, but attempt to regard it as a *strict* rather than wide duty.

3. RESPECT AND LOVE AS COMPLEMENTARY PRINCIPLES

(. . .) As concerns meritorious duties to others, the natural end that all human beings have is their own happiness. Now, humanity could indeed subsist if no one contributed anything to the happiness of others while not intentionally detracting anything from it; but this is still only a negative and not positive agreement with *humanity, as an end in itself*, if everyone does not also try, as far as he can, to advance the ends of others. For if that representation is to have *full* effect in me, the ends of a subject that is an end in itself must, as much as possible, also be *my* ends. (GMS IV: 430)

Treating humanity as an end in itself requires more than merely *refraining* from violating humanity in the person of others. We are also required to *advance* the happiness of others, as a commission following from the requirement to treat humanity as an end in itself. The requirement to respect persons as ends in themselves will not have "full effect" (*alle Wirkung*) on agents unless they also positively promote the permissible ends of others.

What Kant means by "full effect" is not entirely clear. Is Kant making a psychological claim about human beings and suggesting that merely avoiding harm would somehow undermine our ability to respect persons as ends in themselves? It is possible to interpret the "full effect" of the representation of humanity as an end in itself in a holistic sense, meaning the full implications of the idea of treating persons who are also *finite* rational beings as ends in themselves.

Helping others without respect for their rights is a violation of duty and cannot count as a duty at all. While the negative duty not to harm others is a *necessary* condition for the possibility of treating humanity as an end in itself, merely refraining from harming others *is not sufficient* for treating persons as ends in themselves, insofar as they are also finite beings with needs. Since we are finite beings who necessarily want to be happy (who have both moral and non-moral ends), treating persons as ends in themselves in its *full sense* implies taking into consideration the permissible non-moral ends we happen to have. It follows that duties of respect and of love cannot be isolated from each other. While respect (*Achtung*) imposes *constraints* on duties of love (*Liebespflichten*), duties of love *complement* respect for persons by reminding us of the *needs* of finite rational beings, beyond mere respect for rights (MS VI. 448).

> Love and respect are the feelings that accompany the carrying out of these duties [meritorious duties and duties which are owed]. They can be considered separately (each by itself) and can also exist separately (one can love one's neighbour though he might not deserve but little respect, and can show him the respect necessary for every human being regardless of the fact that he would hardly be judged worthy of love). But they are basically always united by the law into one duty, only in such a way that now one duty and now the other is the subject's principle, with the other joined to it as accessory. (MS VI: 443)

Although it is our duty to help others, being dependent on another person's beneficence is also to a certain extent humiliating. We must therefore help others in a way that is compatible with their own dignity as human beings. Kant suggests for instance that we make our help seem a small service of love in order to avoid humiliation to the person helped (MS VI: 449) and recommends that beneficence be done in secrecy (*im Verborgenen*, MS VI: 453 ll. 28–30). Another limitation respect imposes on our practice of beneficence is that we should not try to make others happy by imposing on them our own ideal of happiness. *Respect for persons* requires us to observe the right of every person to determine her own conception of happiness. "Forcing a gift" on someone else cannot be called beneficence (MS VI: 454).

Although Kant believes that greater respect for rights would be more efficient in making the world a better place than relying on beneficence, duties of love are not a mere *compensation* for our lack of respect. This idea is reflected in Kant's identification of love of humanity (as a practical ideal and not as pathological affect) with an ideal of *moral beauty*:

> Would it not be better for the well-being of the world generally if human morality were limited to duties of right, fulfilled with the utmost consciousness, and beneficence were considered morally indifferent? It is not so easy to see what effect this would have on human happiness. But at least a great moral adornment, philanthropy (*Menschenliebe*), would then be missing from the world. This is accordingly, required by itself, in order to present the world as a beautiful moral whole in its full perfection, even if no account is taken of the advantages (of happiness). (MS VI: 458)[29]

The analogy between benevolence/beneficence (note that Kant conflates both concepts in the quoted passage) and beauty holds in two main aspects: both are *disinterested* and have to do with an ideal of *perfection*. To acknowledge the "beauty" of morality is to appreciate it for its own sake, regardless of any advantages to oneself.[30] However, insofar as disinterestedness applies to all actions from duty (including those of respect) the specific "beauty" of our duty of love to others must be another aspect. The beauty of beneficence is that it extends right and strict ethical duties beyond the strictly required (the *moral minimum*) into the domain of *excellence* or *perfection*.[31] As Kant stresses, while the rights of human beings are "holy," i.e., strictly required, kindness is an (non-optional) "extra" (XXVII: 432), something we add "as a beautiful ornament" to what is strictly required. Further, a virtuous action is the more perfect (and the more *beautiful*) the closer we bring our duty of love (a wide duty) to narrow duty.

In the next section I provide an interpretation of the *latitude* of wide duties by analyzing Kant's reinterpretation of Horace's adage *insani sapiens nomen habeat; aequus iniqui –ultra quam satis est virtutem si petat ipsam* (the wise man has the name of being a fool, the just man of being iniquitous, if he seeks virtue beyond what is sufficient," MS VI: 433n.) and his criticism of Aristotle's doctrine of the mean. In discussing the latitude of wide duties I shall also engage with Kant's correspondence with Maria von Herbert, in which Kant differentiates lying from reticence. As we shall see, latitude does not apply to one's commitment to the moral principle. But since there is no upper limit to the extent we may realize moral ends, depending on the circumstances prudence is morally permitted to shape the degree to which an agent may choose to comply with wide duties.

4. ON CONTRADICTORY AND CONTRARY MAXIMS

Perfect duties give us laws for actions and give more or less clear instructions as to what is morally required: I must either omit or perform a certain action. For wide duties of virtue, on the contrary, there are no such determinate limits.[32] We can always be more virtuous than we are, since the extent to which we should comply with the duty is not specified (MS VI: 392). However, failing to perform an action which would count as promoting the moral end in question is not *vice,* as long as the agent remains sincerely committed to the end. As Kant observes, the German *Tugend* comes from *taugen* (to be fit for some function); *Untugend*, however, means not *vice* (*Laster*) but *lack of fitness* (*zu nichts taugen*).

Only imperfect duties are, accordingly, duties of virtue (*die unvollkommenen Pflichten sind allein Tugendpflichten*). Fullfillment of them is merit (*meritum*) = +a; but failure to fulfill them is not in itself culpability (*demeritum*)

=-a but rather mere deficiency in moral worth = 0, unless the subject should make it his principle not to comply with such duties (MS VI: 390).

There is no upper limit to the compliance with meritorious duty: one can do too little, but one can never do too much when it comes to virtue. This becomes clear when examining Kant's criticism of the Aristotelian doctrine of the mean (MS VI: 404 note, 409 and 433 note). As Kant reads Aristotle, virtue and vice are matters of degree. While virtue consists in achieving the right measure in one's actions, vice is either doing too much or too little. Kant argues that the doctrine of the mean is superficial and cannot provide us with any determinate guidelines for action.[33] The difference between vice and virtue lies not in the degree or *quantity* but in the *quality* of the agent's maxims. It is the relation of a specific maxim to the moral law and not the reference to some quantitative standard of excellence that determines virtue and vice. Avarice and thrift, for instance, are based on different, opposing maxims (MS VI: 404, note).

Although the cardinal virtue for Kant is *courage* (moral strength or the firm resolution to put moral law into practice, MS VI: 408–9),[34] Kant also stresses the need for *moderation* in matters of virtue. However, moderation is not finding the "right measure" between two vices but in the avoidance of moral fanaticism (enthusiasm), which turns human virtue into tyranny (MS VI: 408–9).

Kant is often not content with showing only that his moral theory is superior to its alternatives; he is also keen to integrate what he finds useful in them by reinterpreting the rejected theories and making them compatible with his own theory.[35] Although Kant rejects a quantitative understanding of virtue, he offers his own reinterpretation of Horace's maxim, instead of simply rejecting it as wrong: "insani sapiens nomen habeat; aequus iniqui—**ultra quam satis est** virtutem si petat ipsam" ("The wise man has the name of being a fool, the just man of being iniquitous, if he seeks virtue **beyond what is sufficient**" (Kant's emphasis, Mary Gregor's translation). This verse is quoted twice in the *Metaphysics of Morals* (MS VI: 409 and VI: 433, note).

According to Kant, if Horace's verse were taken *literally*, it would be "utterly false" (MS VI: 433, note); for going "beyond what is sufficient" would mean that one can be "too just" or "too virtuous." However, claiming that virtue or justice can be excessive would be as absurd as "making a circle too round or a straight line too straight" (MS VI: 433, note).

Virtue is a matter of having adopted a maxim of ends fit to be universalized: decisive is the relation of the agent's *maxim* to the *moral law*. One's maxim can only be either permissible or impermissible; having different "degrees" of morality in this case is not an option, although one can do more or less in compliance with the duty. This idea might sound strange at first when considering that virtue involves merit and thus "adds up" to strict moral requirements. Kant's point is that virtue *itself* is not defined by the degree of merit of the agent (which is not fixed and can vary greatly), but by her maxim or principle of action. Although an agent may devote more time to helping others and has greater merit than someone who does less, insofar as they both sincerely adopted a maxim of beneficence, they are equally *committed* to a virtuous maxim. It follows that one cannot be *too virtuous*, although one may be *insufficiently committed* to the moral end, to the point of no longer sincerely having the end as one's own. One cannot do too much when it comes to permissible actions or to strict duties either. Therefore, if there is something the wise and the just person can be said to do in *excess*, this cannot be located in their maxim of virtue or of justice.

In order to explain what the wise and the just could possibly do "too much," Kant introduces the distinction between *contradictory* (*contradictorie oppositis*) and *contrary* maxims (*contrarie oppositis*). Truthfulness (*Wahrhaftigkeit*) and lying (*Lüge*) are contradictory maxims: the permissibility of the one entails the impermissibility of the other. In contrast, candor (*Offenherzigkeit*) and reticence (*Zurückhaltung*) are merely *contrary* maxims. They can both be consistent with a maxim of truthfulness but differ in that they allow a variation in the degree of disclosure compatible with truthfulness. As we shall see, this variation depends on how one makes use of the latitude characteristic of a maxim of uprightness (*Aufrichtigkeit*). I will argue that for Kant uprightness is the second best alternative to the ideal of complete open-heartedness (*Offenherzigkeit*), which cannot be realistically expected of human beings.

Consider the difference between telling a lie and being reticent. Reticence is the ability to communicate only what is true while *not telling everything*. At first, it does not seem to be a virtue but only a *prudential* measure, which can nevertheless, to a certain degree, be reconciled with a genuine commitment to truthfulness. For this, the agent's maxim of action must be permissible: she must have a permissible (prudential?) reason not to disclose certain details, while refraining from lying in her account of the events. In contrast, an agent who tells *the whole truth* without reserve will be just as committed to truthfulness as the reticent person, but she may be going against her interests or the interests of someone else by revealing all the details of a circumstance, when it would perhaps have been permissible for her to be silent about certain information.[36]

Kant's considerations about lying and reticence seem to have been inspired by a peculiar letter he received from a young Austrian noblewoman in 1791. Maria von Herbert was only 20 years old when she wrote to the 70 year old philosopher, seeking moral guidance. Her brother, Baron Franz Paul von Herbert, was the owner of a lead factory in Klagenfurt and an ardent follower of Kant's philosophy. Despite general opposition to Kant's critical philosophy in conservative Austria, von Herbert's house became a centre for the discussion of Kant's philosophy.[37] Maria was also acquainted with Kant's theory. In her letter she raises interesting philosophical issues, namely, whether retaining information would amount to lying and if one can be reproached for being reticent to a beloved person.

> Great Kant,
>
> As a believer calls to his God, I call upon you for help, for solace, or for counsel to prepare me for death. The reasons you gave in your books were sufficient to convince me of a future existence—that is why I have recourse to you—only I found nothing, nothing at all for this life, nothing that could replace the good I have lost. For I loved an object that seemed to me to encompass everything within itself, so that I lived only for him. (. . .) Well, I have offended this person, because of a protracted lie (*langwierige lug*), which I have now disclosed to him though there was nothing unfavorable to my character in it - I had no viciousness in my life that needed hiding. The lie was enough, though, and his love has vanished. He is an honorable man, and so he doesn't refuse me friendship and loyalty. But that inner feeling that once unbidden led us to each other, it is no more. O my heart splits into a thousand pieces. (. . .) Now put yourself in my place and either damn me or give me solace. (Letter 614 from Maria von Herbert to Immanuel Kant, 1791)

The letter seems to have touched Kant. He wrote a very sensitive reply in "sermon form" to Maria's first letter, which was sent to Austria in the Spring of 1792. In this letter, Kant argues that we must differentiate moral from prudential failure. Although we have a duty to abstain from lying, we are not morally required to reveal details which could harm us from a prudential point of view.[38] The problem is thus the following: while ideal love and friendship require complete openness and are incompatible with distrustful reticence,

> . . . there is in man an element of improbity (*Unlauterkeit*), which puts a limit on such candor, in some men more than in others. Even the sages of old complained of this obstacle to the mutual outpouring of the heart, this secret distrust and reticence, which makes a man keep some part of his thoughts locked within himself, even when he is most intimate with his confidant: "My dear friends, there is no such thing as a friend!" (. . .) This reticence, however, this want of candor—**a candor that, taking mankind en masse, we cannot expect of people, since everyone fears that to reveal himself completely would make him despised by others**—is still very different from that lack of sincerity that consists in dishonesty in the actual expression of our thoughts." (Letter 510 from Kant to Maria von Herbert, 1792, my emphasis)

As Kant explains in his reply, reticence "does not corrupt one's character," but merely limits the full expression of one's commitment to truth. Lying, in contrast, is a sign of corruption in one's attitude to morality and a positive evil. A lie can be harmless, but it is nevertheless a violation of a perfect duty to oneself, whereas reticence takes into account the imperfection of human nature and the fact that disclosing everything would expose oneself to the manipulation or spite of others. Kant suggests to the young woman that she ask herself whether her feelings of regret are due to her moral failure (i.e., a lie) or mere lack of prudence (i.e., disclosing more than morally required and suffering the consequences). While in the first case the beloved's reaction would be justified, the second, Kant argues, would only prove that the nature of his love "was more physical than moral" and thus would have ended soon by itself.

An agent who is committed to truthfulness can, to a certain extent, determine how much to disclose in her account of the events without violating duty. At first, reticence and candor seem to be defined merely with reference to prudence, as a (permissible) prudential measure or lack thereof. However, Kant takes reticence and candor to be *virtues themselves*.

> Between truthfulness and lying (which are *contradictorie oppositis*) there is no mean; but there is indeed a mean between candor and reticence (which are *contrarie oppositis)*, since one who declares his thoughts can say only what is true without telling the *whole truth.* Now it is quite natural to ask the teacher of virtue to point out this mean to me. But this he cannot do; **for both duties of virtue** have a latitude in their application *(latitudinem)*, and judgment can decide what is to be done only in accordance with rules of prudence (pragmatic rules), not in accordance with rules of morality (moral rules). (MS VI: 433n)

As Kant writes in the footnote in MS VI: 433, "both duties of virtue have a latitude in their application" (*beide Tugendpflichten haben einen Spielraum der Anwendung*). "Both duties of virtue" in this case must refer to candor and reticence, as those duties of virtue "who allow a middle." That candor is a virtue is not difficult to see; telling *the whole truth* without reserve requires great moral fortitude, which needs to be acquired (Rel. VI: 190). However, it is harder to see how reticence can be a virtue as opposed to a mere permissible prudential measure, unless the incentive for keeping some information is a moral one.

In the *Religion*, Kant draws the distinction between uprightness (*Aufrichtigkeit*) and open heartedness (*Offenherzigkeit*).[39] Although *Aufrichtigkeit* is like "Astreia, who fled earth to the heavens,"[40] it is nevertheless something we can require from human beings, that is, that everything we say is said with truthfulness. Complete open-heartedness (*Offenherzigkeit)*, in contrast, is to reveal the whole truth one is aware of, without reserve. But this, Kant argues, requires great moral strength, since an open-hearted moral agent will be more exposed to temptations and forced to make sacrifices (Rel. VI: 190). In contrast, uprightness (*Aufrichtigkeit*) means to communicate only what is true without disclosing *everything one knows*. In this sense, there seems to be no difference between uprightness (*Aufrichtigkeit*) and reticence (*Zurückhaltung*): Kant's definition of the two concepts is nearly identical. There is however a great difference in meaning between the two terms. *Aufrichtigkeit* highlights the correctness of one's conduct, while *Zurückhaltung* emphasizes the *restraint* in one's disclosure (the German *zurückhalten* means "to hold back," while *aufrechten* means "to straighten"). One could argue that *Aufrichtigkeit* is a moral term, while *Zurückhaltung* has more of a prudential connotation. Surprisingly, Kant says in the passage of the *Metaphysics of Morals* that *Zurückhaltung* in disclosure is a *virtue*. How can we make sense of this claim?

If we assume that the agent's motivation for holding back information instead of being completely open hearted is a moral one, understanding how reticence can be a virtue poses no major difficulty. For instance, if I am careful not to mention the sensitive details of a certain event, insofar as morally permissible, in order to protect a friend's privacy, it seems that my reticence is not only consistent with a maxim of truthfulness but has moral worth itself. The question is whether reticence would be an independent virtue or just one way to comply with my duty of beneficence to others (after all, I am helping my friend). However, if we grant Kant for the sake of the argument that my reticence would be a virtue in itself, would reticence still be a virtue if my motivation were the protection of my own reputation against the malice and prejudice of others, that is, a *prudential motive*, as it seems in the case of Maria von Herbert?

As Kant stresses in MS TL VI: 433n., "both duties of virtue (candour and reticence) have a latitude in their application *(latitudinem)*, and judgment can decide what is to be done only in accordance with rules of prudence (pragmatic rules), not in accordance with rules of morality (moral rules). In other words, what is to be done cannot be decided after the manner of *narrow* duty *(officium strictum)*, but after the manner of *wide* duty *(officium latum)*." A person who protects her privacy by being silent about some events (and would be doing so for prudential reasons) would be making use of the latitude of the duty of candour (*Offenherzigkeit*) in order to protect herself against possible abuse or manipulation by others.

If we follow the *Religion*, absolute *Offenherzigkeit* is the *moral ideal* we ought to realize in ideal circumstances. However, given the human tendency to manipulate and even to *despise* open hearted agents, open heartedness would make agents easy prey for the malice and contempt of others. This is why Kant says what we can *demand* from human beings is not complete open-heartedness, but merely uprightness. Kant is thus taking into consideration the non-ideal conditions for the application of the moral ideal. Although uprightness is only "the second best option" to absolute open-heartedness, it is rare enough (it seems to have "fled the earth to the heavens").

It is important to note that reticence for Kant is not merely a means to protect one's interests, but that given the limitations of human nature, it is necessary for maintaining one's *worth* as a human being in relation to others. Reticence is thus not only compatible with a maxim of truthfulness but also with *the right of humanity in one's person*, that is, the duty "not to let oneself become a mere means for other people but to be at the same time an end for them" (MS VI: 236). In the *Doctrine of Right*, Kant associates this duty with the first Ulpian formula *honeste vive*: be an honourable human being! (*sei ein rechtlicher Mensch*! MS VI: 236 ll. 24). If we assume that *honeste vive* or the duty of rightful honor is an *internal juridical* duty, that is, a non-coercible duty of right because it lacks the relation to the rights of other agents,[41] the agent's incentive for avoiding making herself a tool for others does not have to be the motive of duty; her fear of the social consequences of exposing herself to others, for instance, would equally satisfy the requirement of maintaining rightful honour as long as she *de facto* avoids vulnerability to others. However, as all juridical duties, *honeste vive* is also an *indirectly ethical duty*, that is, it equally allows the possibility of ethical motivation.[42]

In a world of social conventions detrimental to women and where disclosing sensitive details makes us if not vulnerable then perhaps despised by others, open heartedness is not always compatible with maintaining one's worth as a human being in relation to others. Maintaining one's worth as a human being has a social dimension in Kant's view: it is a worth one must maintain *in relation to others* (MS VI: 236). Even a scoundrel still has dignity (*Würde*) insofar as he is a rational being. Maintaining one's worth as a human being, however, requires not only being free of guilt, but also the preservation of one's good reputation and the good opinion of others. Therefore, even when the agent's motivation for being reticent is merely prudential, she is nevertheless not letting herself become a mere tool to others and is maintaining her worth as a human being.

It is important to stress that reticence presupposes an unconditional commitment to truthfulness: it would turn into *lying* if it did not. Reticence is thus none other than *Aufrichtigkeit*, that is, the "second best" option for human beings, given the fact that the moral ideal of openheartedness would be incompatible with *honeste vive* in most circumstances. Therefore, prudence is allowed to shape the way we comply with the duty of truthfulness and will lead us to adopt a maxim of reticence instead of candour.

When reticence is motivated by mere prudential reasons but is nevertheless required for maintaining rightful honor and does not violate any other strict duty to others, it can be seen as compliance with a juridical duty to the self. However, when reticence is motivated by *the awareness that it is also a duty to maintain rightful honor,* it becomes a virtue: the agent is making the right of humanity in her person also the motive of her conduct (and positively adopting a moral end).

5. DOING GOOD AND DOING TOO MUCH

Duties of virtue have to do with our moral *perfection* and not with what is strictly due to other persons. Because duties of virtue involve the realization of moral ends, they do not prescribe an upper limit for compliance: it is always possible to do more and become more perfect than we are. At first sight, this seems to imply a maximization requirement (to do as much as we can). Kant however explicitly rejects such a requirement to maximize virtue. The reason is that perfection is an unachievable task for the finite beings we are.

Kant believes that our commitment to morality requires recognizing the possibility (or at least the "non-impossibility")[43] of completely fulfilling moral requirements (the achievement of moral perfection). This is because adopting an end requires committing oneself to its realization, but one cannot commit oneself to something one thinks impossible. Since the achievement of moral perfection would require an infinite amount of time and we are *finite* rational beings, practical reason allows us to postulate the immortality of the soul as the condition for the realization of moral perfection and consequently for the *coherence* of our commitment to morality. Only if we assume that we can continuously improve morally (and this would mean beyond this life), can we make sense of the requirement that we ought to strive for perfection. However, to strive to achieve perfection *in this finite life* at all costs is not only vain, but also morally reprehensible: it would be fanaticism and not human virtue. Although this is not at first obvious in the passage, I take this to be Kant's point when he writes about the fantastically virtuous in the *Doctrine of Virtue*:

> The human being can be called fantastically virtuous who allows *nothing to be morally indifferent* (*adiaphora*) **and strews all his steps with duties, as with mantraps**; it is not indifferent to him whether I eat meat or fish, drink beer or wine, supposing that both agree with me. Fantastic virtue is a concern with petty details (*eine Mikrologie*) which, were it admitted into the doctrine

of virtue, **would turn the government of virtue into tyranny**. (MS VI: 409, my emphasis)

At first, it seems that the problem with the "fantastically virtuous" is only one of wrong judgment: she takes situations to be morally relevant when they are not. Although it is true that she treats morally irrelevant situations (*adiaphora*) as relevant ones, it is important to note that by "strewing his steps with duties as with mantraps" such an agent "turns the government of virtue into *tyranny*." Kant's point in the passage seems to be not merely that the agent is making a wrong judgment when he treats "petty details" as morally relevant. She seems to be doing something *reprehensible*: she transforms a life governed by virtue into a tyranny. But why is being concerned about petty details in moral matters a kind of tyranny, as opposed to being just silly or mistaken?

It is important to note that in this passage Kant is talking about a *person* (*Phantastisch-tugendhaft aber kann doch **der** genannt werden* . . . , my emphasis) and not of "fantastic virtue," as in Mary Gregor's translation. Further, Kant accuses the fantastically virtuous person not explicitly of misjudgement but of "*micrology*" (*Mikrologie*). In other passages, Kant associates micrology with "useless precision" (*unnütze Genauigkeit* IX: 046), "subtlety in the smallest details" (*Subtilität im Kleinen,* IX: 049) or also "hair-splitting" (*Kleinigkeitskrämerei,* MS VI: 440). Above all, *micrology* is a form of *pedantry* (*Pedantarei,* Cf. IX: 046). I interpret the fantastically virtuous' attitude as an attempt to create *opportunities* for virtue artificially, not so much due to misjudgement but as a kind of *pedantry* in moral matters.

In the casuistical questions at MS VI: 426, Kant asks the reader when treating wide obligation in a strict manner would amount to *purism*, i.e., "a pedantry regarding the fulfillment of duty." Characteristic of purism or pedantry in the fulfilment of duty is the denial of some latitude to one's animal inclinations, even when giving leeway to these inclinations would not endanger one's moral integrity. And this is exactly why the fantastically virtuous is not merely mistaken, but a *moral pedant*.

The fantastically virtuous person moralizes the morally indifferent (*adiaphoron*). But what leads her to do so? It seems that she attempts to *maximize* virtue by treating all her decisions as matters of strict duty even when it would be morally permissible for her to act on the basis of her inclinations and to further her happiness. She wants to be morally perfect at any costs and this is why she goes about strewing duties around her as mantraps. Presumably, she would attempt to moralize not only morally indifferent choices (*adiaphora*), but also the *latitude* of wide duties, which could otherwise be used to satisfy her needs and inclinations without detriment to morality. In this case, she would also be moralizing the *permissible* (*licitum*) and not only the morally indifferent (*adiaphoron*). The opposite of the fantastic virtuous would be the judicious man (the *prudens*), who does not expect to achieve moral perfection at all costs in this life and therefore allows some space for the satisfaction of his needs and inclinations. On this point, we are able to connect the passage about the fantastically virtuous in MS VI: 409 with the previously mentioned footnote at MS VI: 433 concerning "doing too much" in moral matters.

> In fact, *sapiens* here means only a judicious man (*prudens*), who does not think fantastically of virtue in its perfection. This is an ideal which requires one to approximate to this end but not to attain it completely, since the latter requirement surpasses man's powers and introduces a lack of sense (fantasy) into the principle of virtue. (MS VI: 433, note)

Although bringing wide duty closer to narrow duty is a virtue in some circumstances, completely disregarding one's happiness for the sake of maximizing virtue (*purism*) would be to introduce a fantastic idea of virtue, unfit to be applied to rational beings as *finite beings with needs*. Prudence, which is also a normative standard for human beings (though not independent from the agent's inclinations and only insofar as it is subordinated to morality) is thus often *permitted* to dictate limits to our compliance with moral ends, as long as these limits neither violate moral requirements nor imply abdicating any moral ends we ought to adopt. Therefore, when one is said to "do too much" in moral matters, this can only be the case from the perspective of *permissible prudential considerations*, that is, when one sacrifices his or her happiness beyond what is strictly morally required. However, one can never do too much from the perspective of virtue itself (since this would amount to *falling short* of virtue and not to an excess of virtue proper).

The next chapter is a digression into questions arising from Kant's distinction between perfect and imperfect duties. Although Kant identifies beneficence with imperfect duties, allowing certain latitude for choice, there are clearly circumstances in which this latitude is not given, for instance, in Singer's famous "drowning child" example. In this case, not to help is not an option, although there seem to be circumstances where it is clearly permissible not to help. Some commentators have therefore argued that the distinction between perfect and imperfect duties must be superfluous: it plays no role in practical deliberation when determining when there is a strict obligation to help. If the distinction is meaningless, the worry arises that the duty of beneficence may be far more demanding than Kant realized. In a world of acute and urgent need, one could argue that the obligation to help is a narrow one: there is no latitude for choosing whether or not to prevent someone's death by starvation or preventable diseases.

NOTES

1. When talking about ethics or virtue, I shall talk interchangeably of ethical duties, duties of virtue, imperfect duties and duties of commission, although we must bear in mind that there are also perfect duties included in the *Doctrine of Virtue*. Similarly, I shall speak of juridical duties, duties of right, perfect duties and duties of omission, bearing in mind that there is also wide right (the tribunal of conscience, *Gewissensgericht*, MS VI: 235, l. 10f.).

2. See Timmermann, *Kant's Groundwork of the Metaphysics of Morals. A Commentary*, Cambridge University Press, 2007, p. 79.

3. Timmermann, *Kant's Groundwork of the Metaphysics of Morals. A Commentary*, p. 78.

4. For further interpretations of how the contradiction tests should be understood, see Christine Korsgaard, "Kant's Formula of Universal Law," In: *Creating the Kingdom of Ends*, Cambridge University Press, 1996 and Onora O'Neill, *Acting on Principle: An Essay on Kant's Ethics*, Columbia University Press, 1975.

5. The publicity criterion appears in Kant's political writings, prominently in *Perpetual Peace* (ZeF VIII: 381–3; see also the *Metaphysics of Morals* RL VI: 349). There is a clear correspondence between the unfitness of a maxim to be made public and a contradiction in conception. See also MS RL §43 at VI: 311, where public right is defined as the sum of laws which need to be promulgated generally (*die einer allgemeinen Bekanntmachung bedürfen*) in order to bring about a condition of public justice.

6. Kant is careful not to conflate the perfect duty not to harm others or violate their rights with the imperfect duty to help (that is, to further their permissible ends or happiness).

7. As Timmermann observes, here there is also an implicit reference to the stoic ideal of indifference ("what is that to me? MS VI: 457), which Kant rejects as a permissible maxim of ends. *Kant's Groundwork of the Metaphysics of Morals. A Commentary*. Cambridge University Press, 2007, p. 86 note 77.

8. Schopenhauer argued that egoism is the tacit regulative principle for the possibility of *willing* the universalization of a maxim: I can only want what is to my best advantage. A. Schopenhauer, *Kleinere Schriften II*, Zürcher Ausgabe, Band VI, pp. 195–6.

9. We must also be benevolent toward the misanthropist (as long as her ends are permissible). See MS VI: 402.

10. Wolfgang Kersting, "Der Kategorische Imperativ, die Vollkommenen und die Unvollkommenen Pflichten," *Zeitschrift für philosophische Forschung*, 1983, p. 414.

11. Onora O'Neill observes that in this way Kant justifies the reciprocity of the duty to help without implying that actions must be reciprocated in the merest detail. Onora O'Neill, *Acting on Principle. An Essay on Kantian Ethics*. Columbia University Press, 1975, p. 88. From the reciprocity of the duty of beneficence, it does not follow that if I help *you*, you must help *me* in return and that no one would have a reason to further the permissible ends of the misanthropist.

12. As a further argument for the duty of beneficence, Kant appeals to the *publicity criterion*: if made public, a maxim of self-love would undermine itself. If others knew of my intention, they would be justified in not helping me and this is something I cannot want from the perspective of self-love (MS VI: 453, §30. See also ZEF VIII: 381, where the publicity criterion is used to test the permissibility of political maxims). Kant also makes a teleological claim in the same passage, namely, that since we are rational beings with needs, nature's intention in putting us together in the same dwelling place must have been that we help each other. The suggestion seems to be that the impossibility of universalizing a maxim of self-love is that it goes against nature's purpose. However, the moral argument for the duty of beneficence, which is the main justification for beneficence, works independently of this controversial teleological assumption.

13. From Kant's claim that we "only" have an indirect duty to pursue one's own happiness and a direct duty to promote the happiness of others, Michael Slote suggests that Kant devalues the agent's happiness in regard to the happiness of others. For Slote, the way we value our own happiness is also a mark of virtue. Slote, *From Morality to Virtue*, Oxford University Press, 1992, pp. 4–57. For a discussion of Slote's misunderstanding of Kant, see Thomas E. Hill, "Happiness and Human Flourishing" In: *Human Welfare and Moral Worth, Kantian Perspectives*. Oxford University Press, 2002.

14. Bernard Williams, "Persons, Character and Morality," In: *Moral Luck*, Cambridge University Press, 1981, p. 19.

15. Although Kant provides a conceptual distinction between both duties, in some passages he seems to use both concepts interchangeably, without carefully distinguishing between a benevolent attitude and doing good to others.

16. As an additional limitation, helping others must always be done according to the beneficiary's own conception of what would count as help, i.e., her own conception of happiness. Imposing on others what we take to be good for them, according to our own conception, would be a form of paternalism, which Kant vehemently rejects (MS VI: 454).

17. *"Denn im Wünschen kann ich allen gleich wohlwollen, aber im Thun kann der Grad nach Verschiedenheit der Geliebten (deren Einer mich näher angeht als der Andere), ohne die Allgemeinheit der Maxime zu verletzen, doch sehr verschieden sein"* (MS VI: 452, ll. 5ff.).

18. *"Es wird aber unter einer weiten Pflicht nicht eine Erlaubnis zu Ausnahmen von der Maxime der Handlungen, sondern nur die der Einschränkung einer Pflichtmaxime durch die andere (z.B. die allgemeine Nächstenliebe durch die Elternliebe) verstanden, wodurch in der That das Feld für die Tugendpraxis erweitert wird"* (MS VI: 390, ll. 9–14).

19. Do special duties of love to particular persons, for instance, duties to one's relatives, "trump" one's general duties of love to others? "Trumping" is perhaps not the correct way to explain the relationship between duties of love to particular persons and to humanity in general. For instance, it is not the case that caring for one's child will always preclude caring for anyone else, although in certain circumstances giving priority to one's child intuitively seems to be in order. Kant thinks that we are

permitted to limit our maxim of beneficence in general by other maxims of indirect duty. But to limit a maxim of duty by another does not mean that one duty must "trump" the other. Kant's picture is instead one of "expanding the field" for the practice of virtue, suggesting that different adopted maxims of imperfect duty can coexist with each other.

20. Cicero, *De officiis*, I, 16.

21. Katja Maria Vogt, "Duties to Others: Demands and Limits,." In: Monika Betzler, *Kant's Ethics of Virtue, Walter de Gruyter, 2008, p. 242.*

22. The distinction between merit and indebtedness, as well as the subordination of merit (in the form of imperfect duties) to indebtedness (perfect duties) is implicit, although not further developed in the *Groundwork*.

23. As Ludwig frames it, *Rechtspflichten sind alle diejenigen Pflichten, denen man Genüge tun **kann**, ohne sie **aus Pflicht** zu befolgen.* Bernd Ludwig, "Die Einteilung der Metaphysik der Sitten im Allgemeinen und die der Metaphysischen Anfangsgründen der Tugendlehre im Besonderen." Forthcoming in: . . . Andreas Trampota, Oliver Sensen and Jens Timmermann (eds.), *Kant's Tugendlehre. A Comprehensive Commentary*, De Gruyter, 2013, p. 2 (emphasis by the author).

24. Bernd Ludwig argued that perfect duties to the self are based on the right of humanity in one's own person and are consequently *juridical* duties. They are subsumed under duties of virtue because they lack the relation to the rights of other agents. That they are juridical duties is also confirmed by the fact that perfect duties to the self do not require compliance from the motive of duty: in order to avoid letting myself become a means to the purposes of others, it is enough to avoid putting oneself in a position which could make the agent vulnerable to others. Bernd Ludwig, "Die Einteilung der Metaphysik der Sitten im Allgemeinen und die der Metaphysischen Anfangsgründen der Tugendlehre im Besonderen." In: . . . Andreas Trampota, Oliver Sensen and Jens Timmermann (eds.), *Kant's Tugendlehre. A Comprehensive Commentary*, De Gruyter, 2013.

25. As Kant stresses, meritorious duty (*verdienstliche Pflicht*) *binds* the beneficiary. Buying flowers for a friend to celebrate her new job is such an example. Getting flowers from me is something my friend cannot *claim* as a right. It is an act of kindness I freely chose to do. This is why doing my friend this kindness also puts her under an obligation to me. In contrast, duties that are owed to others involve only the obligation not to take away what belongs to another (MS VI: 448). Because I give the other person what is her *right*, she does not need to feel indebted to me. Paying back money I borrowed from you is such an example. I am not *obliging* you when I pay you back, but merely doing what I owe you.

26. Kant defines "Jesuitism" in the context of his criticism of European colonialism as the rhetoric of justifying any means by the "good ends" they promote. As a form of speech, Jesuitism aims at veiling injustice: it is a *Schleier der Ungerechtigkeit*, MS VI: 266, ll. 25.

27. Cf. similar claims in Moral Collins, XXVII: 415–6.

28. I explore the consequences of systematic injustice for Kant's account of beneficence and justice in chapter 6.

29. Cf. similar idea in Practical Philosophy Herder XXVII: 53: "I cannot say, as an absolute injunction, Thou shalt love! This love is that of wishing well, or of pleasing well. The latter is also non-moral, but wishing well presupposes a morality of beauty: the idea of the beautiful in the action is the means thereto."

30. Cf. GMS IV: 441–2, where Kant says that moral sense theory is closer to morality than a theory based on the principle of happiness, for it *immediately* attributes to virtue "the delight and high esteem we have for her," thereby showing that it is tied by her *beauty* and not by any advantages.

31. Although Kant discusses three duties of love (*Liebespflichten*) in the *Doctrine of Virtue*, namely, beneficence, gratitude and sympathy (MS VI: 452–8), insofar as the last two are conceived as a *support* to the duty of beneficence, it is it is plausible to conclude that beneficence is if not the *only* duty of love *proper*, then the most important duty of love, providing the rationale for the other ones.

32. A version of this section was published as Pinheiro Walla, Alice, "Virtue and Prudence in a Footnote of the Metaphysics of Morals (MS VI: 433n)," *Jahrbuch für Recht und Ethik = Annual Rreview of Law and Ethics*, vol. 21 (2013), pp. 307-23.

33. Although Aristotle talks of the right decision as being a mean between extremes, what one should do according to Aristotle is determined by the *orthos logos* (the correct reasoning or decision), i.e., what the wise (*phronimos*) would do in a given situation (see Aristotle, *Nichomachean Ethics*, II.6, 1136b). If so, the fact that the right ethical decision is a "mean" between two extremes seems to be secondary in Aristotle's account. Ursula Wolf tried to make sense of the doctrine of the mean by arguing that the mean Aristotle has in mind refers to the agent's *affects* and not to the practical judgment concerning what one should do in a given situation (Wolf, "Über den Sinn der Aristotelischen Mesotheslehre" in: O. Höffe, *Nikomachische Ethik*, Akademie Verlag, Berlin 2010). My interest in Kant's criticism of the doctrine of the mean is mainly the way it sheds light onto Kant's conception of the latitude of imperfect duties. I shall not engage with the question of whether it does justice to Aristotle's position.

34. Kant also calls this strength *moral apathy*. However, it is not indifference or lack of inclination, but a condition in which respect for the law is the stronger incentive (MS VI: 408–9).

35. For instance, Kant also tries to accommodate the heteronomous theories he rejects in Groundwork II within his theory of autonomy. See my discussion in chapter 2 and Lewis White Beck, *A Commentary on Kant's Critique of Practical Reason*. University of Chicago Press, 1960, p. 107.

36. "Telling the whole truth" does not have to include every irrelevant true detail (doing this would not only take too much time but also render the narrative uninformative) but disclosing all possibly relevant information one has knowledge of.

37. While Kant's philosophy became widely popular under Joseph II, Kant's writings were banned from Austrian schools and universities from 1798 until 1861. Wilhelm Berger and Thomas Macho (ed.) *Kant als Liebesratgeber. Eine Klagenfurter Episode*. Verlag des Verbandes der wissenschaftlichen gesellschaften Österreichs, 1989, p. 6.

38. In her article "Duty and Desolation," *Philosophy,* Vol. 67, No. 262, 1992, Rae Langton sees Kant as reproaching Maria von Herbert for deceiving her lover while she "may have had a duty to lie" in order to save her relationship (p. 504). Langton argues that Kant sees no principled distinction between lying and reticence (p. 491), which is clearly a wrong interpretation of the point Kant is making in his reply. For a criticism of Langton's article and an account of the distinction between lying and reticence in Kant's reply to Maria von Herbert, see James Edwin Mahon, "Kant and Maria von Herbert: Reticence vs. Deception," *Philosophy,* Vol. 81, 2006.

39. In the *Religion* Kant uses the same term for candour / openheartedness as in the *Metaphysics of Morals*, namely *Offenherzigkeit*. However, in the *Religion* he distinguishes *Offenherzigkeit* from *Aufrichtigkeit* (uprightness), while in the *Metaphysics of Morals* the distinction is between *Offenherzigkeit* and *Zurückhaltung* (reticence).

40. O Aufrichtigkeit! du Asträa, die du von der Erde zum Himmel entflohen bist, wie zieht man dich (die Grundlage des Gewissens, mithin aller inneren Religion) von da zu uns wieder herab? Ich kann es einräumen, wiewohl es sehr zu bedauern ist, **daß Offenherzigkeit (die ganze Wahrheit, die man weiß, zu sagen) in der menschlichen Natur nicht angetroffen wird. Aber Aufrichtigkeit (daß alles, was man sagt, mit Wahrhaftigkeit gesagt sei) muß man von jedem Menschen fordern können,** und wenn auch selbst dazu keine Anlage in unserer Natur wäre, deren Cultur nur vernachlässigt wird, so würde die Menschenrasse in ihren eigenen Augen ein Gegenstand der tiefsten Verachtung sein müssen. **Aber jene verlangte Gemüthseigenschaft ist eine solche, die vielen Versuchungen ausgesetzt ist und manche Aufopferung kostet, daher auch moralische Stärke, d. i. Tugend (die erworben werden muß), fordert,** die aber früher als jede andere bewacht und cultivirt werden muß, weil der entgegengesetzte Hang, wenn man ihn hat einwurzeln lassen, am schwersten auszurotten ist. - Nun vergleiche man damit unsere Erziehungsart, vornehmlich im Punkte der Religion, oder besser der Glaubenslehren, wo die Treue des Gedächtnisses in Beantwortung der sie betreffenden Fragen, ohne auf die Treue des Bekenntnisses zu sehen (worüber nie eine Prüfung angestellt wird), schon für hinreichend angenommen wird, einen Gläubigen zu machen, der das, was er heilig betheuert, nicht einmal versteht, und man wird sich über den Mangel der Aufrichtigkeit, der lauter innere Heuchler macht, nicht mehr wundern (REL IV: 190).

41. See Bernd Ludwig, "Die Einteilung der Metaphysik der Sitten im Allgemeinen und die der Metaphysischen Anfangsgründen der Tugendlehre im Besonderen," In: . . . Andreas Trampota, Oliver Sensen and Jens Timmermann (eds.), *Kant's Tugendlehre. A Comprehensive Commentary*, De Gruyter, and my discussion in section three, especially footnote 167.

42. Ibid., pp. 8–9.

43. When you cannot provide a positive *proof* for a certain claim, it is enough to show that the claim is *not impossible*, that is, that nothing rules it out as eventually the case.

Chapter Five

Excursus: Kant's Moral Theory and Demandingness

This chapter is a digression into some difficulties arising from Kant's distinction between perfect and imperfect duties and his claim that perfect duties have normative priority over imperfect ones.[1] Firstly, I discuss the intuition that imperfect duties are able to "trump" perfect ones under certain circumstances, for instance, in cases where we have a duty of rescue. If this intuition is correct, Kant's distinction between perfect and imperfect duties seems to be superfluous, since the structure of these duties does not seem to help us determine when there is a *strict* obligation to help. Further, the duty of beneficence may be far more demanding than Kant realized. In a world of acute and urgent need, one could argue that the obligation to help becomes a strict one.

I sketch a Kantian account of duties of rescue, which I take to be compatible with Kant's moral theory. I argue that there is in fact no "trumping relation" between imperfect and perfect duties but merely that "latitude shrinks away" in certain circumstances. Against possible demandingness objections, I explain why Kant thought that imperfect duty must allow latitude for choice and argue that we must understand the necessary space for pursuing one's own happiness as *entailed* by Kant's justification of one's duty to promote other's happiness. Nevertheless, becoming *worthy of happiness* still has priority over one's own happiness when circumstances are such that we cannot secure our own happiness without seriously neglecting more pressing needs of other persons. I conclude that Kant's moral theory calls for complementation by the political and juridical domain. Implementing just political institutions and creating satisfactorily well-ordered societies create an external world which is friendlier to our attempts to reconcile moral integrity and a happy human life.

1. IS THE DISTINCTION BETWEEN PERFECT AND IMPERFECT DUTIES RELEVANT?

Perfect duties are injunctions to refrain from or to perform certain acts. They are strict requirements concerning more or less clearly specified actions. All act tokens falling under the description of the duty are *binding* duties: they should either be performed or refrained from. If one has a perfect duty not to wrong others, one must refrain from performing all the act tokens matching the description "wronging others" or perform all those act tokens whose non-performance would imply harming others. Thus, it is not up to the agent to choose whether to perform or refrain from performing a strictly required act token: refusing to do what is strictly required amounts to a violation of duty. This is made explicit by Kant's *contradiction in conception test* of the *Groundwork* (GMS IV: 421–23).

Imperfect duty, in contrast, may leave some latitude for choice. This means that an unlimited amount of act tokens A1, A2, A3 . . . may fall, for instance, under the duty of beneficence, but doing a specific act instead of others does not imply a violation of duty, only, to use Kant's own expression, "lack of merit" (*demeritum*, MS VI: 390) in regard to the act tokens which were not performed.

Kant's paradigmatic imperfect duty is the duty of beneficence. Even though it is possible to think of a world in which a maxim of indifference would be a universal law, Kant argues that as rational agents we cannot consistently *will* that such a maxim become a universal law (GMS IV: 423). Recognizing imperfect duties seems necessary for two reasons. Firstly, not recognizing them would imply making morality excessively demanding, perhaps even unbearable for human beings. No matter how much we do in matters of beneficence, we are never "done" with it. It is therefore not possible to release oneself forever (or even temporarily) from the duty by doing a "sufficient" amount of beneficent acts. Secondly, Kant scholars such as Marcia Baron have shown that imperfect duties can help us not only demystify the idea of *supererogation* but ultimately *replace* that notion by that of imperfect duties.[2] Supererogation has been regarded with suspicion by moral theorists, who believe that accepting that some morally worthy actions are "beyond duty" can be used as an excuse for ignoring moral requirements.[3]

According to Kant, perfect duties must always be given priority over imperfect duties. Since we are not obliged to act on every possible act token falling under an imperfect duty, foregoing one opportunity to comply with an imperfect duty for the sake of satisfying a strict requirement does not amount to a conflict of duties. In contrast, choosing to comply with an imperfect duty when this presupposes violating a strict requirement would amount to a positive violation of duty and undermine the moral worth of one's conduct. If helping you would require stealing something or murdering an innocent, then I must not help you.

The normative priority of perfect over imperfect duties seems to contradict some common moral intuitions. For instance, it seems absurd to think that one should not save persons from a burning house if doing so would require using the neighbor's garden hose without her permission, or that I should not save a drowning child because that will entail breaking a promise. Many instances of beneficence intuitively seem more pressing than certain instances of respect for private property or other perfect duties.[4] These are cases when we would have a *duty of rescue*. Kant however does not seem able to derive duties of rescue from his contradiction in the will test. Our duty to help is an imperfect one: it comes with a latitude for choice which seems out of place in emergency situations, when another person's life is at stake. Kant seems either to have ignored duties of rescue or to have conflated them with duty of beneficence in general.

If we take these intuitions seriously, it seems that it is not the specific structure of the duty which determines our judgment of what to do in a certain circumstance. This raises the suspicion that practical deliberation can do without the distinction between perfect and imperfect duties. A second, more serious worry follows from the first one: if imperfect duties do not always allow us latitude for choice, it could be that we are wrong when we think it is permissible to forego an opportunity to help. If the pressing needs of others can make the duty to help stronger than some perfect duties and we are living in a world of urgent need, then it is possible that we are being more lax about the duty of beneficence than we are aware of.

Kant himself did not seem to think his conception of beneficence could be overdemanding precisely because he believed in the distinction between perfect and imperfect duties. However, he believed that *perfect duties* could be very demanding, depending on external circumstances. I will discuss the demandingness of perfect duties in the last section of this article and argue that it can be minimized with the institution of just political institutions. In the following, I will concentrate on Kant's understanding of the duty of beneficence and make the case for the following claims: (1) the distinction between perfect and imperfect duties is not superfluous; (2) it is possible to give a Kantian account of duties of rescue without undermining this distinction; (3) the latitude of imperfect duties can deflect demandingness objections against a Kantian duty of beneficence.

Most cases which rule out latitude for compliance with imperfect duties are instances of the duties of aid or rescue, which Kant does not explicitly distinguish from beneficence in general. Kant argues in the *Doctrine of Right* that the concept of right "does not signify the relation of one's choice to the mere wish (hence also to the mere **need**) of the other, as in actions of beneficence or callousness" (RL VI: 230, my emphasis). As stressed before, Kant seems unable to account for the stringent requirement to help in emergency situations; he treats emergency situations in the same way as instances of the duty of beneficence. If there is a *juridical* duty of rescue, that is, if the duty of rescue is institutionalized by one's state, the case would be settled for Kant. The duty of rescue would be a *perfect* duty whose "ground of obligation" could be considered more stringent than the duty to respect private property, for instance. However, I will explore the possibility of a *moral* argument for duties of rescue and will put this possibility aside.

Daniel Statman has argued that when a perfect duty is "overridden" by an imperfect duty in accordance to our common intuitions, the imperfect duty in question must actually be a perfect one. If saving persons from a fire requires us to use the neighbor's garden hose without her permission, saving them not only has priority over respecting private property, but is a perfect duty. While this view at first seems to leave Kant's understanding of perfect duties as more fundamental than imperfect ones intact, Statman goes on to argue that the characterization of a duty as perfect or imperfect is done *ad hoc*, "on the basis of the weight of the conflicting duty, instead of independent considerations concerning the nature of the duties at stake."[5] In other words, it is not the specific "logical structure" of a duty which determines which action should be given priority in a certain situation.

Although under certain circumstances it may *seem* that imperfect duty overrides perfect duty, I will argue that it is only the *stringency* of these duties which may vary under exceptional circumstances. The subordination of imperfect to perfect obligation, however, is maintained and still plays an important regulative function for practical judgment. This is the subject of the next section.

2. WHY LATITUDE MATTERS AND WHEN IT SHRINKS AWAY

While in the first formulation of the categorical imperative in the *Groundwork* Kant used the termini perfect and imperfect duties,[6] at the transition from the first to the second formula, Kant changes his terminology. He now speaks of *necessary* or *owed* duty (*nothwendige Pflicht gegen sich selbst*, IV: 429, l. 15, *nothwendige oder schuldige Pflicht gegen andere*, Ibid., l. 29) and of *contingent* or *meritorious* duty (*zufällige/verdienstliche Pflicht gegen sich selbst*, IV: 430, l.10). It might seem puzzling that Kant associates the distinction strict/wide duty with the predicates *necessary/contingent*. Given Kant's standard definition of duty as the necessity of an action from respect for the law (GMS IV: 400 l.18), one might wonder how a duty can ever be contingent. According to Timmermann, wide duties are contingent not because they depend on an existing inclination of the agent (in which case they would no longer be duties, but a hypothetical commands), but because token duties depend on particular occasions to apply (for instance, from the fact that someone else is in need). They are not "less obligatory" than perfect duties.[7]

Contingent duties are dependent on the specific circumstances in a way necessary or strict duties are not. The necessity of acting on a certain act token identified by the agent as a beneficent action will depend on the specific circumstances, for instance, the degree of need involved, her position to give help, whether there are other persons responsible or more able to help, etc. Depending on how pressing the conjunction of all these factors is, one has either an opportunity to act beneficently or no latitude at all. As I will stress later, latitude refers to the *stringency* of the duty and not to the choice of means available to the agent.

Kant often equates the distinction pairs *strict/wide* with *juridical/ethical*, perhaps giving the impression that they are synonymous. Although juridical duties which can be externally coerced are strict,[8] ethical duties can be both strict and wide (although wide duties are the paradigmatic ethical duties). There are also variations in the wideness of different imperfect duties. The duty to work towards greater moral perfection is presumably stricter than the duty to develop one's talents (MS VI: 446) just as the ethical duty of respect for others is more strict than the ethical duty of love (MS VI: 449–450). The distinction strict/wide thus seems to refer to the *type of necessity* or the *stringency* of the obligation in question, whereas the juridical/ethical distinction addresses the aspect of *necessitation* (*Nötigung*), i.e., whether only *internal* or also *external* necessitation (i.e., coercion) is possible.[9] The stringency of wide duties can thus vary depending on the context, a feature belonging to the *latitude* of these duties. Therefore, Kant's distinction between perfect and imperfect duties is less rigid than Kant's critics assume and could accommodate variations in stringency without undermining itself.

When there is no latitude for choice? My view is that latitude shrinks away when refusing to help would amount to *giving up* one's commitment to beneficence *altogether.* While bypassing opportunities to help is mostly compatible with a maxim of beneficence ("sorry, I don't have time to help you with your garden right now, but next time!"), there are circumstances when acting otherwise would necessarily imply that the agent has altogether given up a maxim of beneficence. Making use of the latitude of wide duties is permissible in Kant's account as long as one remains sincerely committed to the moral end. Certain circumstances, however, put the sincerity of one's commitment to the moral end *under proof.* Under these circumstances the duty to help acquires a *stringency* that is identical to that of perfect duties.

This is because even though beneficence is an imperfect duty, the requirement to adopt a moral end is itself a strict one: what is "in the manner of imperfect duty" is *discharging* the duty, that is, the promotion of the end of beneficence. As rational finite beings we are strictly required to adopt the happiness of others as our end, but since this involves the furtherance of an end[10] (and not simply the omission or commission of certain acts), we need latitude for choice, so that we can comply with other duties and have the necessary space for the satisfaction of permissible needs and non-moral interests.

As Kant notes, "if the law can prescribe only the maxim of actions, not actions themselves, this is a sign that it leaves a latitude (*latitudo*) for free choice (*freie Willkür*) in following (complying with) the law, that is, that the law cannot specify precisely in what way one is to act and how much one is to do by the action for an end that is also a duty" (MS VI: 390). The ways in which I can comply with my maxim of beneficence seem open to me. Because I can choose when, how and how much to comply, foregoing act tokens which would fall under the description "beneficence" are not violations of duty; they just reflect the fact that I have chosen to comply with my duty of beneficence in a different way; insofar as I remain sincerely committed to the moral end, it poses no greater difficulties.

Now, I do not claim that the way one should help becomes determinate in emergency cases, while it is otherwise indeterminate. What is clear in the circumstances is only that help we must, here and now. The requirement to help is stringent in the sense that under the circumstances we cannot choose whether to help or not (although we could still decide between one act token or another, say, ringing up the ambulance, screaming for passers-by to assist you with the injured person or applying your first aid knowledge by yourself). It is important not to confuse the latitude / stringency of the duty with the possibility of choosing the means to help. Even perfect duties allow for choice in the means of compliance (for instance, I can pay my debt by cheque, debit or with any combination of paper money and / or coins, even though using only coins is likely to drive the creditor mad). If that is the case, what makes a duty stringent or gives rise to latitude is not simply the availability of different means to discharge the duty.

My duty not to lie is stringent and not complying with this duty here and now amounts to a violation of duty. It is not permissible to lie to you now because I shall be discharging my duty of truthfulness to someone else tomorrow after breakfast. Stringency has to do with the question *when* to discharge the duty. We cannot put off compliance with the thought that we are going to discharge it later in this or that way.

In contrast, beneficence does not *always* impose a stringent obligation to act in a particular circumstance. But it *can* become stringent. Stringency in the case of beneficence signalizes that not to act here and now would be incompatible with the description of an agent who is committed to the end of beneficence. While perfect duties are *always* stringent across different scenarios, imperfect duties can vary in stringency depending on the circumstances. If so, when does beneficence become stringent, to the point of leaving us no latitude for choice?

It is important to remember that the commitment to any end excludes certain actions and attitudes as incompatible with one's commitment to that end. If I have decided to further my musical talent and become a professional pianist, any activities compromising my ability to play are off the list. For instance, becoming a hobby boxer or chopping wood in my free time would show that I no longer take serious my end to become a professional pianist. Since not helping someone in great need at very little cost to ourselves when possible is incompatible with having adopted the end of beneficence, not helping would amount to giving up the moral end of beneficence. Stringent occasions for help are therefore situations in which voluntary, conscious non-compliance would undermine our commitment to a moral end. Just as the pianist who irresponsibly hurt his fingers, you can no longer say you are sincerely committed to beneficence. This of course excludes cases of ignorance or inability to offer help.

But what if some perfect duty prohibits or imposes constraints on one's conduct in an emergency situation? For instance, if helping the victims of a car crash nearby makes it necessary that I break into your house and take whatever I need to help the victims? Intuitively, one might think that I would be morally permitted to violate private property (whether this is legally the case is another matter), but not to murder you if you are in the house and refuse me entry. Strictly speaking, we are not *permitted* to violate perfect duty; we might be merely *excused* to do so, given the circumstances. I would be violating a perfect duty if I broke into your house and used your phone to save the victims of the car crash, but the point is that from a moral and maybe also from a legal perspective I may be retrospectively *excused* for doing so.[11]

Perfect duties are not "trumped" by the imperfect ones in emergency situations. They are *violated*, but with an *excuse,* namely that the circumstances were such that although our duty to help is very stringent, perfect duties did not allow us to comply with imperfect duty. However, there is a point when violating perfect duties is no longer excusable and this is not only when violating perfect duties would be strictly necessary for complying with the stringent imperfect duty. Although the violation of a perfect duty must be strictly needed for saving the victims, saving the victims is not the only duty we have. Our conception of the perfect duties there still imposes constraints on the means "morally available" to us for saving the victims. This shows that the subordination of imperfect to perfect obligation is still maintained at a broader level and plays a regulative function for practical judgment.

It accounts for the intuition that although we may be excused for violating some perfect duty to comply with a duty of rescue, there is a point *we may be excused not to comply with the duty of rescue.*

We can summarize the points made so far as follows:

1. Willfully not acting would be incompatible with the description of an agent who is committed to the end of beneficence. There is no latitude for choice;
2. However, the duty to help is still an imperfect duty because it may be limited by perfect duties;
3. One may choose to violate some perfect duties in order to discharge one's stringent duty to help; given the circumstances, we may be morally excused for doing so;
4. But there is a limit to how far we can violate perfect duties and be excused. Other perfect duties still limit one's conduct and there is no trumping relation.

One might object to the idea of *excusing* a violation of a perfect duty in order to save a person's life. Why not acknowledge that agents are *permitted* and not merely *excused* to violate these duties? Granting an agent a permission to do X entails an express recognition that the agent is justified in violating the norm. In contrast, excusing the agent may suggest that it would be better if the agent had not violated the duty, although her violation can be condoned, given her circumstances (perhaps she was too distressed and not fully accountable for her conduct at the time). Intuitively, there is a great difference between someone who breaks into a house to save someone's life and a person who does the same action to avoid some inconvenience, although her action is excusable. It seems that *excusing* someone is incompatible with the idea that she has done nothing *wrong* in the first place. I will argue that the agent has done something wrong, even though not helping the victim is not an option either.

The notion of permission entails an exception to a rule. Kant acknowledges that there can be "permissive laws of pure reason," namely, under situations where strict compliance with the duty would *undermine* the moral end the same duty is supposed to promote. An example of a permissive law (*lex permissiva*) in the *Doctrine of Right* is the permission to appropriate and keep objects for oneself to the exclusion of others, even if that imposes a unilateral hindrance on their freedom to use that object (MS RL VI: 246–7). Kant thinks that property rights in the state of nature are necessary for a future condition of public distributive justice. Forbidding the appropriation of objects would make the achievement of such a condition and ultimately the protection of individual's freedom impossible. Therefore, we must allow such acts of unilateral acquisition. Another example is the sovereign's deferral of political reforms in line with the notion of a republican constitution when the people is not prepared for them (ZeF VIII: 373). An ethical example can be found in a casuistic question in the *Doctrine of Virtue,* where Kant stipulates whether sexual intercourse for non-procreative purposes should be permitted. He notes that forbidding it might have much worse consequences for virtue than insisting that sex remains attached to its "natural purpose" (MS TL VI: 426).

Positive laws are needed for maintaining a condition of public justice. Once they are laid down in an equally binding manner for all agents, it is not up to individuals to decide for themselves when they should uphold or make an exception to these laws. This would undermine the possibility of public justice. Kant himself acknowledges that strictly adhering to positive laws will sometimes generate unfair outcomes. The "strictest right is the greatest wrong" when our sense of equity seems completely impotent in face of the blindness and insensitivity of law systems to the facts of life. Kant's point is however that we need an omnilateral system of laws which would collapse if everyone took the liberty to reinterpret the law subjectively. However, while we have a duty of justice to obey the law, courts of justice can decide to excuse agents for violations in emergency cases or to formulate clauses permitting the violation under certain conditions.

There is a clear difference between taking your coat by mistake and taking your coat because I want it for myself. None of these intentions can make your property right in that coat disappear, although they will be relevant for accessing your action retrospectively. Now, if I take your coat to save the life of someone dying of cold, it is still the case that I have violated your property right in that coat. Your right does not disappear nor is it "trumped." We might however agree that I should be excused for that action.

3. WHY LATITUDE MATTERS

While some Kant scholars interpret latitude as allowing the agent to decide when, how and how far to comply with imperfect duty,[12] other scholars have adopted a more rigoristic interpretation of imperfect duties, in which the notion of latitude for choice is restricted. Timmermann, for instance, interprets latitude of choice as restricted to the possibility of choosing the *means* to satisfy duty in a certain situation, since the choice of means falls outside the scope of moral deliberation. Latitude thus only applies to rules of skill (technical imperatives) related to one's duty.[13] According to Timmermann, we have a *strict* duty to help when there is only one permissible course of action open to the agent in a given situation. In this case, it is not possible to choose the means to beneficence "according to one's preferences," that is, there is no latitude for choice.

Timmermann's interpretation is problematic. Imagine someone going out to work in the morning who finds a severely injured person lying on the pavement (a pedestrian who was hit by a car on the nearby road). It is clear to the agent that she has no option other than to help. Nevertheless, she might still be unsure what means to take, although help she must: what should she do first, call the ambulance straight away or perhaps first see that the person is not choking on her own blood? Should she perhaps first cover the injured person's body with a warm blanket, since this is a cold January morning, and then call for help? Or should she perhaps just start screaming for help as loud as she can, so that the neighbors will come and perhaps make a better decision? Latitude in Kant's account refers to the *stringency of the duty* relative to the circumstances and not to the range of possible means for complying with the duty. What is "not an option" in this case is *indifference* to the injured person's condition rather than any specific way of helping. When the duty is especially pressing, latitude for doing *anything else which is not helping* shrinks away, even though we are still dealing with an imperfect duty. On the other hand, it is possible that helping in a certain case is only *effective* through a particular action. If I am dying of thirst, the only useful thing you could possibly do is to give me some water. If you *know this* and choose instead to make a generous bank transfer on my behalf, it seems that you were not really committed to helping me. Your duty is to try to help me effectively. But this is a "technical" aspect of my action and not what latitude is all about.

One of the problems which recent, more rigoristic approaches to latitude seek to address is the worry that acknowledging latitude for choice in the case of imperfect duties would lead not only to a minimalistic, self-indulgent conception of morality, but also to the dangerous belief that compliance with imperfect duty may be considered *supererogatory*. Doing anything that goes beyond what is strictly owed to others would be considered "good but not required." As Marcia Baron notes, "one can puff up with self-satisfaction at having done something extra for someone; it is not as easy to feel smug and superior about doing what, one believes, anyone in those circumstances is morally required to do."[14] This view is a good expression of Kant's critical attitude in regard to the romantic ideals recommending extraordinary heroic acts (cf. KpV V: 155).

Since in Kant's moral theory moral worth depends on whether an action is morally required and has been done from the motive of duty, the idea of something being morally good but not required seems a conceptual impossibility, at least in Kant's theoretical framework. Although not ill founded, Kantian concerns about admitting the category of supererogation should not lead us to adopt an excessively restrictive understanding of the latitude of imperfect duties, against Kant's own intention. Once we understand the role the notion of latitude is intended to play in Kant's account of duty, these worries will be dispelled.

Let us have a closer look at what the rigoristic interpretation says about the pursuit of one's own happiness and imperfect duty. Timmermann's interpretation might suggest that we may pursue our happiness only when there is no other duty to be discharged. As soon as one perceives an opportunity to help, one has a *stringent* duty to help, unless other moral principles speak against it. Latitude is only about which means to take in order to help: but if no perfect duty speaks against it, help we must. But my question is: since one has a duty to actively *promote* a moral end (in this case, the happiness of others), should we not *look* for opportunities to help when no opportunity presents itself? The world is full of persons in need, many of them in urgent need and I know this. As Timmermann puts it, moral goodness is "infinitely precious."[15] The question is thus: how can my happiness, which is merely *permitted*, ever compete with what is *morally necessary*?

Here we can enumerate all those aspects of Kant's moral theory which permit us to limit compliance with beneficence and perhaps clear Kant's moral theory of the charge of being overly demanding: firstly, we must take into account the indirect duty to promote one's happiness, since a certain degree of satisfaction with one's condition keeps us from temptations to violate duty. Secondly, we should only adopt the permissible ends of others (although it seems implausible to assume that not having to help sloths, bank robbers, murderers, and exploitative people would considerably reduce opportunities to help). Thirdly, we should avoid making others dependent; we should only help until agents can restore their ability to provide for themselves. There is also the duty to cultivate one's talents, which would permit (if not *require*) us to invest some resources in our person. Additionally, Timmermann argues that one should not let the morally lax free ride on our good works (even though he acknowledges that in Kant's account no one would be exempt from duty if others happen not to do their share). Despite these limiting conditions, it seems that we have still not justified *why* we are not giving up our commitment to the happiness of others when we *recognize* an opportunity to help and deliberately forego it, despite the fact that we are *always under the obligation to help*.

In order to solve this problem, we must recall why we have a duty to help others in the first place. Kant assumes that we all naturally want to be happy. Happiness can be presupposed as an actual end for all dependent rational beings, insofar as imperatives apply to them (GMS IV: 415 ll. 28–37). Since we all naturally want to be happy, this cannot be a duty, unless for some reason we cease to feel the natural concern for our wellbeing most healthy persons have (in which case, duties to the self remain).[16] Kant concentrates on the "normal" scenario, which is that we pursue happiness most of the time from *inclination* and not from duty. The condition for the permissibility of the pursuit of one's own happiness is that we also adopt the happiness of all others as our end. This means that a person who sincerely adopts the happiness of others as her end is *permitted* to be beneficent to herself (MS TL § 27 at VI: 451).

Marcia Baron argued that these considerations do not rule out a "sterner" view of the latitude of imperfect duties. The quotation at VI: 451 means only that "we are all equals and there is no ground for regarding as morally irrelevant one's own happiness."[17] In her view, what will lead us to adopt a more restrictive view of the latitude of imperfect duty is the duty of *self-perfection*. According to Baron, the duty to improve oneself morally will influence the way we carry out the duty to promote each other's happiness. As she puts it, "the full spirit of the [imperfect duty of making the ends of others my own] is not brought out until that duty is seen as shaped and 'stiffened' by the duty to improve oneself morally."[18] By self-scrutiny, the agent will become alert to the fact "that she has a tendency to avoid friends when they are ill or depressed or in mourning" and has the opportunity either to improve herself or to be beneficent in different ways. Baron's interpretation may suggest that agents who make use of the latitude of imperfect duties are not perfecting themselves when they could do so, and are failing to live up to certain moral standards. No significant role seems to be assigned to the notion of latitude in moral life (apart from the view that it ought to be restricted by self-perfection). It is also important to note that self-perfection in Kant's account is "narrow and perfect in terms of its quality but it is wide and imperfect in terms of its degree, because of the frailty *(fragilitas)* of human nature." In regard to its object, the moral ideal one ought to realize, it is narrow, but in regard to the subject, whose duty it is, it can only be considered an imperfect duty to the self (MS VI: 446). Although more strict than other wide duties, self perfection focuses on the *purity* of our motives and does not necessarily imply that we should maximize opportunities of making ourselves more perfect and thereby reduce latitude for compliance with beneficence.[19]

Since beneficence to oneself is not a duty, but merely a *permission* entailed by the adoption of the happiness of others as one's end (MS TL VI: 451), it is necessary that the principle commanding beneficence to others involves *latitude* for compliance. We have the duty to adopt the happiness of others as our end because we naturally want our own happiness. If commitment to the principle would exclude the possibility of pursuing our own happiness,[20] a maxim of benevolence would be *self-contradictory*. We *must* acknowledge latitude because while there is no upper limit to the demands of wide duty, the promotion of our own happiness is *not morally required.* We are required to promote the moral end of beneficence and self-perfection *ad infinitum*, not because we must *maximize* virtue, but because we are *always* under obligation and can never "be done" with the duty by doing a certain amount of obligatory acts (not even by doing the best we can our whole life long).[21] Latitude creates the required space for the satisfaction of the agent's most important needs compatible with a genuine commitment to the promotion of the happiness of others, what Kant calls one's true needs. A permissible pursuit of happiness must thus *necessarily* be embedded in the context of our moral commitment to the happiness of others, in the form of latitude for choice *granted* to the agent by the principle of beneficence. To deny genuine latitude for choice in the case of the duty of beneficence is thus to undermine its very *raison d'être*.

When we deliberately forego an opportunity to comply with the duty of beneficence to pursue our own happiness, this is not necessarily morally objectionable; this is not because we are making "exceptions" to the duty of beneficence in the name of inclination. We are invoking a permission, which is implicitly built into the principle of beneficence, qua wide duty. This permission is expressed in the way we *integrate* obligation in and *structure* our lives and not on an *ad hoc* basis: our different maxims of imperfect duty, personal projects and preferences all shape the way we lay out (or interpret) the duty of beneficence in advance. It is therefore possible to have more than one correct answer to the same moral problem. Moreover, *different agents* may have *different (correct) answers*. As Barbara Herman argues, "having made certain decisions about how to live one's life, say, ones that require the focused development of special talents, one may have closed off, morally speaking, certain ways of living with others. That is, such decisions affect not just obligations but permissions as well. We can now understand why it is that how often and how much I might offer help could in a sense be up to me and it still be the case that 'I don't feel like it' is not a reason for not helping."[22]

4. A FEW REMARKS ON THE TRAGIC SIDE OF KANT'S MORAL THEORY

In this paper, I have focused on the demandingness of Kant's account of the duty of beneficence.[23] I have not discussed the demandingness of perfect duties in his account. That perfect duties can also be demanding is exemplified by several examples in Kant's works. For instance, Kant stresses that one must not give false testimony even if one's own life may be endangered by complying with the duty (whether one will act as duty commands is another story, KpV V: 30, 155–6). As Kant often stresses, we must do what duty commands regardless of the impact on our non-moral interests (however, when one can avoid bad consequences, there is no reason why one should be imprudent).[24]

Kant seems to have thought that the latitude characteristic of beneficence would preclude demandingness. But if conditions are as dire as to make the need around agents more pressing than furthering their less urgent non-moral interests, then similarly to emergency situations, latitude may shrink away. I will argue that possible sources of demandingness are the same for perfect and imperfect duties in Kant's account. If one's conception of happiness includes only permissible ends, the incompatibility between moral demands and the agent's happiness will always be *contingent*. The fact that morality can become very demanding is therefore not intrinsic to moral demands, but depends on how friendly or unfriendly external circumstances are in regard to moral agency.

Kant regards morality as the condition for the permissibility of happiness (in Kant's words, for the "worthiness to be happy"). Although for Kant there is a necessary conceptual link between morality as worthiness to be happy and happiness proper, "morality meets happiness" only in a contingent way in the world (KpV V: 124). The best moral agent may end up being a very unhappy person, while an immoral agent may enjoy a much more pleasant life. Kant's moral theory does not exclude the possibility of moral agents having to sacrifice their happiness completely when circumstances are very dire. This is because *worthiness to be happy* must always be given normative priority over happiness, when being moral *and* securing one's happiness is contingently impossible. All that Kant seems to offer in those circumstances are reasons to hope that God exists and will compensate us for our morally motivated sacrifices in an afterlife. Since this hope cannot be confirmed theoretically, the Kantian agent's only consolation must remain an unwarranted object of faith (KpV V: 125).

Telling the truth, keeping one's promises and being kind and helpful to others are all aspects of everyday life in well ordered societies. Instead of being a moral burden, these 'basic' obligations are more or less integrated into the lives of most agents and play a crucial role in structuring social life. However, under circumstances of political turmoil or instability (civil wars or in extremely unjust or malfunctioning polities) it can become exceptionally hard if not altogether impossible to comply with the simplest of these everyday duties without sacrificing one's happiness completely. Under less well ordered conditions, compliance with the most trivial moral requirements can make moral agents vulnerable to violence or manipulation by others. Although moral requirements remain the same in both ordered and badly ordered societies, it is clear that the particular social and political context makes a difference to whether morality will be too demanding or not.

Just political institutions are not meant to distribute rewards "proportional to one's moral worth," as God would presumably do in the afterlife in Kant's account of "moral faith." Nevertheless, just societies can create conditions of greater or lesser security and stability under which moral agency does not exclude human happiness and flourishing.[25] Although just institutions would not completely rule out eventual clashes between moral requirements and the possibility of a happy life, the point is that morality is not *intrinsically* incompatible with human happiness. Since overdemandingness is mostly due to contingent factors (for instance, whether there are princes who try to force subjects to give a false testimony by threatening death, cf. KpV V: 30, 155–6), reducing these factors is a political task which may not be achieved within the span of one's life but needs not to be relegated to the afterlife.

Kant suggests a similar idea in the *Conflict of the Faculties* when he identifies moral progress not with the increase in the human capacity for morality or moral intentions, but with the development and expansion of political institutions. Political institutions would "increase the *effects* of morality," that is, actions in external accordance with duty (*legality*, SF VI: 91). Kant does not say explicitly that just political institutions create favorable conditions for moral agency, but this is nevertheless a clear presupposition of his view of moral progress.

> Gradually violence on the part of the powers will diminish and obedience to the laws will increase. There will arise in the body politic perhaps more charity and less strife in lawsuits, more reliability in keeping one's word, etc., part out of love of honour, partly of well-understood self-interest. And eventually this will also extend to nations in their external relations toward one another up to the realization of the cosmopolitan society, without the moral foundation in mankind having to be enlarged in the least; for that, a kind of new creation (supernatural influence) would be necessary. (SF VII: 91–2)

The charge of demandingness has been regarded by moral philosophers as a serious objection against a moral theory. While a Kantian account of morality does not need to deny the possibility of demandingness, it can nevertheless withstand demandingness objections by pointing out that it is not its conception of morality that needs revision, but the political conditions under which agents must act. Although unfortunate circumstances do not free us from the call of duty, we are confronted with the political task of creating a world which is friendlier to rational ideals: a world in which moral agents can finally be at home.

In the next and final chapter, I will analyze the status of happiness in Kant's political and legal philosophy and address the question of economic justice in the Kantian state (which Kant subsumes under the "happiness" of individuals). I will defend the view that the main reason it seems difficult to accommodate welfare legislation in Kant's theory of state is not that welfare legislation promotes the happiness of individuals or some other material end, but that juridical decision making must rely on certain principles.

NOTES

1. A version of this chapter was published as Pinheiro Walla, Alice, "Kant's Moral Theory and Demandingness," *Ethical Theory and Moral Practice,* Vol. 18, No. 4, 2015, pp. 731–43.

2. Marcia Baron, "Kantian Ethics and Supererogation," *The Journal of Philosophy,* Vol. 84, 1987 and Susan Hale, "Against Supererogation." *American Philosophical Quarterly,* Vol. 28, 1991.

3. Catherine Wilson, "On Some Alleged Limitations to Moral Endeavor." *The Journal of Philosophy,* Vol. 90, 1993.

4. Daniel Statman, "Who Needs Imperfect Duties"? *American Philosophical Quarterly,* Vol. 33, No 2, April 1996. Our intuition is also against Kant's notorious claim that one should never lie, not even to save someone's life (*On a supposed right to lie from Philanthropy,* VIII: 427), which has often been transformed into a "Nazi at the door scenario." Most discussions of the theme however result from a misunderstanding of the juridical context of Kant's claim in the text. See Helga Varden, "Kant and Lying to the Murderer at the Door . . . One More Time: Kant's Legal Philosophy and Lies to Murderers and Nazis." *Journal of Social Philosophy,* Vol. 41 No. 4, Winter 2010 and Allen Wood, *Kantian Ethics,* Cambridge University Press 2008, chapter 14.

5. Daniel Statman, op. cit., p. 216.

6. Timmermann, *Kant's Groundwork of the Metaphysics of Morals. A Commentary,* p. 97, footnote 98.

7. Ibid., p. 97.

8. The exception is wide duties of right, which cannot be externally enforced. See MS VI: 233.

9. See Mary Gregor, *Laws of Freedom,* p. 97.

10. Another way of talking about the adoption of a morally required end is to talk about the adoption of a *maxim* of promoting obligatory ends (as opposed to a maxim of indifference or of neglect of one's natural talents). This is the way Kant formulates the first principle of ethics: act according to a maxim of ends (*Maxime der Zwecke*) which it can be a universal law for everyone to have (MS VI: 395). The maxim of ends of ethics is contrasted to the maxim of actions characteristic of the domain of right (*Recht,* cf. VI: 230 ll. 29–30).

11. Depending on the existing laws of a society I may be legally sanctioned for violating private property or contracts, even if addressing emergency situations.

12. H. J. Paton, *The Categorical Imperative. A study in Kant's Moral Philosophy,* Mary Gregor, *Laws of Freedom,* Blackwell, 1963, and more recently Thomas E. Hill,

"Meeting Needs and Doing Favours" In: *Human Welfare and Moral Worth, Kantian Perspectives*. Oxford University Press, 2002.

13. Jens Timmermann, "Good but Not Required? Assessing the Demands of Kantian Ethics," *Journal of Moral Philosophy,* Vol. 2, No. 1, 2005.

14. Marcia Baron, *Kantian Ethics almost without Apology*, p. 37

15. Timmermann, op. cit., p. 23.

16. See my article "Local desire satisfaction versus long-term wellbeing in Kant's *Grundlegung*," unpublished manuscript. Belgrade Philosophical Annual (2015) issue 28. pp. 31–44.

17. Marcia Baron, op. cit. p. 93.

18. Marcia Baron, op. cit. p. 100.

19. Cf. Thomas E. Hill, "Meeting Needs and Doing Favours" In: *Human Welfare and Moral Worth*, Oxford University Press, 2002, pp. 209–10.

20. It can be argued that one's happiness could coincide with the happiness of others. I would be pursuing my happiness in that I adopt the happiness of others as my end. Although this is possible, it is certainly not the case that one can completely reduce one's own happiness to the happiness of others. This would mean either that the happiness of others would coincide with my conception of happiness or that my happiness could be reduced to mere moral self-approval. Kant seems to rule out the first option as a conceptual impossibility: if I pursue the happiness of others as my own conception of happiness, I am not adopting the moral end of beneficence, but merely taking the means to my own happiness. As for the second, Kant explicitly rules out reducing happiness to moral self-approval (KpV V: 88).

21. Contra Hill, who assumed that by doing a certain amount of beneficent acts, the agent would accumulate a kind of moral "bonus" after which certain acts falling under the duty of beneficence would be considered supererogatory (although in a weak sense). The problem I see with this view is the assumption that one can reach the point of "having done enough," even if temporarily. Thomas E. Hill, "Kant on imperfect duty and supererogation." *Kant Studien*, Vol. 62, No. 1, 1971.

22. Barbara Herman, "The Scope of Moral Requirement," In: *Moral Literacy*, Harvard University Press, Cambridge Massachusetts, 2007, p. 221.

23. A further development of this section was published as "Kant and the Wisdom of Oedipus," *Jahrbuch Praktische Philosophie in globaler Perspektive / Yearbook Practical Philosophy in a Global Perspective*, 2019.

24. Kant is by no means saying that we should not care about our prudential interests when these do not collide with morality. Often, morality allows us to reconcile duty and prudential interests.

25. See Barbara Herman, "Morality and Everyday Life," *Proceedings and Addresses of The American Philosophical Association,* Vol. 74, No. 2, 2000, pp. 29–45.

Chapter Six

Happiness in Kant's Political and Legal Philosophy

In this chapter, I will analyze Kant's reasons for separating considerations of wellbeing (the material ends of agents) from the object matter of public justice, which is the public wellbeing (*salus publica*). In order to understand why happiness is rejected as a principle of external legislation, I shall firstly reconstruct Kant's views on why we need a civil condition and why our external relations with each other must be regulated by a priori legal principles.[1] I then turn to the question of economic and social justice in Kant's theory of the state. Due to its focus on freedom and the protection of private rights, the Kantian state has traditionally been interpreted as a libertarian, minimalist state: it is restricted to regulating the interactions between individuals and not the material outcomes of these interactions. I argue that although the Kantian *Rechtsstaat* is not primarily concerned with material outcomes and patterns of distribution but only with formal relations of right, it can nevertheless recognize the need to redistribute out of considerations of fairness or equity, that is, from the recognition of the non enforceable rights of individuals or private right (Privatrecht) in the state of nature.[2]

For this purpose, I analyze a central passage in the *Metaphysics of Morals* in which Kant argues for the right of the state to tax the poor. The passage is puzzling and at first seems hard to reconcile with Kant's own characterization of the state as based solely on formal principles of right. With recourse to additional passages in the *Metaphysics of Morals* and Kant's lectures, I reconstruct Kant's argument for the state's right to tax to provide for the poor and link it to his scepticism about the status of beneficence as a meritorious duty given systemic injustice: his acknowledgment that social inequality is perpetuated by the system of right itself, in which all members of society partake. I will then establish a parallel between the right of a state to redistribute and Kant's account of wide, non-enforceable rights or equity (*Billigkeit*).

1. WHY WE NEED A CIVIL CONDITION: KANT'S THEORY OF LEGAL OBLIGATION

Right (*Recht*) concerns the formal conditions enabling a mutually compatible exercise of external freedom by a plurality of agents (i.e., a *system* of external freedom). As Kant puts it, Right is "the sum of the conditions under which the choice of one can be united with the choice of another in accordance with a universal law of freedom" (MS VI: 230). Due to the humanity in our person, every human being has a right not to be bound by others in a way she cannot bind them in return (innate equality) and consequently to be their own master (*sui iuris*) (RL VI: 238). This only innate right of all human beings means that, all things equal, no one has a juridical duty to bear the impositions of others on one's exercise of external freedom as long as one's action is compatible with the equal innate right of all others (MS VI:237). Only the voluntary *deeds* of persons can give rise to positive legal obligations toward specified others, but even so, reciprocity remains a fundamental condition that must structure rightful external relations between persons. Any duty to bear restrictions on one's exercise of external freedom must therefore satisfy formal requirements of reciprocity in order to count as rightful and as a genuine legal obligation (something one has a duty of right to bear as opposed to mere violence or coercion). The difference between external coercion and an external obligation (a duty of right) lies on whether one is genuinely *bound* by what is being imposed on her. For this, we need a theory of legal obligation.

Kant provides a theory of legal obligation in the Doctrine of Right. The task of the theory is to spell out the conditions under which it is *morally possible* to impose duties on others externally. The idea of an external duty is particularly puzzling from a Kantian perspective, since it strongly suggests the definition of heteronomy in Kant's moral theory.[3] Not only is someone else imposing something on me externally (a restriction on my external freedom or some action I must perform), but I must be *bound* by it, that is, have a genuine duty to comply. How is legal obligation *morally* possible?[4]

One may think that there is something intrinsically normative about the *content* of subjective rights that justifies imposing external duties on others to respect these rights. However, distinctive about Kant's legal theory is the view that the question of my authority to bind you is not exhausted by the content of my right or by my correct judgment about my right-claim.[5] The authority to bind another and the corresponding legal obligation are not an epistemic question about the correct interpretation or of the strength of reasons to recognize certain rights. Legal obligation in Kant's theory requires a system of *reciprocal* constraints, which means that all constraints imposed on the external freedom of others are symmetric. This is why Right (*Recht*) is defined as "the sum of the conditions under which the choice of one can be united with the choice of another in accordance with a universal law of freedom." This formal structure ensures that no one is bound by another in a way she could not, at least in principle, bind her in return.

All obligation is ultimately *self-imposed* (*omnis obligatio est contracta*).[6] Ethical obligation binds us because the moral law arises from our own practical reason. This is why even though we may struggle to want what morality requires of us (subjectively), moral obligation is nevertheless *self-imposed* (objectively). Similarly, if duties of right are to qualify as genuine obligations, they must somehow also qualify as "self-imposed." However, we are no longer in the domain of internal freedom and ethical duties, but are considering the exercise of freedom in space and time and the possibility of obligation that is imposed by another, not by one's own will. Therefore, the question of bindingness acquires a different configuration in the domain of external freedom. I defend the view I will call the "mirrowing thesis" of legal normativity. According to the mirroring thesis, legal obligation must "replicate" the formal structure of self-legislation in Kant's ethical writings. This means that the form of self-legislation in the ethical domain is "transposed" into the domain of external freedom by adopting a principle that is significantly similar to the categorical imperative but is suitable to the domain of external freedom as opposed to one's internal *Gesinnung* or ethical attitudes. It follows that legal obligation cannot be correctly understood as an application of Kant's categorical imperative to the domain of external freedom. Instead, the universality constraint on adopted maxims is translated in the domain of external freedom as the "omnilaterality" of public law and public institutions; the rule of law is therefore the "externalised version" of autonomy of the will.[7] Just as subordinating our wills to the moral law is a necessary condition for moral autonomy, public laws under a civil condition, under which all citizens are *equally* bound, are formally required for the moral possibility of imposing external juridical duties on each other.

Although all persons are born with the only original right ("freedom as independence from the necessitating choice of others, as long as it can coexist with the equal right of others according to a universal law"),[8] it is possible to *acquire* further subjective rights through voluntary exchanges and agreements with others, particular relations to other persons such as being the parent or spouse of someone, or by taking possession of a piece of land or objects which were previously ownerless (*prima occupatio/apprehensio*). These private rights are valid independently of whether a state or any juridical institutions are in place, although, as Kant stresses, possession is only *provisionally* rightful until the implementation of a condition of distributive justice. A "provisional" right means that although we can already recognize private rights in the state of nature and they provide a *lawful ground* (*gesetzlichen*

Grund) for obligation (MS RL 6: 237), the full conditions for legal obligation (omnilaterality) are still outstanding. Rights in the state of nature therefore require the implementation of a condition of public law for the possibility of fully fledged legal obligation, although Kant argues that one must already *treat* them as if they were fully fledged, peremptory ones (MS RL 6: 267). Therefore, a civil condition (of which states are the most common embodiment, but in principle not the only possibility) is necessary not only to protect the entitlements "imported" from the state of nature into the civil condition, but to change the *modality* of subjective rights from a contingent "presumption of right" into a necessary, i.e., peremptory right (MS RL §9 at VI: 257). According to this interpretation, Kant can be understood as providing a *modal theory of legal obligation*. Distinctive of this reading is that a condition of distributive justice[9] is required first of all for altering the modality of subjective rights. This means that instead of having rights that are merely given (the category of reality), they become necessary (the category of necessity) under a condition of public justice. All other functions such as protecting and enforcing rights are still important and are by no means excluded, but are nevertheless *secondary* when it comes to establishing the moral possibility of legal obligation. We have thus a duty to enter a lawful condition with others (*exeundum esse e statu naturali*).

Although the concept of a juridical right analytically implies an authorization to coerce (MS VI: 231–3), coercion is only *rightful* if it is consistent with the freedom of all agents (i.e., "in accordance with a universal law"). This means that rights must not be enforced by private persons *unilaterally* or by other private persons on their behalf. Rightful enforcement of rights (or rightful *coercion*) must be omnilateral and thus have a *public* character. Because they represent all persons under the law, only *public institutions* have the authority to lay down public laws, determine what is in accordance with the law in case of disputes, and enforce its interpretation of rights in a way that is genuinely binding to all those below it. The *public* character of a condition of distributive justice, legal certainty and not least positive laws bring about a system that is independent from the arbitrary choice of one person over another and therefore reproduces the universality of ethical self-legislation (although only for persons under its jurisdiction).

2. HAPPINESS AND THE KANTIAN STATE

In *On the Common Saying,* Kant argues that considerations about the happiness of subjects should not be allowed to guide legislation and policy making in the state. Happiness is an indeterminate idea; it is unfit as a basis for universal legislation, be it internal or external legislation. For the same reason that happiness is disqualified as a principle of morals in the foundational ethical works, happiness must be ruled out as the organizing principle of a civil condition. Since people differ in their thinking about happiness and how each would have it constituted, their wills in respect to it cannot be brought under any common principle and so under external law harmonizing with everyone's freedom. (TP VIII: 290)

Although happiness is disqualified as the basis for external laws, it is nevertheless the matter of one's exercise of external freedom: "each may seek her happiness in the way that seems good to her, provided she does not infringe upon that freedom of others to strive for a like end which can coexist with the freedom of everyone in accordance with a possible universal law." This is why no one should try to make another person happy according to one's own (and not the other person's) conception of happiness (TP VIII: 290). Right must thus abstract from the material ends of individuals and focus merely on the form of external interaction because this is the only way to respect each person's right to determine and pursue unhindered one's own conception of happiness. In contrast, a government which tries to "make its subjects happy" by adopting a so-called "principle of benevolence" towards its subjects, would be imposing a specific conception of happiness on individuals and consequently violating the original liberty to choose one's own ends. If the content of individual pursuits must be left to agents themselves to determine, the principle of happiness must be excluded from lawmaking.

> A government established on the principle of benevolence toward the people like that of a father toward his children –that is, a **paternalistic government** (...), in which the subjects, like minor children who cannot distinguish between what is truly useful or harmful to them, are constrained to behave only passively, so as to wait only upon the judgment of the head of state as to how they **should be** happy and, as for his also willing their happiness, only upon his kindness - is the greatest despotism thinkable. (TP VIII: 290–91)

Kant's rejection of happiness as a legislative principle is a result of his concern to avoid state paternalism (TP VIII: 302) and has a specific historical background. It is a direct response to 18th century German theorists such as Samuel Pufendorf and Christian Wolff who conflated law with the promotion of happiness. Wolff's *cameralism* made the case for an excessively controlling government, on the assumption that individuals alone are not able to determine what is best for them. Their happiness and the choice of the means conducive to it should thus be wholly determined by the state.[10] This corresponds precisely to the definition of a despotic state in Kant's legal theory. Kant distinguishes between tyrannical and despotic states or governments.

Tyrannical is a violent, oppressive government (TP VIII: 382). A despotic government may not be felt as oppressive, but does not respect the division of powers within the state; has not only its pertaining executive power, but also seeks to exercise legislative power (MS VI: 316–7). Kant assumes that a despotic state's encroachment upon the division of powers is always motivated by the attempt to promote happiness through public means: the state either wants to force a specific conception of happiness onto its subjects or permits state officials to use the commonwealth to advance their own interests. Although in contrast to a tyrannical government a despotic governemnt could be conceived as benevolent toward its citizens it nevertheless subverts its public character by turning the *res publica* ultimately into an private instrument of a particular individual or group of individuals, despite its alleged good substantive end. It is no less acceptable than a tyrannical state.[11]

Kant bases the notion of the civil condition on three a priori principles: civic freedom, equality and independence (*Freiheit, Gleichheit, Selbständigkeit*, TP VIII: 290). Civil freedom is the aforementioned right to pursue one's own conception of happiness unhindered, as long as it does not hinder the freedom of others. Civil equality is the equality of all subjects before the law and entails that nobody should have the authority to bind others legally in a way that others cannot bind her in turn (cf. MS 6:314). Although natural differences in physical and intellectual ability, external goods and private rights give rise not only to inequality but also to material *dependency* of some individuals on others, Kant insists that material inequalities do not impinge upon the formal equality of individuals as juridical persons. Civil equality is thus consistent with social or economic inequality. However, it is important to stress that in Kant's account civil equality imposes an important constraint on legislation: no one can be denied the opportunity to raise herself to where her talents, industry and fortune can bring her (TP VIII: 292). Equality of opportunity is therefore presupposed in Kant's account of civil equality as equality before the law. Examples of laws which would be ruled out for violating civil equality are those granting hereditary privileges of rank. Hereditary privileges entail the alleged prerogative of one class to restrict access to certain opportunities (public offices, access to the higher ruling rank) on the basis of birth. However, "since birth is not a deed of the one who is born, he cannot incur by it any inequality of rightful condition and any other subjection to coercive laws than merely that which is common to him along with all others, as subjects of the sole legislative power" (TP VIII: 293). The privileged class would be imposing an obligation on members of other classes to abstain from opportunities despite equal qualification or aptitude, which they cannot impose on the privileged class in return. This violates reciprocity and the principle of equality of persons before the law. Civil equality thus prohibits a particular kind of asymmetry: the greater normative authority (the power to obligate) of some persons over others within the juridical system, although not of all kinds of asymmetries in society.¹² It is important to note that Kant's criticism is aimed primarily at the idea that some individuals as *private persons* could have greater authority to bind others juridically. His focus is thus on "normative power" instead of relations of domination. From a Kantian perspective, the idea of domination can be said to *follow* from the asymmetry of normative authority as its effect. The strength of Kant's account is that instead of aiming to eradicate power asymmetries as patterns of social relations it tackles instead the *form* of external relations. These can reveal certain interactions as incapable of genuinely binding those subject to it. And where there is no authority to bind there is no juridical duty to bear. As a theory of legal obligation, Kant's legal theory shows that relations of domination are in their very structure normatively impossible. No private persons have greater normative authority over other private persons because nothing in our normative starting position (the only original right) warrants such an asymmetry. There is simply no normative basis for asymmetries of normative power among equals before the law; these relations simply lack any genuine authority to impose a legal obligation although when embodied in the positive laws of a given state persons have a duty to obey them because they have a more general duty to uphold the civil condition. Civil equality in this case functions as a normative guide for future reforms: the positive laws in the Kantian state ought to be brought closer to the idea of equality of persons under the law.

Kant introduces a regulative device for determining the compatibility of legislation with the a priori principles of right: the idea of an *original contract* (*ursprünglicher Vertrag*) or the *united will of the people*. The original contract is neither a historical fact nor implies *actual* consent from the members of a commonwealth. It is instead an idea of reason which has "undoubted practical reality" since legislators must create laws *as if* they could have arisen from the united will of a whole people and to regard every member of society *as if* she had voted for such a will (TP VIII: 297).¹³ "If a public law is so constituted that a whole people cannot give its consent to it [. . .] it is unjust; but if it is only possible that a people could agree to it, it is a duty to consider such a law just, even if the people is at present in such a situation or frame of mind that, if consulted about it, it would probably refuse its consent" (Ibid.).

The idea of a general will can help identify normative constraints or the rightful limits of state legislation. For instance, legislation prohibiting the possibility of future reforms on the constitution of churches would be incompatible with the notion of a united will of the people insofar as it would negate the possibility of improving institutions in the future or making progress in one's views over time (MS RL §C at VI: 327 and TP VIII: 304). Incompatible with the united will of all would also be the alleged right of a sovereign to take away a public office from someone for arbitrary reasons (MS RL §D at VI: 328) and granting special privileges to a certain group while others are forced to carry the burdens of war (TP VIII: 297n). Kant also argues for "freedom of the pen" (intellectual freedom and freedom of expression, "the sole palladium of the people's rights") as constitutionally protected means for expressing public dissatisfaction about the government and a constructive way for heads of state to be instructed about how they can improve arrangements for the state.

The state must ensure that subjects are not legally barred from raising themselves where their talents, industry and luck can bring them by imposing constraints on legislation and making it compatible with civil equality, but it has no duty to *promote* the social ascent of the lower class beyond this formal requirement. The same applies to the more controversial principle of the civil condition: civic independence (*Selbständigkeit*). In *On the Common Saying*, this is the ability to be one's own master (*sui iuris*) insofar as it requires financial independence from others. This material independence is the necessary condition for the right to co-legislate and to be a full *citizen* (*Staatsbürger*), as opposed to a mere bourgeois (*Stadtbürger*) and co-beneficiary of state protection (*Schutzgenosse*). Being one's own master means to serve no one other than the commonwealth (TP VIII: 295). One must be neither a child nor a woman and have some property (which can also be understood as an art, science or craft) which one can *alienate* as a source of income instead of having to sell one's physical powers to another person. In the later *Doctrine of Right*, Kant substitutes the distinction between citizens and bourgeois of the *Common Saying* for the distinction between active and passive citizenship (MS RL §46 at VI: 314). The condition for political participation (voting for legislation) is now *civil personality*, the capacity not to be represented by another in matters of right (MS RL §46 at VI: 314).[14] Being fit to vote presupposes the *will* not to be just a part of the commonwealth, but also an active member of it, i.e., "a part of the commonwealth acting from his own choice in community with others."[15] In contrast, individuals who need to be under the direction or protection of other individuals do not possess civil independence. This includes apprentices in the service of a merchant or artisan, domestic servants (as opposed to civil servants), all women ("*alles Frauenzimmer*") and other persons whose preservation and subsistence depend on the arrangements of others (except when this is the state itself). Kant's concern seems to be that dependent persons will not be able to vote in expression of their own best judgment, but would be manipulated into voting for the interests of their guardians or masters. This is perhaps why Kant compares the existence of those who lack civil personality with mere inherence (*Inhärenz*, MS RL §46 at 314, l. 26), that is, the dependence of a property on its underlying substance, to which it belongs.[16]

Kant has been strongly criticized both for his exclusion of women from the right to citizenship[17] and for basing citizenship on a material criterion (private property or financial independence from others).[18] Although the juridical subordination of women to their fathers or husbands is by no means an invention of Kant's legal philosophy but the norm in 18th Century Europe, basing the right to vote on something which is *no deed* of the person (being born a woman) is radically incompatible with the principles of Kant's legal theory. Let us recall Kant's argument against hereditary privileges of rank: "since birth is not a deed of the one who is born, he cannot incur by it any inequality of rightful condition and any other subjection to coercive laws than merely that which is common to him along with all others, as subjects of the sole legislative power" (TP VIII: 293). The same argument disqualifies gender as a rightful criterion for political participation.

Similarly, basing citizenship on property (be it internal, as knowledge or *knowhow*, or external, as land or goods) also blatantly contradicts the purely *formal* character of the civil union. As Ludwig observes, Kant offers no explicit explanation why independence should be a criterion for active citizenship. Kant's major concern is *conservative*, namely, to argue for the *compatibility* of the exclusion of passive citizens from the right to vote with the principle of civil equality. However, it is striking that Kant derives both the principles of civil freedom and civil equality directly from innate right, without recurring to the distinction between active and passive citizens. Further, the exclusion of passive citizens from voting seems incompatible with the justification of the state. *Volenti non fit injuria*; "when someone makes arrangements about another, it is always possible for him to do the other wrong; but he can never do wrong in what he decides upon with regard to himself" (MS VI: 313–4). Excluding some citizens from the right to vote would undermine this principle. The introduction of civil independence as a criterion for the ability to participate in legislation seems to be an "alien body" (*Fremdkörper*) within Kant's legal theory.[19] A possible solution to this problem would be to assume that only those with civil personality would be in the position to vote in accordance with the regulative idea of right as proceeding from the general will of the people. In other words, active citizens would not simply defend the interests of the property owning class with their vote, but adopt the "as if" perspective in decision making for the commonwealth.

Some scholars have tried to derive a state duty to help the poor from the principles of civil union, more precisely from the principle of civil independence. Jacob Weinrib argues that state aid for the poor is an implication of the duty of states to enable the conditions for civil independence. Just as parents have a duty to support their dependent children (whom they have brought into the world without their consent) the state has a duty to enable the independence of subjects whom the institution of a property regime has made dependent on the private wills of others. Since excluding citizens from legislation is incompatible with the idea of original contract, the legitimacy of the state according to Weinrib requires that dependent citizens have the possibility of becoming independent ones. This entails both institutional reforms that enable persons to become independent and state aid to the poor. Since the poor in this case would be dependent on the state and not on private persons, it would qualify for civil personality in Kant's standards. Kant would therefore be free from the accusation of economic prejudice.[20]

Here are some difficulties with this account. Firstly, we have the problem that not all forms of dependence have been created by the state. The state can be said to be (or, more extremely, held) responsible for poverty-related dependence, since it has instituted a property regime. A poor person can no longer satisfy her basic needs by walking into another's orchard and taking whatever food she needs, as would be perhaps possible in the state of nature. She is now dependent on the property of others for her subsistence and in this sense is coerced by the state to remain poor. But what about other forms of dependence? As Kant stresses in "What is Enlightenment," minority (*Unmündigkeit*), i.e., dependence on the guidance of another, is often due not to lack of understanding (and one could add, of resources) but to fear of making use of one's own understanding. In this sense, minority can be said to be self-incurred. "It is so comfortable to be a minor!" (WA VIII: 35). A "minor" in this sense does not have civil personality either, as he or she would have to be represented by another in matters of right (MS RL §46 at VI: 314). It is not clear whether the state would have a duty to eliminate this type of dependence too in order to enable self-incurred minors to achieve political participation.

Secondly, it is not clear why dependence on state aid would make subjects independent in the sense required for being one's own master, as opposed to depending financially on parents or partners. After all, it is just another form of dependence, though one which does not rely on the private will of others. True, Kant explicitly argues that being dependent on the state does not count as dependence, as opposed to being fed and protected by another private person (MS RL VI: 314). However, as becomes clear from the context of the passage, Kant does not have in mind persons living on state aid, but those who are able to *provide for their own existence*[21] and *are only dependent on the state*. A closer look at the original German will help us clarify this point.

> Der Geselle bei einem Kaufmann, oder bei einem Handwerker; der Dienstbote (nicht der im Dienste des Staats steht); der unmündige (naturaliter vel civiliter); alles Frauenzimmer, und überhaupt jedermann, der nicht nach eigenem Betrieb, sondern nach der Verfügung Anderer (**außer der des Staats**), genötigt ist, seine Existenz (Nahrung und Schutz) zu erhalten, entbehrt der bürgerlichen

Persönlichkeit, und seine Existenz ist gleich nur Inhärenz. (MS RL § 46 at VI: 314, my emphasis)

An interpretation of the passage depends upon how we read the parenthesis "außer der [Verfügung] des Staats." *Everyone* in the commonwealth is dependent on the state, rich and poor alike; the specific difference in this case is whether one is responsible for one's own preservation and thus independent "from the absolute will of another **alongside him or above him**" (*neben oder über ihm*, MS RL §49 at VI: 317, my emphasis) for one's subsistence.[22] Kant's requirement to *serve* no one other than the commonwealth, as a criterion for independence does not amount to being *dependent* on no one other than the commonwealth, in a material sense. Only when a person becomes able to provide for herself (perhaps after having being initially helped by the state, given her initial disadvantage) is she on the way to become her own master.

Finally, *making* persons independent would be impermissible, as in Kant's conception this would be just another form of state paternalism (despotism). As Kant stresses in "What is Enlightenment," freeing oneself from the walking cart (*Gängelwagen,* WA VIII: 35) of another's "supervision" and learning to walk freely by following one's own lights is a task that only the agent herself can perform; waiting for someone else to make us think for ourselves would just be to have a new guardian. Analogously, waiting for another person or the state to make us independent would be just as absurd. This is why Kant stresses the element of *choice* in wanting to become a citizen: citizenship should be open to all those members who *want* to be independent and have political participation. Thus, the duty of the state is to secure equality of opportunity for those who want to become independent: "Being fit to vote presupposes the independence of someone who, as one of the people, **wants** to be not just a part of the commonwealth but also a member of it, that is, a part of the commonwealth **acting from his own choice** in community with others" (MS VI: 314).

Another difficulty is that basing state provision for the poor on a duty to enable civil equality *presupposes* the controversial distinction between passive and active citizens. It is only because citizens can be excluded from the right to vote that the state has a duty to enable citizens to work their way up. In a society which recognizes a universal right to vote, the duty to help the poor or the state duty to secure the conditions for civil independence would no longer exist. The strategy to transform the "alien body" in Kant's legal philosophy into a virtue by attempting to derive substantive principles of justice from it ultimately fails.

Additionally, there is no textual evidence for the assumption that the state has a direct *duty* to aid the poor. In the relevant passage, Kant speaks about the state *right* to tax the rich to support the poor: "to the supreme commander (*Oberbefehlshaber*) there belongs **indirectly**, that is, **insofar as he has taken over the duty of the people**, the right to impose taxes on the people for its own preservation (...) (MS RL §C at VI: 325–6, my emphasis). Commentators have often overlooked the fact that the state is said to have a *right* to redistribute and that the duty in question belongs in fact to *the people*, not to the state. For a reason not made explicit, the state then *takes over* the duty from the people. It is also not clear whether the state *is obligated* to take over this duty of the people or if it is merely *permitted* to do so. Weinrib's interpretation links Kant's discussion of the state right to tax in §C at VI: 325–8 with Kant's discussion of citizenship and civil independence in §46 at VI: 313–6.[23] There is however no textual evidence that the state right to tax the rich follows from the state duty to ensure access to civil independence, or that the state has a duty to ensure civil independence at all.

Despite scholarly efforts to derive material principles of justice from the principles of Kant's legal theory, it is not possible to derive *directly* a legal obligation to promote social justice (understood as redistribution of wealth) from Kant's juridical concepts of right, freedom and equality. Kant explicitly acknowledges "reasons of state" for reducing social inequality (in order to avoid social tensions which could threaten the stability of the system, TP VIII: 269), but there seems to be no direct duty of the state to reduce economic inequality. This has led to the traditional interpretation of Kant's state as a *minimal state* or a version of classic liberalism's *"night watchman."* According to this reading, the legitimate function of the state consists merely in ensuring the protection of individual freedom, without interfering in the society's economic patterns of distribution. This reading therefore assumes that Kant's political theory not only lacks the theoretical resources for establishing a duty of the state to intervene in the economy or social distribution, but would even be overtly *against* any intervention of this kind. A clear statement of this interpretation can be found in Wolfgang Kersting's work:

> (...) Kantian equality is totally indifferent towards the economic structure of society and the distribution of goods, means and socio-economic power laid down by it. Kant's legal and political equality lacks all economic implications and social commitments; it cannot be used to justify the welfare state and to legitimise the welfare state programmes of redistribution. (...) The promotion of social equality and the increase of economic justice are not considered a necessary political aim by Kant's political philosophy.[24]

As Kersting acknowledges, it is still possible to sketch a justification of the welfare state compatible with Kant's political theory, but this could only be based on a derivative or instrumental argument for economic justice. Other scholars have considered a merely derivative argument for state intervention in the distribution of wealth not only unsatisfactory, but also incompatible with fundamental aspects of the Kantian theory.[25] In the next section, I will present an alternative interpretation to both positions. I argue that although the Kantian *Rechtsstaat* is not concerned with material outcomes and patterns of distribution but only with *formal* relations of right, it can nevertheless recognize the need to redistribute from considerations of equity or *fairness*, that is, from the recognition of the non-enforceable rights of individuals.

3. THE RIGHT OF THE STATE TO REDISTRIBUTE

To the supreme commander there belongs **indirectly**, that is, insofar as he has taken over the duty of the people, the right to impose taxes on the people for **its own preservation**, such as taxes to support organizations providing for the poor, foundling homes and church organizations, usually called charitable or pious institutions.

> The general will of the people has united itself into a society which is to maintain itself perpetually; and for this end it has submitted itself to the internal authority of the state in order to maintain those members of the society who are unable to maintain themselves. For reasons of state (*von Staats wegen*) the government is therefore **authorized** to constrain the wealthy (*die Vermögenden*) to provide the means of sustenance to those who are unable to provide for even their most necessary natural needs. The wealthy have acquired an **obligation to the commonwealth**, since they owe their existence to an act of submitting to its protection and care, which they need in order to live; **on this obligation the state now bases its right** to contribute what is theirs to maintaining their fellow citizens." (MS 6: 325–6, my emphasis)[26]

The above passage belongs to Kant's account of the *Right of the State* (*Staatsrecht*) in the public right section of the *Doctrine of Right*. More precisely, it is part of the "general remark on the juridical effects that follow from the nature of the civil union" (*Allgemeine Anmerkung von den rechtlichen Wirkungen aus der Natur des bürgerlichen Vereins*). In this passage, Kant speaks not of a duty, but of a right which belongs to the supreme commander (*Oberbefehlshaber*) indirectly, as *Übernehmer der Pflicht des Volks* (as "overtaker" of the duty of the people). It is important to note that here Kant is explaining a right pertaining to the *executive* power of the state. Following Bernd Ludwig's rearrangement of the public right section of the *Rechtslehre*, Kant explained in the previous sections the rights of the three powers of the state, as personified by the legislator (*Gesetzgeber*, RL §46), the commander (*Regent*, first half of §49, in the Ludwig edition §48) and the judge (*Richter*, second half of §49, in the Ludwig edition §49), the so-called *trias politica*

(MS RL §45 at VI: 313); the "general remark" is clearly connected to these sections: §A refers to the former discussion of the right of the *legislator* in §§ 51–52, while §§ B-C refer to the rights of the executive power (*Beherrscher, Oberbefehlshaber*) in the first half of §49, as the power which applies physical power to enforce the verdicts of legislative and judiciary in the state.[27]

Since the role of the *Oberbefehlshaber* is not to make laws but to *enforce* the laws of the *Gesetzgeber* and the verdicts of the *Richter*, there is good reason to understand *Übernehmer* in the sense of *Ausführer* (executor) of the duty of the people (whatever that duty is).[28] Kant is therefore not saying that the supreme commander has a *duty* to provide for the poor, but that it has the *right* to tax the rich to support the poor, as the executive power in the state. The function of the supreme commander is thus to *enforce* the duty of the people. The translation of *Übernehmer* as "taking over" the duty of the people is thus misleading. It suggests that the duty of the people has been somehow *transferred* to the supreme commander, who is now the bearer of that obligation. In a similar vein, Allen Rosen argued that the ruler takes *over the duty of benevolence* of the people (by which Rosen must mean *beneficence*), since "no other duty fits the description." The ruler has a duty of benevolence toward his subjects which is derived "without reducing or eliminating" individuals' ethical duty of benevolence. The right to tax is thus derived *indirectly* from the duty of benevolence of the people, Rosen argues.[29]

But which duty of the people (*Pflicht des Volks*) is the *Oberfehlshaber* enforcing by taxing the rich? It cannot be the duty of beneficence of individuals: as an ethical duty, beneficence implies the free adoption of the moral end (the happiness of others) by individual agents. Beneficence cannot be coerced from outside by the state and still remain a virtue. However, since Rosen argues that the state *itself* has a duty of beneficence, I assume it would be taxing individuals as a means to comply with *its own duty*, and not to make individuals comply with *theirs*.

There are still several problems with the interpretation of the Kantian state as having duties of virtue to its subjects. Firstly, even if the *Oberhaupt*, who is a public person, is also the bearer of duties of virtue as a private person, one should not confuse the *ethical motivation* of the *Oberhaupt* to comply with the regulative idea of Right (which is always *uncoerced*, since there is no higher authority above him) with the assumption that the *Oberhaupt* qua representative of the people has only duties of *virtue* toward the people. Whatever duties the *Oberhaupt* as a public person has toward the people, these must be understood as juridical duties, although *non coercible* ones. A benevolent *Oberhaupt*, that is, one which uses state means to make people happy, is a form of despotism in Kant's account. This does not apply to the *moral Oberhaupt*, who guides himself by the idea of the general will, even though he is not externally coerced to do so. I shall discuss this view in the next section, in conjunction with Kant's criticism of Hobbes in *Theory and Practice*.

Kant argues that the general will of the people has united itself into a society, which is to perpetuate itself. For the sake of perpetuating civil society, the general will of the people has subjected itself to state power to maintain those members of society who cannot support themselves. For "a reason of state" (*Von Staatswegen*), which seems to follow directly from the previous claim about the united will of the people, the government is entitled (*berechtigt*) to constrain the rich to provide for the preservation of the poor. Kant then adds that the *existence* of the rich is at the same time an *act of subjection* to the protection and providence of the Commonwealth (*gemeinen Wesen*) to which they have obligated themselves (*wozu sie sich verbindlich gemacht haben*). The state thus bases its right to contribute what belongs to the rich to the preservation of their fellow citizens on the fact that the state has enabled the existence of the rich and that the rich have an obligation toward the state.[30] Provision for the poor itself, on the other hand, seems to follow from the idea of a united will of the people. But what exactly does this mean?

In the *Common Saying*, provision for the poor was included among the state policies of "public happiness" such as population control, restrictions on imports or any other incentive to flourishing (TP VIII: 299). Since these policies aim to improve the strength and stability of the commonwealth and not to "make people happy against their will," the state is *permitted* to implement laws aimed at public happiness. In the above passage of the *Doctrine of Right* (from the section on "The Right of States"), Kant seems to be making the same claim, namely, that the preservation of the *state* itself requires maintaining those members of society who are not able to meet their basic needs. However, a closer look at the original passage shows that provision for the poor is not thought of as a means to preserve the state, but the *people*. The actual aim of taxation of the rich is the preservation of members of the state, and not a mere means to the perpetuation of the state.

Mary Gregor's translation is ambiguous and could be interpreted as if "its own preservation" refers to the *state*, instead of to the *people*. However, Kant was himself aware of the ambiguity in his text and added parentheses to show that "its own preservation" refers to the people (*des Volks*) and not to the state (*Dem Oberbefehlshaber steht indirect, d.i. als Übernehmer der Pflicht des Volkes, das Recht zu, dieses mit Abgaben zu seiner (**des Volks**) eigenen Erhaltung zu belasten.* MS VI: 326, my emphasis). This is reinforced further in the same passage: "This can be done either by imposing a tax on the property or commerce of citizens, or by establishing funds and using the interest from them, **not for the needs of the state** (for it is rich) **but for the needs of the people**" (MS 6: 326, my emphasis).

In contrast to the clearly instrumental argument in the *Common Saying*, the passage of the *Metaphysics of Morals* does not reduce provision for the poor to the perpetuation of the civil order. As Kant observes, the state has a right to charge the people with the duty of not knowingly letting abandoned children perish, despite the fact that these children are "an unwelcome addition to the population." There is no indication that saving and providing for "unwanted" children is an instrument for the preservation of the commonwealth.

Kant argues that providing for abandoned children should be done in a way that offends "neither rights nor morality." One possible way would be to impose a special tax on wealthy unmarried people (*Hagestolzen beiderlei Geschlechts* (*worunter die vermögenden Ledigen verstanden werden*)) "who are partly to blame for there being abandoned children" (MS VI: 326–7). *Hagestolz* is an old term for someone who remains unmarried *by choice*, although he or she has the financial means to start a family. Although later the term became restricted to older unmarried persons (50 years old onwards), usually male,[31] Kant clearly has the original definition in mind.[32] *Hagestolze* traditionally met with strong social disapproval and were also disadvantaged in terms of rights, as remaining unmarried was not only against the states' interest in high birth rates, but also associated with indecent behavior. In Prussia there was special legislation concerning inheritance rights of wealthy unmarried people (*Hagestolzenrecht*).[33]

As Kant notes, children were abandoned either out of necessity or out of shame (*Not oder Scham*). The assumption seems to be that the *Hagenstolze* would be averse to marriage but not to sexual life, they would be at least partially responsible for children born "out of wedlock" and abandoned for reasons of "social decency." By mentioning the taxation of unmarried people as a means of social redistribution, Kant could have had in mind precisely the Prussian *Hagestolzenrecht*. However, Kant's judgment on the matter is not that taxing the *Hagestolze* is the uncontroversial rightful way to provide for abandoned children, but that lacking a better solution, i.e., one that violates "neither rights nor morality," taxing wealthy unmarried persons would be the best possible way to do so.

In his influential article "Poverty and Property in Kant's system of Rights," Ernest Weinrib argued that the destitute would not be able to consent to entering the state, since accepting a property regime would imply denying oneself access to the basic means of subsistence.[34] In contrast to the pre-civil condition, in which all resources distinct from someone's body are at everyone's disposal, a property regime introduces the dependence of some on the property of others for their subsistence. Because property entails the danger of some persons being reduced to a mere means to others, it seems incompatible with innate right and the duty of rightful honour (*honeste vive*).

Ernest Weinrib sees in Kant's introduction of a public duty to support the poor the only way to reconcile property with innate right. Because a public duty to support the poor is the precondition for a state in which property is consistent with innate right, unless this duty is fulfilled, the state "forfeits its legitimacy."[35]

Despite the plausibility of Ernest Weinrib's argument, the problem is Kant's insistence that the state's failure to be just *does not undermine its legitimacy*. Only the *republican state* (*the state in the idea*) is a fully legitimate state. Although the "well-being" of the state lies in the greatest possible conformity of the constitution with the principles of right (*salus reipublicae suprema lex est*, MS VI: 318), all existing state forms and consequently all existing states are merely approximations of the ideal republic in which the law alone is "self-ruling" and depends on no specific person (*wo das Gesetz selbstherrschend ist, und an keiner besonderen Person hängt*, MS RL §52 at VI: 340). Nevertheless, existing states must be regarded as legitimate.

The different forms of states are only the *letter (littera)* of the original legislation in the civil state, and they may therefore remain as long as they are taken, by old and long-standing custom (and so only subjectively), to belong necessarily to the machinery of the constitution. But the *spirit* of the original contract *(anima pacti originarii)* involves an obligation on the part of the constituting authority to make the *kind of government* suited to the idea of the original contract. Accordingly, even if this cannot be done all at once, it is under obligation to change the kind of government gradually and continually so that it harmonizes *in its effect* with the only constitution that accords with right, that of a pure republic, in such a way that the old (empirical) statutory forms, which served merely to bring about the *submission* of the people, are replaced by the original (rational) form, the only form which *makes freedom* the principle and indeed the condition for any exercise *of coercion,* as is required by a rightful constitution of a state in the strict sense of the word (MS RL §52 at VI: 340–1).

Kant's theory of the state provides the guiding a priori principles for gradually approximating the ideal *Rechtsstaat*. In principle, every state is able to reform itself and continually evolve as close as possible to the ideal republic (and have in fact a duty to do so). The historical beginning of a state, i.e., whether it was founded upon violence, injustice or is the product of a revolution, does not determine its legitimacy. Despite Kant's vehement rejection of a right to revolution, if a revolution is ultimately successful the people have a duty to obey the new government, regardless of the injustice or violent means behind its access to power (MS VI: 323). Although a revolution is never permissible, the newly instituted government must be nevertheless regarded as authoritative. The distinctive feature of Kant's theory of the state is that state legitimacy is *future oriented:* it lies in the duty to bring existent constitutions as close as possible to the ideal republic.³⁶ A government which does not provide for the poor would be no less legitimate in Kant's account than one which does. Weinrib's account of the state duty to provide for the poor as the condition for the legitimacy of the state fails, at least as an interpretation of Kant's legal theory.

The recent secondary literature on the Kantian state's provision for the poor offers compelling arguments concerning what Kant should have said, given his theoretical commitments, or how specific shortcomings of Kant's legal theory can be overcome.³⁷ In the following section I will present an interpretation of the public duty to provide for the poor based on Kant's account of equity or *Billigkeit* in the Doctrine of Right. I combine Kant's account of equity with passages from the *Metaphysics of Morals* and from Kant's lectures on "general injustice," in which he questions the idea of beneficence toward the poor as a matter of virtue, given that need is often the result of injustice. I argue that although the destitute have a right to *collective* support, unlike *strict right* these equity rights cannot be juridically enforced. This has led to the wrong conclusion that the state or the supreme commander has a duty of virtue toward its subjects. The advantage of this interpretation is that it can account for the intuition that the poor have a right to welfare while preserving Kant's fundamental assumptions about the duties and rights of states.

4. THE COURT OF CONSCIENCE AND THE COURT OF JUSTICE

Consider the following passage from *On the Common Saying*:³⁸

> I will surely not be reproached, because of these assertions, with flattering monarchs too much by such inviolability; so, I hope, I will also be spared the reproach of overstating the case in favour of the people when I say **that the people too has its inalienable rights against the head of state, although these cannot be coercive rights.** (TP VIII: 303, my emphasis)

In this passage, Kant is making an objection against Hobbes, according to whom the head of state has no obligations towards its subjects and therefore *cannot do them wrong* (*de Cive,* Chap. 7, §14). Kant adds that Hobbes would be right if one understood wrong (*Unrecht*) as that kind of violation (*Läsion*) which involves a corresponding right to coerce (*Zwangsrecht*) on the part of the wronged person against the one who wrongs her. However, such a proposition, namely, that subjects have coercive rights against the head of state, would be "appalling" (*erschrecklich* TP VIII: 304). The conclusion we can derive from the above passage is that, contra Hobbes, subjects *have* inalienable rights against the head of state, although subjects cannot *coerce* the head of state to respect these rights. In this sense, the *implications* of Kant's theory may be the same as Hobbes'; for what good is a right which cannot be externally coerced? Why should we recognize such non-coercive rights of the people and which are those rights?

Kant's reason for denying subjects coercive rights against the head of state is that to enforce them would require another coercive power *above the state*. Consequently, the supreme commander would no longer be the supreme commander (MS VI: 319). Because coercive rights against the commander would be self-contradictory and the principles underlying these rights are not suitable for external legislation, Bernd Ludwig concludes that the laws in question cannot be juridical ones. The only motive (*Triebfeder*) the supreme commander could have for bringing the government closer to the idea of the original contract (the united will of the people) would be self-constraint (*Selbstzwang*), i.e., *ethical* motivation. Whether the supreme commander would orient herself by the idea of the rights of the people would thus depend on whether the commander is a *moral* politician (*moralischer Politiker*, see TP VIII: 372). Natural right is thus the "doctrine of virtue of the government."[39]

However, as Kant stresses in the passage quoted above, subjects have *rights* against the head of state even if they are non-enforceable ones. Ludwig argues that such rights are not addressed in the *Doctrine of Virtue* because they are insignificant to one's ethical duty and the person to whom the ethical duty is directed.[40] Since ethical duties must rely on the ethical motive alone, they cannot be claimed from outside with appeal to the notion of a corresponding right. The notion of rights is therefore superfluous to ethics. Although this is correct, it begs the question.

Public right must be regarded as *ius strictum*, that is, it must include only those laws which can be externally enforced. However, Kant acknowledges that there are genuinely *juridical* rights which cannot be externally enforced, i.e., rights in a wider sense (*ius latium*, MS VI: 234). Identifying the rights of subjects against the head of state as wide rights makes better sense of Kant's objection against Hobbes than assuming an ethical duty of the head of state. Further, it is only when individuals have rights that they can be said to be *wronged* in a legal sense.[41] Having the theoretical resources for identifying where states can *wrong* their subjects is of great importance for the improvement of existing governments even if subjects cannot legally coerce respect for their rights. As I will show in this section, this is precisely the reason why Kant acknowledges non-coercive rights of the people against the head of state. In contrast, no one is wronged if I fail to comply with my duty of benevolence toward them. True, I fail to treat them as ends in themselves, but

I am not using them merely as means to my ends. (See GMS IV: 430 ll. 9–13 and my discussion of the Formula of Humanity in chapter 4, section three.)

Kant's discussion of wide rights appears in the context of his distinction between the "wavering principles" of *ius aequivocum* (ambiguous right) and the "firm basic principles" of strict right, which are the principles of the state. As Kant stresses, "without making incursions into the domain of ethics, there are two cases which lay claim to a decision about rights" (*ohne ins Gebiet der Ethik einzugreifen, gibt es zwei Fälle, die auf Rechtsentscheidung Anspruch machen,* MS VI: 233). These are equity or fairness (*aequitas, Billigkeit*) and the right of necessity (*Notrecht, ius necessitatis*), both are instances of ambiguous right. However, only equity happens to be a true matter of right (i.e., "right without coercion") whereas necessity is "coercion without right" and consequently no genuine right at all.

Ius aequivocum is a *vitium subreptionis* (German: *Erschleichung*): a confusion between what is empirical and what a priori in a certain representation, in this case, the binding verdicts of a public court of justice (positive law) and "Right in itself," which can be recognized privately by reason (natural law).

Kant's classification of equity as "ambiguous right" does not disqualify equity as a genuine source of rights: it is not a matter of beneficence or kindness to others, but based on the principle of right (which pertains to external freedom) and not on the principle of ethics (which is concerned with internal freedom).[42] Equity is "ambiguous" due to the tendency to confuse *what is right in itself* as opposed to what is *laid down as right*, that is, statutory law. While as private individuals we can recognize what is "the fair thing to do" in a given situation, a public court of law must follow and is bound by statutory laws for its verdict.

> The question here is not merely what is *right in itself*, that is, how every human being has to judge about it on his own, but what is right before a court, that is, what is laid down as right. [. . .] It is a common fault (*vitium subreptionis*) of experts on right to *misrepresent*, as if it were also the objective principle of what is right in itself, **that rightful principle which a court is authorized and indeed bound to adopt for its own use (hence for a subjective purpose)** in order to pronounce and judge what belongs to each as his right, although the latter is very different from the former. (MS VI: 297, my emphasis)

A condition of public right requires that rights conflicts be settled by a public court of justice and not by the private persons themselves, as in the state of nature. The interesting (and confusing) aspect of Kant's theory in this respect is that although judgments of rights in the state of nature are "private," they are nevertheless said to be *objective* ("right in itself"), whereas the decision of a public court of justice, despite its public, authoritative character, is said to be *subjective*. "Subjective" in this case refers to the *principles* a court of justice is constrained to apply in its judgment, for statutory laws are *empirical* principles, as opposed to purely rational principles of right. Although a judge as a private person may be able to recognize the equity claims of a certain person, in her *public* role as a judge her judgment is constrained by different principles. Ideally, the verdict of reason and the verdict of a court of justice should overlap; however, due to procedural constraints and other contingent aspects that are sometimes inevitable in a system of public law, these verdicts may contradict each other.

The right of necessity (*Notrecht*) is the "seeming" right to take the life of an innocent in order to save one's own life. Kant uses as an example the classic plank of Carneades: someone pushes another shipwrecked person from a plank in order to save herself from drowning. In contrast to other theorists who recognize a right to self-preservation, Kant argues that such an action can never be in accordance with right, even if it is necessary for one's own survival. The agent is guilty not only from an ethical, but also from a *juridical* perspective: she is *wronging* an innocent person. The true reason why such actions from "necessity" are nevertheless not punished by law is that it is not possible to *deter* them with threats of punishment (MS VI: 236).

Even if penal law were to punish with death whoever kills an innocent to save her life, this would not have the intended deterrence effect since a "threat of an ill that is still *uncertain* (future death by a judicial verdict) cannot outweigh the fear of an ill that is *certain* (imminent drowning)." No punishment threatened by the law could be greater than imminent death (MS VI: 235–6). Unless an agent is *ethically motivated* to spare the life of an innocent at the cost of her own survival, she would have no sufficient *prudential* reasons for sparing the unfortunate innocent person, at least psychologically. The *infeasibility* of deterring anyone in such a condition creates the illusion that killing an innocent to preserve one's life is a right. This is why the right of necessity must be included under *ius aequivocum*: actions motivated by necessity are taken for rights because of a confusion between what is *not prohibited* by statutory law (subjectively) and what would be prohibited by "right in itself" (again, Kant departs from his natural law predecessors in which he denies that there is a right to self-preservation at the cost of an innocent life). Although from the perspective of objective right the innocent person's right is being violated, a court of justice will not punish such a violation.

Equity claims are *genuine* juridical rights although not *coercive* rights.[43] They are juridical because they are based on the principle of right and non-coercive because no judge can be appointed to render a public decision concerning this right (MS VI: 234). Kant gives the example of a trading firm (*Maskopei*)[44] whose terms are that partners are to share profits equally.

However, one partner has worked more than the others and therefore loses more when the company meets with reverses. By equity, the hard working partner would be entitled to more compensation than the other partners. Another example is the domestic servant whose agreed wage loses value due to inflation (*verschlechterte Münzsorte*, MS VI: 234). Equity would require that the servant be compensated accordingly. However, Kant argues that a court of justice could reject both equity claims. This is because the judicial decision depends on certain conditions being available (MS VI: 296). A judge is constrained to guide her decision by what is stated in the contract (*Declaration*). In *Maskopei*, there was no clause in the contract concerning the possibility of inflation; the judge has thus no *determinate* conditions to make a decision in this regard.[45] We thus have a case in which our conception of what would be just (equitable) in a given situation, i.e., the verdict of *the court of conscience*, departs from what the *court of justice* must regard as just (legally binding) in the same case.

Although the *court of conscience* declares that the more strictly we apply the statutory right, the more we *wrong* the person who has an equity claim (*summum ius summa injuria*), the court of justice is not allowed to proceed otherwise if it is to preserve its public character and ultimately its authority to bind. Equity is thus "a mute divinity who cannot be heard" (MS VI: 234) by a public court of justice, although it can always be heard by "the court of conscience," i.e., by reason in private judgment. The only possibility to address the equity claim in *Maskopei* and in *verschlechterte Münzsorte* is that the partners in the trading company and the servant's employer voluntarily agree to recognize these equity claims and waive their right to enforce the precise terms of the contract. Although required by equity, the compensation paid to the diligent worker and to the servant would depend on the good will of the other parties. Ex post, it is possible to include such clauses in contracts, as to avoid such disparities between equity and the application of law; equity claims would then, by definition, no longer be equity claims.

The ambiguity of wide right lies therefore on a tendency to conflate reasoning according to *commutative* justice and the reasoning distinctive of *distributive* justice. Natural law can be recognized by everyone *a priori* as what is right *in itself*, before the "court of conscience" (*forum poli*: the marketplace or also the court of heaven, MS VI: 235). Statutory right, in contrast, is based on existing civil constitutions and therefore on empirical principles (MS VI: 297). Given its public character, a court of justice (*forum soli*, the earthly court)[46] is not allowed to make use of "guesses" or presumptions concerning what is right in itself, but must be bound by the terms of contracts and existing regulations (although the latter can and should be improved to render the legal system more equitable). But what does Kant mean when he says a judge would be "guessing" when judging an equity claim?

In *Naturrecht Feyerabend*, Kant argues that if the intentions (*Gesinnungen*) of agents could be made public independently of what they *declared*, i.e., if we could know with certainty what the parties *actually intended* when making a contract, equity would no longer go unheard (see XXVII: 1328, 1333 and 1359).[47] This suggests that the problem with equity is epistemic. A public judge would have to "guess" people's original intentions, while having no appropriate evidence. But this is implausible. Anyone can understand that it is a disadvantage to lose money when a currency is depreciated and that no reasonable person would have agreed to those terms if she expected inflation. She would have no reasonable incentive to work more hours for the company if she knew it meant a greater loss for herself at the end. If so, what is actually left for a judge to guess?

I take Kant to mean that the difficulty is not to correctly identify if there is an equity claim or not, which is reasoning according to the principles of commutative justice, but the fact that, despite equity, the court must engage in another form of legal reasoning for the decision to be externally binding. A court of justice must reason according to distributive justice. As Kant explains in *Maskopei*, the judge would not have determinate information (*data*) to decide *how much* according to the contract the person should be compensated (*keine bestimmten Angaben (data) hat, um, wie viel nach dem Kontrakt ihm zukomme, auszumachen*, MS VI: 234). The problem is thus not indeterminacy concerning the possible intentions of the involved parties, but the need for public standards for decision making, which enable public justice to function *most readily* and *surely*. This idea is further developed in Kant's discussion of "subjectively conditioned acquisition through the verdict of a public court of justice." In this rarely analyzed section of the Doctrine of Right, Kant discusses the different standards for determining the rightful owners of objects in the state of nature and in the civil condition.[48] If I bought a horse which had been previously stolen, according to the rules of commutative justice (which is justice in private exchange and contracts), the previous owner would have a right to recover the horse since I am only the putative owner of the horse. In the civil condition, in contrast, the previous owner would only have a right against the *seller* of the stolen horse and could only claim compensation for the loss but not recover the horse. This is because I would be considered the true owner of the horse, having bought it in accordance with the rules of the market (MS VI: 302). Since having to investigate the title of possession of every seller before buying something would be very impractical, if not impossible. Therefore, relevant for determining rightful acquisition in a condition of distributive justice is that acquisition be *formally* correct, as specified in accordance with statutory laws (MS VI: 301).

So it is only for the sake of a court's verdict (*in favorem iustitiae distributivae*) that a right to a thing is taken and treated not *as it is in itself* (as a right against a person) but as it can be *most readily* and *surely judged* (as a right to a thing), and yet in accordance with a pure a priori principle.—On this principle various statutory laws (ordinances) are subsequently based, the primary purpose of which is to set up conditions under which alone a way of acquiring is to have rightful force, conditions such that a judge can assign to each what is his *most readily and with least hesitation*. (MS VI: 302)

The reason one must give priority to what is "laid down as right," as opposed to what we can recognize as right in itself, is that a well functioning system of public laws requires legal certainty.[49] Unless judges constrain their verdicts to the application of statutory laws, a condition of public justice would be made superfluous and replaced by the principles of private right. Therefore, the civil condition for Kant is not merely the use of state coercion for enforcing pre-civil rights; it also requires the introduction of a system of positive laws, whose institution may at times lead to divergent results from what we recognize as just according to common sense judgments about justice. This is the price we pay for living under a condition of distributive justice.

5. STATE PROVISION FOR THE POOR AS AN IDEAL OF JUSTICE

What I have others must do without: - my powder takes away the flour of others (. . .) The sum of welfare does not increase in accordance with the proportion of earnings: and I am always unjust when I take away a considerable part of their welfare, since I only add a little to my own. (Praktische Philosophie Herder, XXVII: 51, my translation)[50]

Kant is well aware of the historical and political sources of social inequality, which creates both the needy person, who must depend on the beneficence of others for her subsistence, and the "benefactor," who is in a wealthier position and able to help. I will concentrate on statements in Kant's works in which dispels the illusion that beneficence is a matter of virtue instead of a duty of indebtedness. Although most of these passages can be found in Kant's lectures and notes, there are also clear statements in Kant's mature published works, which shows that he did not abandon or revise his position. Consider the following "casuistic question" in the *Doctrine of Virtue*:

Having the resources to practice such beneficence as depends on the goods of fortune is, for the most part, a result of certain human beings being favored through the injustice of the government, which introduces an inequality of wealth that makes others need their beneficence. Under such circumstances, does a rich man's help to the needy, on which he so readily prides himself as something meritorious, really deserve to be called beneficence at all? (MS VI: 454)

Given the systemic character of economic inequality, the duty of beneficence in the context of poverty alleviation becomes problematic. While it is an ineliminable feature of our human condition that we are vulnerable and dependent on each other and must thus regard ourselves as "united by nature in one dwelling place so that [we] can help each other" (MS VI:453), poverty-related dependence involves injustice in which we all partake to different degrees. As a result of the injustice of actual governments, some are disadvantaged while others are benefited; helping others in need must thus be understood as a matter of *strict* rather than wide duty. We often fail to recognize this due to the complexity of systematic injustice: not only because the historical sources of injustice lie often in the past and are deeply entrenched in social life and structures, but because no particular individuals can be identified as perpetrators.

> One may take a share in the general injustice, even though one does nobody any wrong by civil laws and practices. So if we now do a kindness to an unfortunate, we have not made a free gift to him, but repaid him what we were helping to take away through a general injustice. For if none might appropriate more of this world's goods than his neighbour, there would be no rich folk, but also no poor. Thus even acts of kindness are acts of duty and indebtedness, arising from the rights of others. (Moral Collins, XXVII: 416)

And again:

> If we have taken something away from a person and do him a kindness when in need, that is not generosity but a poor recompense for what has been taken from him. Even the civil order is so arranged that we participate in public and general oppressions, and thus we have to regard an act we perform for another, not as an act of kindness and generosity, but as a small return of what we have taken from him in virtue of the general arrangement. All acts and duties, moreover, arising from the right of others, are the greatest of our duties to others. (Moral Collins, XXVII: 432)

It is important to stress that the right in question is not a right to the beneficence of others (there is no such right in Kant's theory). The needy have a right to compensation for the injustice underlying their condition. In the lack of better means, the charity of others "fills the gap" and provides alleviation, although from the perspective of the benefactors their actions are meritorious, meaning that the benefactors regard themselves as complying with a duty of virtue instead of addressing the rights of those they are helping. Kant's social criticism is that economic dependence is largely a side effect of civil society. His critique of charity is that it is an inadequate means to compensate for systemic injustice. It is also morally objectionable to treat the rights of others (which are a source of strict duties) as a matter of generosity and good will. However, it is not possible to identify who should satisfy the claims of the poor (*who is responsible? Who wronged them?*) and to what extent these claims must be satisfied (*how much compensation is owed to them?*). Past historical injustice could have a significant contribution to the present generation's disadvantage, just as inheritance rights enable wealth to be conserved over several generations perpetuating inequality between members of society (TP VIII: 293, ll. 14–9). Since the amount of compensation would depend on the extent of suffered wrongs, a person could be thus entitled to more compensation than the mere provision for her basic needs. Compensation would thus require determining how and to what extent a person has been the victim of systematic injustice, which seems in many cases if not impossible to retrace then at least extremely costly and time consuming to implement.

The indeterminacy of these rights has led to the view that a person who cannot provide for her most basic needs has *no right to subsistence* and that her survival must instead be the object of the beneficence of others. If someone cannot claim a right to be helped *from me*, it does not entail that she has no right to subsistence at all. The diffusion of responsibility in this case can only be addressed as a matter of a *social, collective* duty. I take this to be "the duty of the people" Kant is talking about in MS VI: 325–6.

There is a strong similarity between the impossibility of claiming subsistence rights against the state (when no welfare programs are in place) and satisfying equity claims in a court of justice; both are based on rights we can recognize privately through reason (as objective) but which fall out of the scope of public statutory laws. Both are matters of *wide right*. Strict right cannot address social inequality as *material* injustice unless it is made into a policy of the state; it can only address *formal* inequality before the law, according to what is publicly specified in statutory laws ("laid down as right"). This is not because the only function of the Kantian state is to apply the pure principles of Right, but because distributive justice cannot appeal to the principles of commutative justice to compensate for systemic injustice, since this would require investigating how each person came to be disadvantaged in society. We therefore have an *ambiguous right scenario* in which (1) our private intuitions about justice may depart from what is considered just by the positive system of law (2) we tend to confuse what is *formally* just with what is just *objectively*. While equity tells us that victims of systemic injustice have a right to compensation, strict right does not see poverty and destitution as a violation of rights (no one is harming or taking away anything from the poor; no one is excluding them from opportunities of working their way up). The interesting aspect of Kant's theory of right is that while we must commit ourselves to a public system of justice as a necessary condition for civil society, we nevertheless have the resources for recognizing rights which cannot be properly addressed by public justice. These rights provide us guidance in improving our current systems of law.

Although in existing governments legislation must be made *as if* it can be regarded as originating from the united will of the people[51] (that is, even if the people itself cannot *actually* agree with the law), in the *ideal* republic legislation would be directly derived from the will of the people: what they must or cannot choose for themselves as rational beings. Provision for the poor would thus be a necessary law of the *republica noumenon*, provided there were citizens who could not provide for themselves as a consequence of the social contract. However, unlike the Hobbesian state, the rationale of the Kantian state is not *self-preservation*, but the realization of Right.[52] Providing for the poor belongs to the primary tasks of neither the executive power nor the Kantian state. However, insofar as the executive power is bound to execute the laws from the united will of the people, and the united will of the people *must commit itself to the preservation of its members*, the head of state has a right to provide for the poor, in the name of the people. This is a right governments *ought* to exercise if they are to be closer to the ideal just state, but failure to redistribute does not undermine their legitimacy.[53] We can therefore conclude that although the Kantian state does not have to be a welfare state, the duty to approach the ideal just state will require the adoption of welfare policies. The duty to maintain its poor belongs to the people as a collective and only indirectly to the Kantian state.

The institutionalization of aid is more appropriate than individual beneficence in addressing the problem of basic subsistence needs. When helping others, we are morally required to avoid humiliating those helped and creating dependence; begging, a practice Kant considers not only debasing but also "closely akin to robbery," since it is meant to manipulate the feelings of other persons, ought to be avoided.[54] Contributions for the poor should be collected neither by voluntary contributions, assets gradually accumulated nor pious institutions, but by legal levies only. Pious institutions make poverty "a means of acquisition for the lazy" and impose an unjust burden on the people (MS VI: 326), perhaps because relations of dependence are regarded as occasion for some to display charity and piety, and not as a social and economic problem for which society as a whole is responsible. Institutions ought to be regularly reformed in order to adapt to the needs of the time, to avoid dependency and begging and to ensure that taxation of the wealthy is *just*.[55]

166   Chapter Six

This is only possible if collection of contributions and provision for the poor has a public, institutional character. By creating an entitlement to welfare support, the state makes it possible to *select* the candidates for help on the basis of genuine need and vulnerability. The most vulnerable and destitute in society would no longer have to humiliate themselves begging for help and their needs can be treated as they ought to, namely as matters of *right* (cf. *Erläuterung Achenwall* XIX; 378 N. 8000).

However, not being able to determine exactly the extent to which a person has been affected by general injustice, it is not possible to determine how much one should be compensated. As with equity cases, an official determining whether a person is entitled to state aid would have to appeal to what is certain by the standards of statutory law. All we have before us is the degree of concrete disadvantage (one's ability to provide for herself), but often no record of the systemic disadvantages suffered by agents and their ancestors. Granting at least basic aid to the poor would not impair the functioning of a system of distributive justice, although we would still be very far from giving what is due to each person. Basic welfare would thus be a proxy for the actual compensation due to each person for systemic injustice and discrimination.[56]

In this chapter, I analyzed Kant's reasons for excluding the happiness of individuals as a principle for external legislation. I also explained how Kant nevertheless accounts for a right of the state to redistribute. I argued that although the Kantian *Rechtsstaat* is not concerned with patterns of distribution but only with formal relations of right, it can nevertheless recognize the need to redistribute from considerations of equity or fairness, the domain of right Kant calls *Billigkeit*. Kant recognized social inequality as the result of systemic injustice and did not regard helping the poor only as a duty of virtue of individuals, which is an inadequate way to address systemic disadvantage. I supported my interpretation with passages of Kant's lectures and of the *Metaphysics of Morals* in which Kant questions the character of the duty of beneficence as a meritorious duty. The problem is that although the poor have a right to aid, unlike strict right, these rights cannot be determined with the precision required by a court of justice. This has led to the wrong conclusion that the state or head of state has a duty of virtue toward its subjects and the poor no right to aid.

NOTES

1. External freedom also (and importantly) requires positive laws, which are empirical principles. However, as we will see, positivistic elements in Kant's legal theory are ultimately required by *Vernunftrecht*. I interpret Kant as defending a specific kind of legal positivism for non-positivistic reasons, which I will elaborate in this section.

2. Pinheiro Walla, Alice. "Honeste Vive: Dignity in Kant's Theory of Juridical Obligation." Adam Cureton and Jan-Willem van der Rijt (eds.). *Human Dignity and the Kingdom of Ends: Kantian Perspectives and Practical Applications*, Routledge, 2021.

3. Legal duties are paradigmatically external and relational. However, *honeste vive*, the very first legal duty corresponding to the only innate right is internal and non-relational (it binds the right-holder herself). For my account of honeste vive as an internal juridical duty, see "Honeste Vive: Dignity in Kant's Rechtslehre." In Adam Cureton and Jan-Willem van der Rijt (eds.), *Human Dignity and the Kingdom of Ends: Kantian Perspectives and Practical Applications*, Routledge, 2021.

4. I am using "moral" as opposed to the idea of natural necessity, as expressed by the laws of nature. It does not mean that the account of legal obligation I will develop here is ethical.

5. Pinheiro Walla, Alice. "Honeste Vive: Dignity in Kant's Theory of Juridical Obligation." Forthcoming in Adam Cureton and Jan-Willem van der Rijt (eds.). Human Dignity and the Kingdom of Ends: Kantian Perspectives and Practical Applications, Routledge, 2021.

6. Preparatory Works to the Doctrine of Right XXIII: 219.

7. Reference to author's published work. Honeste Vive, "Dignity in Kant's Theory of Juridical Obligation." Adam Cureton and Jan-Willem van der Rijt (eds.), *Human Dignity and the Kingdom of Ends: Kantian Perspectives and Practical Applications*, Routledge, 2021.

8. "Freiheit (Unabhängigkeit von eines Anderen nöthigender Willkür), sofern sie mit jedes Anderen Freiheit nach einem allgemeinen Gesetz zusammen bestehen kann, ist dieses einzige, ursprüngliche, jedem Menschen kraft seiner Menschheit zustehende Recht. - Die angeborne Gleichheit, d. i. die Unabhängigkeit nicht zu mehrerem von Anderen verbunden zu werden, als wozu man sie wechselseitig auch verbinden kann; mithin die Qualität des Menschen sein eigener Herr (*sui iuris*) zu sein, imgleichen die eines unbescholtenen Menschen (*iusti*), weil er vor allem rechtlichen Act keinem Unrecht gethan hat" (MS 6: 237–8).

9. *Lex iustitia distributivae* or a condition of distributive justice is a term Kant uses for the civil condition or justice under public institutions. According to Byrd and Hruschka, Kant takes over Hobbes' distinction between commutative and distributive justice and parts with the scholastic conception of justice as an individual virtue (*Commentary*, appendix to chapter 2, p. 71). The idea of distributive justice in Kant's legal theory is that public institutions have the authority to determine and enforce rights, i.e., to administer the law. It should not be confused with the way current political philosophers understand distributive justice, namely, as the (re)allocation of resources according to a conception of just or fair distribution. While Kant's conception of distributive justice focuses on a legal procedure and application of public laws, contemporary distributive justice focuses instead on outcomes.

10. Samuel Pufendorf, *De iure naturae et gentium*, 1688, I, 1; Christian Wolff, *Institutiones iuris naturae et gentium*, 1750, I, 2, §45. See also A. Kaufmann, *Welfare in the Kantian State*, Oxford University Press, 1999, chap. 2 and Otfried Höffe, "Der Kategorische Rechtsimperativ," in: *Metaphysische Anfangsgründe der Rechtslehre*, Akademie Verlag, 1999, p. 51.

11. How should the people proceed in the case of a despotic or tyrannical (violent) government? Kant argues that a constitution which allows a right to revolution would be self contradictory and this is why there can be no such right. Someone who limits the authority of the state must have a public character: they must have equal or more political power than the supreme commander; but then, the supreme commander would not be the supreme commander, but the one who resists her. But the more important question is *quis iudicabit*, namely, who ought to decide what is right in a dispute between the people and the sovereign (MS VI: 320). However, an additional, pragmatic reason for Kant's rejection of a right to revolution, also evident from his political writings, is the pragmatic concern that a right to limit or overturn the state would be used as an excuse by some individuals to manipulate the state and its legislation for their own private purposes. Often, the true motive behind revolutions and of legislation allowing a right to limit or overturn the government is the interest of politicians to secure their own advantage through political power. Their abuse of power is masked by the rhetoric of "the rights of the people" against the state: "The people, in being represented by its deputies (in parliament), has, in these guardians of its freedom and rights, men who have a lively interest in positions for themselves and their families, in the army, the navy and the civil service, that depend on the minister, and who are always ready to play into the government's hands (. . .).—Hence a so-called moderate constitution, as a constitution for the inner rights of a state, is an absurdity. Instead of belonging to right it is only a principle of prudence, not so much to make it more difficult for a powerful transgressor of the people's rights to exercise at will his influence upon the government as to disguise his influence under the illusion of an opposition permitted to the people" (MS VI: 319–20).

12. Allen Wood, *Kantian Ethics*, Cambridge University Press, 2008, p. 194. Unlike Wood I understand "power" not in Focauldian terms, but as a Hohfeldian legal relation (the authority to impose a corresponding liability on another person).

13. In the ideal state, namely, in the *Republic*, the law is self-governing (*selbstherrschend*, MS VI: 341). Only in the Republic is there no need for a ruler distinct from the people (as the people rules itself) and laws can be regarded as *actually* proceeding from the will of the people. In real states, which are (in the best case) only *approximations* of the ideal Republic, the regulative principle for the rightfulness of legislation is the "as if" (*als ob*). The idea of an original contract provides no independent material criterion of justice and expresses only the form of rightful relations itself: it is the thought that obligation must be thought as *reciprocal*, in order to be compatible with civil freedom and equality. Bernd Ludwig, *Kants Rechtslehre*, p. 168, see also notes 148 and 150.

14. The capacity to be one's own master (*sui iuris*) is identified in the *Doctrine of Right* with the innate Right (MS VI: 237–8), whereas Selbständigkeit (civil independence) is not being dependent on the choice (Willkür) of another for one's existence and subsistence (MS VI: 314).

15. "[Die Fähigkeit der Stimmgebung] *setzt die Selbständigkeit dessen im Volke voraus, der nicht bloß Teil des gemeinen Wesens, sondern auch Glied desselben, d.i. aus eigener Willkür in Gemeinschaft mit anderen handelnder Teil derselben sein will.*"

16. Kant's examples of those who lack civil personality are the woodcutter I hire to work in my yard; the blacksmith in India, who goes into people's houses to work on iron with his hammer, as compared to the European carpenter or blacksmith who can put his goods for sale to the public; the private tutor as compared to the school teacher and the tenant farmer (*Zinsbauer*), as compared to the leasehold farmer (*Pächter*) (MS RL §46 at VI: 314–5).

17. Susan Mendus, "Kant: an honest but narrow minded Bourgeois?" in: Howard Williams (ed.), *Kant's Political Philosophy*, University of Wales Press, 1992. See also Helga Varden "Kant on Women," *Pacific Philosophical Quarterly*, 2015.

18. See Luke Davies. "Kant on Civil Self-Sufficiency" *Archiv für Geschichte der Philosophie*, 2021; Kate A. Moran, "Kant on Traveling Blacksmiths and Passive Citizenship," *Kant-Studien*, vol. 112, no. 1, 2021, pp. 105–26 and A. Pinzani and N. S. Madrid, *The State Looks Down: Some Reassessments of Kant's Appraisal of Citizenship*, In: A. Faggion, A. Pinzani, N. Sanchez Madrid (eds.), *Kant and Social Policies*, Palgrave Macmillan, 2016.

19. Bernd Ludwig, *Kants Rechtslehre*, Meiner, 1988, pp. 162–3.

20. Jacob Weinrib, "Kant on Citizenship and Universal Independence," *Australasian Journal of Legal Philosophy*, 33, 2008.

21. (. . .) das Attribut der bürgerlichen Selbständigkeit [welche darin besteht], seine Existenz und Erhaltung nicht der Willkür eines Anderen im Volke, sondern seinen eigenen Rechten und Kräften, als Glied des Gemeinen Wesens, verdanken zu können (. . .) (MS RL §46 at 314).

22. According to Kant, a patriotic government is one that does not treat citizens as children, but as members of a family and, at the same time, as citizens. This makes it possible that "each is in possession of himself" (*jeder sich selbst besitzt*) and not dependent upon the will of another alongside him or above him. (MS RL §49 at 317)

23. Jacob Weinrib, op. cit. p. 16, n. 55.

24. Wolfgang Kersting, "Kant's Concept of the State," In: Howard Williams (ed.), *Essays on Kant's Political Philosophy.* University of Chicago Press, 1992, p. 153.

25.See Allen Wood, *Kantian Ethics*, Cambridge University Press, 2002 and "The Final Form of Kant's Practical Philosophy," In: Mark Timmons (ed.), *Kant's Metaphysics of Morals. Interpretative Essays*, Oxford University Press, 2004; Alexander Kaufmann, *Welfare in the Kantian State*, Oxford: Clarendon Press, 1999; Allen D. Rosen, *Kant's Theory of Justice*, Cornell University Press, 1993, and Marcus Willaschek, "Kant on right without Ethics. Reflexions on Kant's Conception of 'Strict Right' in the *Metaphysics of Morals*," *European Journal of Philosophy Studies*, 17, 2009.

26. Dem Oberbefehlshaber steht indirect, d.i. als Übernehmer der Pflicht des Volks, das Recht zu, dieses mit Abgaben zu seiner (des Volks) eigenen Erhaltung zu belasten, als da sind: das Armenwesen, die Findelhäuser und das Kirchenwesen, sonst milde oder fromme Stiftungen genannt. / Der allgemeine Volkswille hat sich nämlich zu einer Gesellschaft vereinigt, welche sich immerwährend erhalten soll, und zu dem Ende sich der inneren Staatsgewalt unterworfen, um die Glieder dieser Gesellschaft, die es selbst nicht vermögen, zu erhalten. Von Staats wegen ist also die Regierung berechtigt, die Vermögenden zu nötigen, die Mittel der Erhaltung derjenigen, die es

selbst den nothwendigsten Naturbedürfnissen nach nicht sind, herbei zu schaffen: weil ihre Existenz zugleich als Act der Unterwerfung unter den Schutz und die zu ihrem Dasein nöthige Vorsorge des gemeinen Wesens ist, wozu sie sich verbindlich gemacht haben, auf welche der Staat nun sein Recht gründet, zur Erhaltung ihrer Mitbürger das Ihrige beizutragen. (MS VI:326)

27. See Bernd Ludwig, *Kants Rechtslehre*, Meiner 1988, p. 164. Ludwig has rearranged §§ 45–50 of the *Right of the State (Staatsrecht)* and set the *Allgemeine Anmerkung* in conformity with its title, at the end of *Staatsrecht* section. § 60 was made into an extra *Anmerkung* (§F) at the end of the Right of the State since it clearly functions as a transition to what comes next, i.e., the law of peoples (*Völkerrecht*). For a description of Ludwig's major changes of the text, see Ludwig, op. cit, pp. 79–81.

28. According to the *Grimm* dictionary of the German Language, *Übernehmer/übernehmen* can be understood both in a wide or narrow sense. In the wide sense: entrepreneurs, negotiatores, operis conductores [Apinus gloss. novum (1728), 201]. In the narrow sense: der unternehmer, richtiger doch weniger vorkommend übernehmer ist derjenige, welcher gewerbemäszig eine bauarbeit . . . ausführt [Schönermark-Stüber hochbaulex, 856]. *Deutsches Wörterbuch von Jacob und Wilhelm Grimm.* 16 Bde. in 32 Teilbänden, Leipzig 1854–1961, Digital edition of the Trier Center for Digital Humanities, University of Trier, Band 23, Sp. 439.

29. "The *Rechtslehre* passage begins: "Indirectly in as much as he takes over the duty of the people, the supreme commander possesses the right to levy taxes on them for the poor, foundling hospitals and churches; in other words, for what are generally called charitable and pious institutions. Kant says that rulers take over a duty from the people. Presumably the duty he has in mind is benevolence; no other duty fits the description." Allen Rosen, *Kant's Theory of Justice*, Cornell University Press, 1993, p. 179. Toward the end of his chapter on "Justice and Social Welfare" Rosen appeals to the notion of general will and social contract to derive a duty of benevolence of the state toward its citizens.

30. Weil **Ihre Existenz** zugleich ein Akt der Unterwerfung . . . ist . . . **auf welche** der Staat nun sein Recht gründet, zur Erhaltung ihrer Mitbürger das Ihrige Beizutragen.

31. *Deutsches Wörterbuch von Jacob und Wilhelm Grimm.* 16 Bde. in 32 Teilbänden. Leipzig 1854–1961, digital edition of the Trier Center for Digital Humanities, University of Trier, Band 10, Sp. 154–5.

32. Mary Gregor's translation of *Hagestolzen* as "elderly unmarried people" is therefore not appropriate.

33. Katrin Baumgarten, *Hagestolz und Alte Jungfer. Entwicklung, Instrumentalisierung und Fortleben von Klischees und Stereotypen über Unverheiratetgebliebene.* Dissertation, Waxmann, 1997, p. 7.

34. Ernest J. Weinrib, "Poverty and Property in Kant's system of Rights," *Notre Dame Law Review*, No. 78, Vol. 3, April 2003.

35. Ernst J. Weinrib, op. cit, p. 818.

36. See Bernd Ludwig, *Kants Rechtslehre*, Felix Meiner Verlag, 1988, pp. 170–71 and Reinhard Brandt, *Rechtsphilosophie der Aufklärung, Symposium Wolfenbüttel 1981*, Walter de Gruyter, 1982, p. 268.

37. See, for instance, Sorin Baiasu, "Kant's Justification of Welfare," *Diametros* (39), March 2014, pp. 1–28, M. LeBar, "Kant on Welfare," *Canadian Journal of Philosophy* (29), 1999, pp. 225–50; Helga Varden, "Kant and Dependency Relations: Kant on the State's Right to Redistribute Resources to Protect the Rights of Dependents," *Dialogue* vol., 45 2006, pp. 257–84,

38. Partial versions of this and the next section were published as Pinheiro Walla, Alice, "A Kantian Foundation for Welfare Rights," Jurisprudence, 2020 and Pinheiro Walla, Alice, "When the strictest right is the greatest wrong: Kant on Fairness," *Estudos Kantianos* vol. 3, no. 1, 2015.

39. Ludwig, *Kants Rechtslehre*, pp. 172–1 (see also footnote 169).

40. Ludwig, op. cit., p. 173.

41. I am using the term "wronging" (lädieren) in the sense of a violation of right; unfortunately, the use of the term in Kantian secondary literature does not differentiate between failure to live up to ethical duties and rights violations proper.

42. Die Billigkeit (objektiv betrachtet) ist keineswegs ein Grund zur Aufforderung bloß an die ethische Pflicht Anderer (ihr Wohlwollen und Gütigkeit), sondern der, welcher aus diesem Grunde etwas fordert, fußt sich auf sein Recht (. . .) (MS VI: 234) [Equity (considered objectively) is in no way merely a basis for calling upon another to fulfill an ethical duty (to be benevolent and kind). One who demands something for this reason basis his demands on his right, except that he does not have the conditions that a judge needs in order to determine by how much and in what way his claim could be satisfied].

43. "Die Billigkeit ist ein Recht, welches aber keine Befugniß giebt, den andern zu zwingen, es ist ein Recht aber kein Zwangs-Recht [. . .] Denn damit einer mich zu zwingen befugt sey, so muß erstlich die Handlung aus dem Recht des andern gelöst entspringen [**Collins/ Brauer: dem Recht des andern selbst entsprungen seyn**], denn aber muß sie auch auf äußerlich hinreichende Bedingungen der Imputation des Rechts [256] beruhen, diese werden durch Beweise, die äußerlich sufficient sind, dargethan. Coram foro interno ist die Billigkeit strenges Recht, aber nicht coram foro externo. Die Billigkeit ist also ein Recht, wo die Gründe der äußeren Imputation coram foro externo nicht gelten, wohl aber vor dem Gewißen gelten." Moral Mrongovius, XXVII: 1552–3, Moral Collins, XXVII: 433u, Moral Brauer Me 269.

44. "Genossenschaft" in modern German.

45. See Moral Mrongovius, XXVII: 1552–3, Moral Collins, XXVII: 433u, Moral Brauer Me 269.

46. See Höffe, "Der Kategorische Rechtsimperativ," p.51

47. Ich kann bloß nach den Buchstaben, die ich sage, gezwungen werden, wenn ich gleich die Absicht vermuthen kann. Aber wir können die Gedanken der Menschen nicht wissen; sonst würde die Billigkeit auch strenges Recht haben (Naturrecht Feyerabend XXVII:1333)

48. For a discussion of this section of the Doctrine of Right, see Bertani, Corrado. "Equity Presumptions versus Maxim of Distributive Justice in the Metaphysische Anfangsgründe der Rechtslehre, §§ 36–40." In Kant und die Philosophie in Weltbürgerlicher Absicht: Aktendes Xi. Kant-Kongresses 2010, edited by Margit

Ruffing, Claudio La Rocca, Alfredo Ferrarin and Stefano Bacin, 783–96, Berlin: De Gruyter, 2013.

49. Similarly, Byrd and Hruschka argue that the rationale of the rules of distributive justice is to protect the proper functioning of the public judiciary itself. Unless contracts are enforced, distributive justice would lose its meaning. *Kant's Doctrine of Right. A Commentary*, Cambridge University Press, 2010, pp. 225–6.

50. (. . .) was ich habe, müßen andre entbehren: – mein Puder entzieht andern das Meel: (. . .) Nach der Proportion des Erwerbs steigert sich nicht die Summe der Wohlfart: und ich bin stets ungerecht, wenn ich vielen einen beträchtlichen Zusatz zu ihrer Wohlfahrt wegnehme: da ich nur einen unbeträchtlichen meiner eignen zusezze.

51. On Kant's idea of general in Kant's legal and political thought see Marey, Macarena. "The Ideal Character of the General Will and Popular Sovereignty in Kant." Kant-Studien 2018; 109(4): 557–80.

52. Reinhard Brandt, *Eigentumstheorien von Grotius bis Kant*, Frohmann-Holzboog, 1974, pp.180–1.

53. See *Erläuterungen Achenwall*, XIX: 504, N. 7737, "Die idee des socialcontracts ist nur die Richtschnur der Beurtheilung des Rechts und der Unterweisung der prinzen imgleichen einer möglichen Vollkommenen Staatserrichtung, aber nach dieser idee hat das Volk nicht wirkliche rechte. Es scheint nichts natürlicher, als daß, wenn das Volk rechte hat, es auch eine Gewalt habe; aber eben darum, weil es keine rechtmäßige Gewalt etabliren kann, hat es auch kein strictes recht sondern nur ein ideales."

54. *Durch Almosen werden die Menschen erniedriget. Es wäre beßer auf eine andere Art dieser Armuth abzuhelfen, damit nicht Menschen so niedrig gemacht würden, Almosen anzunehmen.* Moral Mrongovius XXVII: 1570) [Through monies persons are humiliated. It would be better to help the poor in another way, so that persons are not humiliated by having to accept monies. My translation].

55. So hat man gefunden: daß der Arme und Kranke (den vom Narrenhospital ausgenommen) besser und wohlfeiler versorgt werde, wenn ihm die Beihülfe in einer gewissen (dem Bedürfnisse der Zeit proportionirten) Geldsumme, wofür er sich, wo er will, bei seinen Verwandten oder sonst Bekannten, einmiethen kann, gereicht wird, als wenn—wie im Hospital von Greenwich—prächtige und dennoch die Freiheit sehr beschränkende, mit einem kostbaren Personale versehene Anstalten dazu getroffen werden. – Da kann man nun nicht sagen, der Staat nehme dem zum Genuß dieser Stiftung berechtigten Volke das Seine, sondern er befördert es vielmehr, indem er weisere Mittel zur Erhaltung desselben wählt (MS VI: 367)

56. For a development of this argument, see Pinheiro Walla, Alice, "A Kantian Foundation for Welfare Rights," *Jurisprudence*, 2020. For a different take on "general injustice" and its implications for the duties of individuals see Kate A. Moran (2017). Neither Justice nor Charity? Kant on 'General Injustice.' *Canadian Journal of Philosophy* 47, no. 4, 2017, 477–98.

Conclusion

Kant's conception of happiness is an important constitutive element of his practical theory insofar as it shapes or indirectly influences several of his conclusions. My aim was to make explicit Kant's underlying assumptions about happiness and the way they relate to central themes of Kant's moral, political and legal philosophy. By bringing these assumptions to the fore, I also hope to have shed light on some puzzling claims and on the scattered, unsystematic remarks Kant makes about happiness and to have provided a more or less coherent picture of Kant's understanding of human happiness.

In chapter 1, I analyzed Kant's apparently contradictory claims that (1) happiness as a necessary end of nature for finite rational beings and that (2) happiness cannot be the highest end of nature for human beings. I distinguished between the formal concept of happiness as the ends-oriented structure of the human will and the material conception of happiness individuals must form for themselves as a guide for the choice of ends and for action. I also analyzed related claims and assumptions Kant makes about happiness such as that happiness is an indeterminate concept and an ideal of imagination; that reason is not the best capacity for achieving happiness and that cultivated persons tend to be unhappier the more they make happiness their highest end. All these considerations were intended as a way to reconstruct Kant's overall idea of happiness as the basis for my discussion in the subsequent chapters.

In chapter 2, I concentrated on the aspect of Kant's moral theory that gives most support to the view that his theory is "hostile to human happiness": his understanding of what counts as an adequate moral theory. I have reconstructed Kant's conception of such a moral theory and his reasons for adopting an anti-eudaimonist position. I concluded that Kant's aim was to show the proper place happiness must occupy in moral theory if we are to account for our common sense understanding of moral obligation in a way that neither falsifies nor corrects our first-personal perspective on moral matters. Further, I argued that Kant's reduction of different types of moral theories to a single category, namely, *heteronomous moral theories*, is motivated by what he recognizes as the underlying "model of the will" shared by these different theories and not simply due to the blatant misconception that all these theories are hedonist. I have also made the case for the view that Kant was primarily addressing his contemporaries and general theoretical models rather than historical sources. Further, by distinguishing between *heteronomy* and *eudaimonism* I showed why Kant did not crudely reduce *ancient* eudaimonist theories to hedonism. I concluded that Kant adopted a non-reductive view of human happiness as illustrated by his critique of the Stoics. Human happiness requires more than moral self-approval.

Although happiness cannot be the foundation of morality for Kant, it nevertheless provides the content of indirect duties to the self and direct duties to others. In chapter 3, I analyzed Kant's view that we have an *indirect duty* to promote our own happiness. For this, I elucidated Kant's understanding of indirect duties before concentrating on the indirect duty to promote one's own happiness. Although Kant claims that one's own happiness cannot be a direct duty because we are naturally motivated to pursue happiness, he nevertheless acknowledges that this natural inclination can become clouded or lost. When the natural inclination to be happy is no longer present, securing our own happiness may become a *direct* duty to oneself, dictated by morality and not by prudence.

In this chapter, also argued that the indeterminacy of happiness (the fact that we can never tell with certainty what will make us happy, as discussed in chapter 1), together with Kant's theory of non-moral choice, make it not irrational to prefer short-term desire satisfaction over long-term wellbeing under conditions of uncertainty. However, morality also provides a *minimal* objective conception of happiness, which we have a direct duty to adopt as an end when we happen to lack the natural inclination for our overall, long-term wellbeing, as illustrated by Kant's discussion of the *gout sufferer* in the *Groundwork*. I show that Kant does not criticize the gout sufferer for being *imprudent*, but for violating *a duty to the self.*

In chapter Four, I concentrated on the way happiness provides the content of duties of love to others and the way it relates to respect for persons. I analyzed Kant's justification for the duty to adopt the happiness of others as our ends (the duty of beneficence) and his claim that, as a wide duty, beneficence allows some *latitude for choice*. To explain what Kant means by latitude, I analyze Kant's reinterpretation of Horace's adage *insani sapiens nomen habeat; aequus iniqui –ultra quam satis est virtutem si petat ipsam* ("the wise man has the name of being a fool, the just man of being iniquitous, if he seeks virtue beyond what is sufficient") and Kant's criticism of Aristotle's doctrine of the mean, which throw considerable light on the relation between morality and prudence in the way we chose to comply with imperfect duties. I also drew on Kant's correspondence with Maria von Herbert, in which Kant differentiates lying from reticence. As Kant's letter makes clear, latitude does not apply to one's commitment to the moral principle. But since there is no upper limit to the extent we may realize moral ends, depending on the circumstances the agent may be permitted to take prudential considerations into account when deciding how to comply with her imperfect duties.

Chapter 5 was an excursus into problems arising out of Kant's duty of beneficence, in particular of Kant's distinction between perfect and imperfect duties. The problem is that imperfect duties seem to be able to override perfect duties under certain circumstances, which gives rise to the suspicion that Kant's distinction between perfect and imperfect duties is *ad hoc*. I have attempted to sketch a possible, although inconclusive answer to that problem, by arguing that there is in fact no "trumping relation" between imperfect and perfect duties but merely that "latitude shrinks away" in certain circumstances. I also addressed the related worry that the duty of beneficence may be more demanding than we tend to think, assuming that we may be mistaken about the imperfect character of the duty of beneficence. I argued that we must understand the necessary space for pursuing one's own happiness as *entailed* by the duty to promote the happiness of others. Nevertheless, becoming *worthy of happiness* still has normative priority over securing one's own happiness when circumstances are such that we cannot secure our own happiness without seriously neglecting more pressing needs of other persons. The "tragic side" of Kant's moral philosophy is that the connection between morality and happiness is contingent: the best moral agent is not necessarily also a happy person. In less ordered societies, this contingent relation tends to be exacerbated to the point of rendering moral agency extremely demanding and moral agents even more likely to be unhappier than unjust, immoral persons. This is why reconciling moral worth and happiness can be seen as a *political task*, to be pursued in *this life*.

The last chapter was devoted to happiness in Kant's legal and political philosophy. Since he subsumes subsistence needs and welfare under the concept of happiness of individuals, I have analyzed his views on state provision for the poor in the *Doctrine of Right* and explored his conception of *equity* or *fairness* (*Billigkeit*) as an alternative to the traditional minimalist and the welfare interpretations of the Kantian state. I argued that although the Kantian Rechtsstaat is not concerned with patterns of distribution but only with formal relations of right, it can nevertheless recognize the need to redistribute from considerations of equity or fairness, the domain of right Kant calls *Billigkeit*. Kant recognized social inequality as the result of systemic injustice and that he did not regard helping the poor as a mere duty of virtue of individuals, but as an inadequate way to address systemic caused disadvantage. I supported my interpretation with passages from Kant's lectures and the *Metaphysics of Morals* in which he questions the characterization of the duty of beneficence as a meritorious duty. The problem is that although the poor have a right to aid, unlike strict right, these rights cannot be determined with the precision required by a court of justice. This has led to the wrong conclusion that the state or the head of state has a duty of virtue toward its subjects and that the poor have no right to aid.

Kant's political liberalism is based on the assumption that it is an innate right of individuals to exercise external freedom unhindered, as long as this exercise is compatible with the freedom of all. The content of these pursuits is left to the discretion of agents themselves and falls outside the scope of state authority. Therefore, the purely formal character of Kant's theory of justice and of the state also aims to protect the formation and pursuit of individuals' conception of happiness. Instead of imposing a conception of happiness on all subjects, the Kantian state enables the unification of a plurality of individual conceptions of happiness into a unified system.

Kant also suggests that it is not merely permissible to coordinate and integrate the pursuit of happiness and moral obligations in our lives, but that we also come to "discover" some of our moral obligations while pursuing our non-moral projects. Some obligations are shaped not only by our specific situation in the world and our relation to particular people, but by the permissible ways of life and goals we have chosen to adopt. Therefore, despite Kant's pessimistic assumptions, human happiness plays a more fundamental role in his moral, legal and political theory than usually acknowledged by Kant's critics and even by Kant himself.

Bibliography

Allison, Henry E., *Kant's Theory of Freedom,* Cambridge University Press, 1990.
———. *Kants Groundwork of the Metaphysics of Morals, A Commentary.* Oxford University Press, 2011.
Anscombe, G. E. M. "Modern Moral Philosophy." *Philosophical Review*, 33, 1958.
Aristotle, *Nichomachean Ethics,* translated and edited by Roger Crisp. Cambridge University Press, 2000.
Baron, Marcia. "Kantian Ethics and Supererogation." *The Journal of Philosophy*, vol. 84, 1987.
———. *Kantian Ethics almost without Apology.,* Cornell University Press, 1995.
Bartuschat, Wolfgang. "Der Moralische Begriff des Rechts in Kants Rechtstheorie." *Jahrbuch für Recht und Ethik/Annual Review of Law and Ethics*, vol. 16 (2008).
Baumgarten, Katrin. *Hagestolz und Alte Jungfer. Entwicklung, Instrumentalisierung und Fortleben von Klischees und Stereotypen über Unverheiratetgebliebene.* Dissertation, Waxmann, 1997.
Benjamin, Walter. "Kant als Liebesratgeber." In: Wilhelm Berger and Thomas Macho (ed.), *Kant als Liebesratgeber. Eine Klagenfurter Episode*. Verlag des Verbandes der wissenschaftlichen Gesellschaften Österreichs, 1989.
Berger, Wilhelm, and Thomas Macho (eds.). *Kant als Liebesratgeber. Eine Klagenfurter Episode*. Verlag des Verbandes der wissenschaftlichen Gesellschaften Österreichs, 1989.
Bertani, Corrado. *Equity Presumptions versus Maxim of Distributive Justice in the Metaphysische Anfangsgründe der Rechtslehre, §§ 36–40*. In: *Kant und die Philosophie in Weltbürgerlicher Absicht: Aktendes Xi*. Kant-Kongresses 2010. Edited by Margit Ruffing, Claudio La Rocca, Alfredo Ferrarin and Stefano Bacin, 783–796. Berlin: De Gruyter, 2013.
Betzler, Monika. *Kant's Ethics of Virtue.* Walter de Gruyter, 2008.
Bittner, Rüdiger. "Das Unternehmen einer Grundlegung zur Metaphysik der Sitten." In: Otfried Höffe (ed.), *Grundlegung zur Metaphysik der Sitten. Ein kooperativer Kommentar*. Vittorio Klostermann, 1989.
Brandt, Reinhard. *Eigentumstheorie von Grotius bis Kant,* Frommann-Holzboog, 1974.

———. *Rechtsphilosophie der Aufklärung. Symposium Wolfenbüttel 1981*, Walter de Gruyter, 1982.

———. "Das Erlaubnisgesetz, oder: Vernunft und Geschichte in Kants Rechtslehre." In: Brandt (ed.), *Rechtsphilosophie der Aufklärung. Symposium Wolfenbüttel 1981*, Walter de Gruyter, 1982.

Byrd, Sharon, and Joachim Hruschka. *Kant's Doctrine of Right. A Commentary.* Cambridge University Press, 2011.

Cohen, Alix. *Kant and the Human Sciences: Biology, Anthropology and History.* Palgrave Macmillan, 2009.

Cicero. *De officiis / Drey Bücher von der menschlichen Pflicht*, translated by Johann Adolph Hofmann and Johann Christoph Gottsched. Felginer & Bohn, 1742.

Crusius, Christian August. *Anweisungen vernünftig zu leben: darinnen nach Erklärung der Natur des menschlichen Willens die natürlichen Pflichten und allgemeinen Klugheitslehren im richtigen Zusammenhange vorgetragen werden* (1744), Gleditsch, 1767.

de Mandeville, Bernard. *An Inquiry into the Origin of Moral Virtue*. In: L. A. Selby-Bigge, *British Moralists*. Clarendon Press, 1897.

de Montaigne, Michel. *Essais de Michel de Montaigne*. J.-V. Le Clerc (ed.) Lefèvre, 1826.

Denis, Lara (ed.). *Kant's Metaphysics of Morals, A Critical Guide*, Cambridge University Press, 2010.

Eberhard, Johann August. *Sittenlehre der Vernunft.* Nicolai, 1781.

Engstrom, Stephen. "The Concept of the Highest Good in Kant's Moral Theory." *Philosophy and Phenomenological Research*, Vol. 52, No. 4 (Dec. 1992), pp. 759–760.

———. The Form of Practical Knowledge. Harvard University Press, 2009.

Flikschuh, Katrin. *Kant and Modern Political Philosophy*. Cambridge University Press, 2004.

Forschner, Maximilian. "Guter Wille und Haß der Vernunft." In: Otfried Höffe, *Grundlegung zur Metaphysik der Sitten. Ein kooperativer Kommentar*, Vittorio Klostermann. Frankfurt am Main, 1989.

Gesang, Bernward (ed.). *Kants vergessener Rezensent. Die Kritik der theoretischen und praktischen Philosophie Kants in fünf frühen Rezensionen von Hermann Andreas Pistorius.* Kant-Forschungen 18, Felix Meiner Verlag, 2007.

Gregor, Mary. *Laws of Reason*. Blackwell 1963.

Grimm, Jacob, and Wilhelm. *Deutsches Wörterbuch von Jacob und Wilhelm Grimm.* 16 Bde. in 32 Teilbänden. Leipzig 1854–1961. Digital edition of the Trier Center for Digital Humanities, University of Trier.

Guyer, Paul. *Kant and the Experience of Freedom*. Cambridge University Press, 1993.

———. "Moral Feelings in the Metaphysics of Morals." In: Lara Denis (ed.), *Kant's Metaphysics of Morals, A Critical Guide*. Cambridge University Press, 2010.

Hale, Susan. "Against Supererogation." *American Philosophical Quarterly*, Vol. 28, 1991.

Herman, Barbara. *The Practice of Moral Judgment*, Harvard University Press, 1993.

―――. "Leaving Deontology Behind." In: *The Practice of Moral Judgment*, Harvard University Press, 1993.
―――. *Moral Literacy.* Harvard University Press, 2007.
―――. "The Scope of Moral Requirement." In: *Moral Literacy.* Harvard University Press, 2007.
Heyman, Steven J. "Foundations of the Duty to Rescue." *Vanderbilt Law Review*, Vol. 43, 1994.
Hill, Thomas E. "Kant on Imperfect Duty and Supererogation." *Kant Studien*, Vol. 62, No. 1, 1971.
―――. *Human Welfare and Moral Worth, Kantian Perspectives*. Oxford University Press, 2002.
―――. "Happiness and Human Flourishing" In: *Human Welfare and Moral Worth, Kantian Perspectives*. Oxford University Press, 2002.
―――. "Meeting Needs and Doing Favors" In: *Human Welfare and Moral Worth, Kantian Perspectives*. Oxford University Press, 2002.
Höffe, Ottfried (ed.). *Grundlegung zur Metaphysik der Sitten. Ein kooperativer Kommentar*, Vittorio Klostermann. Frankfurt am Main, 1989.
――― (ed.). *Metaphysische Anfangsgründe der Rechtslehre*. Akademie Verlag, 1999.
―――. "Der Kategorische Rechtsimperativ." In: *Metaphysische Anfangsgründe der Rechtslehre*. Akademie Verlag, 1999.
――― (ed.). *Nikomachische Ethik* (collection of essays). Akademie Verlag, 2010.
Irwin, Terence. Plato. *Gorgias.* Translated with Notes. Claredon Press, 1979.
―――. "Kant's Criticism of Eudaimonism" In: Stephen Engstrom and Jennifer Whitting, *Aristotle, Kant and the Stoics: Rethinking Happiness and Duty*. Cambridge University Press, 1996.
Kaufmann, Alexander. *Welfare in the Kantian State* Oxford University Press, 1999.
Kersting, Wolfgang. *Wohlgeordnete Freiheit. Immanuel Kant's Rechts und Staatsphilosophie*. Suhrkamp 1983.
―――. "Kant's Concept of the State." In: Howard Williams (ed.), *Essays on Kant's Political Philosophy*. University of Chicago Press, 1992.
―――. "Der Kategorische Imperativ, die Vollkommenen und die Unvollkommenen Pflichten." *Zeitschrift für philosophische Forschung*, 1983.
Korsgaard, Christine M. *Creating the Kingdom of Ends*. Cambridge University Press, 1996.
―――. "Kant's Formula of Universal Law." In: *Creating the Kingdom of Ends*. Cambridge University Press, 1996.
Langton, Rae. "Duty and Desolation." *Philosophy,* Vol. 67, No. 262, 1992.
Ludwig, Bernd. *Kants Rechtslehre*. Felix Meiner Verlag, 1988.
―――. "Kants 'Hypothetische' Imperative." In: Klemme, Ludwig, Pauen and Stark (eds.), *Aufklärung und Interpretation. Studien zu Kants Philosophie und ihrem Umkreis*. Königshausen & Neumann, 1999.
―――. "Die Einteilung der Metaphysik der Sitten im Allgemeinen und die der Metaphysischen Anfangsgründen der Tugendlehre im Besonderen." Forthcoming

in: Andreas Trampota, Oliver Sensen and Jens Timmermann (eds.), *Kant's Tugendlehre. A Comprehensive Commentary.* De Gruyter.

Mahon, James Edwin. "Kant and Maria von Herbert: Reticence vs. Deception." *Philosophy*, Vol. 81, 2006.

Mendus, Susan. "Kant: an honest but narrow minded Bourgeois?" in: Howard Williams (ed.), *Kant's Political Philosophy*, University of Wales Press, Cardiff, 1992.

Mill, John Stuart. *Utilitarianism*, edited by Roger Crisp, Oxford University Press, 1998.

Mulholand, Leslie. *Kant's System of Right*, Columbia University Press, 1990.

Murdoch, Iris. *The Sovereignty of the Good*, Routledge, 1970.

Murphy, Jeffrie G. *Kant: the Philosophy of Right*, Macmillan, 1970.

O'Neill, Onora. *Acting on Principle. An Essay on Kantian Ethics.* Columbia University Press, 1975.

———. *Constructions of Reason. Explorations of Kant's Practical Philosophy.* Cambridge University Press, 1989.

———. "Action, Anthropology and Autonomy," In: *Constructions of Reason. Explorations of Kant's Practical Philosophy.* Cambridge University Press, 1989.

———. "Consistency in Action." In: *Constructions of Reason. Explorations of Kant's Practical Philosophy.* Cambridge University Press, 1989.

———. "Reason and Autonomy in Grundlegung III." In: *Constructions of Reason. Explorations of Kant's Practical Philosophy.* Cambridge University Press, 1989.

Paton, H. J. *The Categorical Imperative.* Hutchinson's University Library, 1947.

Pinheiro Walla, Alice. "Virtue and Prudence in a Footnote of the Metaphysics of Morals" (MS VI: 433n). *Jahrbuch für Recht und Ethik / Annual Review of Law and Ethics,* vol. 21, 2013, pp. 307–323.

———. "Kant's Moral Theory and Demandingness." *Ethical Theory and Moral Practice,* Vol. 18, No. 4, 2015, pp. 731–743.

———. "When the Strictest Right Is the Greatest Wrong: Kant on Fairness," *Estudos Kantianos,* Vol. 3, No. 1, 2015.

———. "Kant and the Wisdom of Oedipus." *Jahrbuch Praktische Philosophie in globaler Perspektive / Yearbook Practical Philosophy in a Global Perspective,* 2019.

———. "A Kantian Foundation for Welfare Rights." *Jurisprudence,* 2020.

———. "Honeste Vive: Dignity in Kant's Theory of Juridical Obligation." In: Adam Cureton and Jan-Willem van der Rijt (eds.), *Human Dignity and the Kingdom of Ends: Kantian Perspectives and Practical Applications.* Routledge, 2021.

Pufendorf, Samuel. *Of the Law of Nature and Nations* (*De iure naturae et gentium*, 1688), Jean Barbeyrac, William Percivale (tr.), printed by L. Lichfield, for A. and J. Churchill, 1710.

Reath, Andrews. *Agency and Autonomy in Kant's Moral Theory.* Oxford University Press, 2006.

———. "Hedonism, Heteronomy and Kant's Principle of Happiness." In: *Agency and Autonomy in Kant's Moral Theory.* Oxford University Press, 2006.

Ripstein, Arthur. *Force and Freedom, Kant's Legal and Political Philosophy.* Harvard University Press, 2009.

Rosen, Allen D. *Kant's Theory of Justice*. Cornell University Press, 1993.
Rousseau, Jean-Jacques, and Heinrich Meier (ed.). *Discours sur l'Inégalité/ Diskurs über die Ungleichheit: Kritische Ausgabe des integralen Textes*. Schöningh, 1997.
Selby-Bigge, L. A. *British Moralists*. Clarendon Press, 1897.
Schneewind, J. B. "Kant against Spurious Principles of Morality." In: Jens Timmermann, *Kant's Groundwork to the Metaphysics of Morals. A Critical Guide.*, Cambridge University Press, 2009.
Schönecker, Dieter, and Christoph Horn (eds.). *Groundwork for the Metaphysics of Morals*. Walter de Gruyter, 2006.
Schopenhauer, Arthur. *Kleinere Schriften II*. Zürcher Ausgabe, Band VI.
Schwartz, Maria. *Der Begriff der Maxime bei Kant. Eine Untersuchung des Maximenbegriffs in Kants praktischer Philosophie*. LIT Verlag 2006.
Sherman, Nancy. *Making a Necessity of Virtue. Aristotle and Kant on Virtue*. Cambridge University Press, 1997.
Sidwick, Henry. *The Method of Ethics*. Hackett, [1907] 1981.
Slote, Michael. *From Morality to Virtue*. Oxford University Press, 1992.
Statman, Daniel. "Who Needs Imperfect Duties?" *American Philosophical Quarterly*, Vol. 33, No 2, April 1996.
Stern, Robert. *Understanding Moral Obligation: Kant, Hegel, Kierkegaard*. Cambridge University Press, 2012.
Stratton-Lake, Philipp. *Kant, Duty and Moral Worth*. Routledge 2000.
Striker, Gisela. "Greek Ethics and Moral Theory." The Tanner Lectures on Human Values, 1987.
Timmermann, Jens. *Sittengesetz und Freiheit, Untersuchungen zu Immanuel Kants Theorie des freien Willens*. De Gruyter, 2003.
———. "Kant on Conscience, Indirect Duty and Moral Error." *International Philosophical Quarterly*, Vol. 46, No. 3, Issue 183, September 2006.
———. "Kantian Duties to the Self, Explained and Defended." *Philosophy*, Vol. 81, 2006, pp. 505–530.
———. *Kant's Groundwork of the Metaphysics of Morals. A Commentary*. Cambridge University Press, 2007.
———. *Kant's Groundwork to the Metaphysics of Morals. A Critical Guide*. Cambridge, 2009.
———.
———. "Kantian Dilemmas? Moral Conflict in Kant's Ethical Theory." Forthcoming in *Archiv für die Geschichte der Philosophie*.
Timmons, Mark (ed.). *Kant's Metaphysics of Morals. Interpretative Essays*. Oxford University Press, 2004.
Tittel, G. A. *Über Herrn Kants Moralreform*. Aetas Kantiana 285. Pfähler, 1786.
Varden, Helga. "Kant and Lying to the Murderer at the Door . . . One More Time: Kant's Legal Philosophy and Lies to Murderers and Nazis." *Journal of Social Philosophy*, Vol. 41, No. 4, Winter 2010.
Vogt, Katja Maria. "Duties to Others: Demands and Limits." In: Monika Betzler, *Kant's Ethics of Virtue*. Walter de Gruyter, 2008.

Weidemann, Hermann. "Kants Kritik am Eudämonismus und die Platonische Ethik." *Kant Studien*, Vol. 92, No. 1, 2001, p. 19–37.

Weinrib, Ernest J. "Poverty and Property in Kant's System of Rights." *Notre Dame Law Review*, Vol. 3, No. 78, April 2003.

Weinrib, Jacob. "Kant on Citizenship and Universal Independence."*Australasian Journal of Legal Philosophy*, Vol. 33, 2008.

White, Lewis Beck. *A Commentary on Kant's Critique of Practical Reason.* University of Chicago Press, 1960.

Willaschek, Marcus. "Kant on Right without Ethics. Reflexions on Kant's Conception of 'Strict Right' in the *Metaphysics of Morals*." *European Journal of Philosophy Studies, Vol.* 17, 2009.

Williams, Bernard. *Moral Luck.* Cambridge University Press, 1981.

———. "Persons, Character and Morality." In: *Moral Luck.* Cambridge University Press, 1981.

———. *Ethics and the Limits of Philosophy.* Harvard University Press, 1985.

Williams, Howard. *Kant's Political Philosophy.* St. Martin's Press, 1983.

Wilson, Catherine. "On Some Alleged Limitations to Moral Endeavor." *The Journal of Philosophy*, Vol. 90, 1993.

Wolff, Christian. *Grundsätze des Natur-und Völkerrechts: Worin alle Verbindlichkeiten und alle Rechte aus der Natur des Menschen in einem beständigen Zusammenhänge hergeleitet werden (Institutiones iuris naturae et gentium, 1750).* Halle und Magdeburg, 1769.

———. Letter to Leibniz (4 May 1715). In: *G.W. Leibniz: Philosophical Essays,* translated by Roger Ariew and Daniel Garber. Hackett Publishing Company, 1989.

Wolf, Ursula. "Über den Sinn der Aristotelischen Mesotheslehre." In: O. Höffe, *Nikomachische Ethik.* Akademie Verlag, 2010.

Wood, Allen. *Kant's Ethical Thought.* Cambridge University Press, 1999.

———. "The Final Form of Kant's Practical Philosophy." In: Mark Timmons (ed.), *Kant's Metaphysics of Morals.* Oxford University Press, 2004.

———. *Kantian Ethics.* Cambridge University Press, 2008.

Index

action:
    aspects of human, 9, 25n9;
        determining ground of the, 29n35.
        See motives;
        dutiful, 23, 62n35, 51, 76–78;
        maxim of. *See* maxims;
        objects of the, 29n35. *See* ends;
        overdetermination of
            moral, 91n21
Allison, Henry E., 26n12, 59n14,
    60n21, 91n28
animals:
        Kant's view on, 72–73,
            89n11, 90n14;
        differences between humans
            and, 15, 19.
        See also animality
Aristotle, 4, 15, 45–46, 106–7,
    119n33, 174
autonomy:
        contrast between heteronomy and,
            48, 59n14, 119n35;
        external version of, 14;
        Kant's conception of morality as,
            3, 28n26, 31–36, 40, 43, 48,
            52–53, 57n2;
        principle of, 35, 58n3, 63n46;
        reason and, 58n4

Baron, Marcia, 122, 130, 132
beneficence:
        benevolence and, 106, 132, 152;
        demandingness of, 115, 121,
            134, 137n21;
        duty of, 3, 71, 88, 93, 95–106,
            111, 115, 116n11, 117–118,
            119n31, 122–34, 152,
            166, 174–175;
        egoistic argument for, 95;
        inclination to, 68;
        inequality and, 152, 156,
            158, 162–65;
        Kant's account of, 4, 68, 95–106,
            115, 117–118, 122–34
        universal maxim of, 3, 63, 68, 71,
            89n7, 95, 137n20
benevolence, 67, 117n15;
        difference between pathological
            love of others and active, 68;
        duty of, 152, 170n29, 171n42;
        maxim of, 132;
        natural inclination to general;
        the State's adoption of a principle
            of, 143–44, 152.
        See philanthropy
Bittner, Rüdiger, 60n21
Broome, John, 27n18

candour, 4, 108, 120n39, 110–11
Cicero, 45, 100
coercion, 68, 101–102, 112, 125, 140–42, 144, 147–48, 152, 155–62
common moral understanding, 28n26, 31–33, 38, 123
conscience:
    duty to cultivate one's, 67–68;
    voice of, 66–68, 78, 89n5;
    moral accountability and, 89n5;
    the court of, 116n1, 160
Crusius, Christian August, 41–43, 60n21

decision-making:
    Aristotle's view on, 119n33;
    juridical, 147, 158–61
dignity, 69–70, 72, 84, 102, 105, 112
duties:
    contrast between ethical and juridical, 3, 74–75, 92n39, 101–102, 118n24, 152, 157;
    imperfect or positive, 27n16, 85, 93, 116n1;
    juridical, 140, 149;
    perfect or negative, 57, 69, 85–86, 102, 104, 118n24;
    self-regarding, 17, 54, 84–88, 102, 118n24, 131, 184;
    strict, 108, 101, 113–14, 125, 129, 164;
    toward other, 3, 117n19, 184;
    wide, 17–18, 106–7, 125, 132.
    See also latitude

Eberhard, Johann August, 44–45
egoism, 43–44, 60n23.
    See also beneficence; maxims.
end:
    moral and morally required, 113, 115, 125–26, 128, 131, 136n10, 152, 175;
    the permissibility of an, 116n11, 131–32;
    commitment to the moral, 127–28;
    finite rational beings natural, 6, 13, 84, 86–87, 104, 173;
    happiness of others as one's own, 131–32, 137n20, 174;
    treating others as means to one's, 157–58;
    agent's material. *See* wellbeing
epicureanism, 23, 44–45, 51, 54;
    Kant on the differences between "beastly" and "true," 61n25
Epicurus, 44, 50–51, 61n25, 62n37
equality:
    civil, 144;
    lack of, 144
equity, 102, 129, 139, 131, 156–161, 164, 166, 175
eudaimonism:
    as a theory about moral motivation, 31, 43, 47–50;
    as an instrumental model of action, 50;
    Kant's objection against, 3, 31, 48, 51, 61n30;
    etiology of, 49–50

freedom:
    civil, 144;
    of choice [*Willkür*], 7–9, 26n12, 24n2, 26n14, 34, 37, 74, 76, 126, 167n8, 168n14–15, 169n21

Garve, Christian, 44–45, 61n28
general will, 145, 147, 151–53, 157, 165, 168n13, 170n29, 172n51
goodness:
    empirical, 53;
    judgment of, 7–8;
    material conception of, 53
    moral, 53, 131;
    objective conception of, 51;
    unconditional or non-subordinated, 33
Guyer, Paul, 77, 91n31

happiness:
    becoming worthy of, 56, 63n47, 121, 134, 175;
    duty to promote one's, 81, 91n25, 91n30, 96, 131, 92n38;
    duty towards others,' 89n9, 91n33, 95–98, 104–5, 117n13, 121, 126, 131–34, 152, 137n20;
    formal concept of 2, 5, 6, 11–12;
    ideal conception of, 2, 5, 9, 16–19, 28n22;
    indeterminacy or uncertainty of, 1–3, 23–24, 81, 174;
    Kant's overall conception of, 6, 22–23;
    material or one's personal conception of, 2,5–6, 13n26,18–19, 21–24, 48, 83, 92n38, 95, 105, 117n16, 131–34, 137n20, 143, 174;
    morality and, 4, 6, 22, 13n26, 115, 117n13, 131–134, 143, 152;
    natural necessity to pursuit, 7–15, 66, 83;
    public legislation and, 4, 139, 142–53, 166;
    rational necessity to pursuit, 16–20.
    See beneficence, duty of
hedonism, 40, 50, 61n30, 174;
    impossibility of, 62n37;
    Kant's, 16–17.
    See also eudaimonism; pleasure
heteronomous theories, 39–45, 119n35.
    See also eudaimonism
highest good, 29n3, 32;
    ancients and modern ideas of, 46–47;
    Epicurean conception of, 55;
    Kant's doctrine of, 54,56, 63n46;
    Plato's idea of, 45;
    Stoic conception of, 54–55.
    See summum bonum

honeste vive, 92n39, 112–113, 154, 167n3
humanity:
    animality and, 28–29n29, 68, 71;
    duty of love of, 66, 98–105, 117n19;
    lack of, 74;
    morality and, 22, 84, 91n27;
    natural purpose of. *See* teleology;
    persons as bearers of, 69, 74, 84, 88, 92n38, 140;
    predisposition to, 71;
    right of, 84, 112–13, 118n24.
    See also personality

imperative:
    categorical, 33–35, 58n4, 62n35, 78, 83, 94, 96, 102, 107, 141, 28n22;
    hypothetical, 10, 26n10, 35, 39, 47, 77–78, 26n10;
    incentives, 23, 26n12, 32, 34, 41, 49, 52, 74–76, 102, 110, 112, 119n34;
    incorporation thesis, 26n12.
    See also moral motivation
independence:
    civil, material and financial, 146–150, 168n14, 169n22.
    See also minority
Irwin, Terence, 51, 55, 61n30, 62n40

Jean-Jacques Rousseau, 20, 28n29

Kersting, Wolfgang, 96, 150–51

latitude, 4, 79, 106, 108, 110–15, 119n33, 121–34, 174–75
legal reciprocity, 140, 144, 168n13
legal theory, Kant's, 140, 149–50
love:
    duties of, 68–69, 77, 84, 93, 98–110, 117n19, 119n31, 125, 174;

maxim of self-, 8, 12, 18, 22, 25,
  36–40, 69, 117n12;
pathological, 68, 89n7, 119n29;
practical, 68, 72, 89n6, 125
Ludwig, Bernd, 26n10, 57n2, 92n39,
  118n23–24, 120n41, 151, 157,
  168n13, 170n27
lying, 4, 106, 108–10. *See* truthfulness

Maria von Herbert, 4, 106, 108–11,
  120n38, 174
material dependency, 144
maxims:
  acting on, 18, 26n12, 54,
    78, 136n10;
  contrast between maxims of ends
    and actions, 136n10;
  definition of, 6–8, 12, 24n3, 25n8;
  difference between practical laws
    and, 25n5;
  non-moral, 8, 62, 97; *See also*
    self-love;
  subjective, 23;
  universal moral 8, 22, 25n5,
    33–35, 39, 62, 134
Mill, John Stuart, 62n37
minority, 143, 148
misology, 20–21
moral apathy, 76, 119n34
moral motivation, 32–33, 38–39,
  102, 113, 157:
  direct, 79, 89, 102, 157;
  egoist, 44;
  eudaimonist view on, 49–51;
  as respect for the law, 36;
  as opposed to self-interested
    action, 49;
  pure or genuine, 67, 70–71, 76,
    81, 102, 113, 157
moral principle:
  commitment to the, 25n9, 73,
    76, 107, 175;
  compatibility between respect for
    the law and the, 32–33;
  formulation of the, 33, 34;

pathological principle as the
  direct opposite of the, 51;
the purity of the, 48, 51, 53;
relationship between highest good
  and, 43, 46, 54–55;
the sources of the, 48;
universal, 80
motive of duty alone, 71, 77,
  130, 132, 157.
  See also moral motivation, pure
    or genuine
motives:
  acting on, 19, 25–26n9, 36,
    47, 112–13;
  being mistaken about one's
    own, 18, 49;
  contrast between ends and, 29n35;
  difference between maxims
    and, 24n3;
  feelings as additional, 71;
  impurity of one's, 49;
  political, 168;
  prudential, 23, 41, 108,
    111, 113, 159,
  secondary, 101–102

nature, ends of, 2, 13–15, 91n32, 173.
  See teleology
necessitation. *See* coercion
obligation:
  legal, 140–45, 150;
  the ground of, 86, 124;
  moral, 31, 35, 42–45, 49, 58, 72,
    141, 173, 176.
  See also principle, moral

O'Neill, Onora, 58n3–4, 116n11
opacity, 18, 29n35-35
overdemandingness, 123, 135

passive citizenship, 147–49
personality:
  civil, 146–48, 168n16;
  moral, 65, 79, 73, 86–88

philanthropy [*Menschenliebe*],
    67, 98, 105
Plato, 45–46
pleasure:
    feelings of displeasure and, 5, 18,
        21, 34, 40;
    in one's perfection, 42;
    moral or disinterested, 59n15, 48;
    as moral self-approval, 50;
    pathological or hedonistic, 17,
        59n15, 47;
    sources of, 20
practical reason:
    antinomy of, 56;
    definition of, 9;
    empirical, 28n29, 52–53, 86;
    heteronomous conception of, 46;
    pure, 22, 27n16, 35–37, 52–56,
        58n2, 58n5–6.
    See also heteronomous theories
political participation, 145–48;
    exclusion of women from, 147
principle:
    moral, 25n9, 32–34, 41–48,
        51–55, 76, 80, 93, 100,
        106, 131, 165;
    self-legislated. S*ee* categorical
        imperative;
    subjective.
    S*ee* maxims
prudence:
    lack of, 12–13, 23, 82,
        87, 134, 174;
    morality and, 174, 30n42, 54–55;
    moral, 66, 70, 78;
    principle of, 168, 27n20, 27n22,
        28n23, 81–82;
    rules of, 83, 87.
    See also imperative, hypothetical
prudential reasoning, 13, 65–66, 88n2
public justice, 116n5, 129, 139,
    142, 161–65
Pufendorf, Samuel, 143

redistribution, 4, 139, 150, 151,
    154, 166, 175
republic, 168n13, 155–156, 165
respect:
    for the law, 29n35, 32, 35–39,
        59n9, 67–68, 71–72, 76, 83,
        92n38, 119n34, 124–25;
    for persons, 102–105, 125, 174;
    towards persons' rights, 143, 157;
    for private property, 123–24
reticence, 4, 106, 108–113, 120n39, 174
right:
    a priori principles of, 145;
    conception of, 123, 139–40, 150;
    domain of, 101–102,
        136n10, 143;
    duties of. *See* juridical duties;
    formal relations of, 139,
        151, 166, 175;
    obligation and, 118n25;
    original or innate, 140–1,
        143, 147–49;
    peremptory or necessary, 142;
    principle of, 74–5;
    private acquired, 129, 139,
        141, 144, 162;
    provisional, 141–42;
    public, 116n5, 151, 157–8;
    rightful enforcement of, 142. *See
        also* coercion, rightful;
    sovereign's, 145, 151. *See also
        trias politica*;
    subjective, 140–42;
    violations of, 116n6, 141, 143,
        159, 165, 171n41;
    wide duties of, 136n8
right to impose taxes, 4, 139, 149–54,
    165, 170n29
right to vote, 148–49. *See* political
    participation
Rosen, Allen, 152, 170n29

Schneewind, J. B., 44, 46–47, 52
Sherman, Nancy, 75–77
Slote, Michael, 117n13

state:
    paternalistic, 117n16, 143, 149;
    ideal, 168n13. *See* Republic;
    Kant's theory of, 139. *See also* legal theory, Kant's
stringency, 4, 124–27, 130
Stoics, Kant's criticism of the, 54–55, 84, 94, 116n7, 174
supererogation, 122, 130
systemic injustice, 4, 139, 163–66, 175

teleology, 2, 6, 13–15, 21–22, 28, 86–87, 117
Timmermann, Jens, 24n1, 28n27, 58n5, 59n16, 61n28, 62n37, 77, 87–88, 21n91, 91n30, 94, 116, 125, 129–31
Tittel, Gottlob August, 44–45
trias politica, 151–52, 156–62, 168, 170n29
truthfulness, 111–13

virtue, 73, 102, 108:
    duties of. *See* duties, ethical;
    excess of, 108;
    fantastic, 113–15;
    over happiness, 55–56;
    Kant's rejection of a quantitative understanding of, 107–8;
    as *fortitude*, 76;
    the practice of, 99
    possibility of, 62n37, 79.
    See also honeste vive
vice, 19, 49, 66, 69, 83, 85–87, 89n10, 102, 106–7, 143

Weinrib, Ernest, 154–56
Weinrib, Jacob, 147–48, 150
wellbeing:
    agent's, 27n20, 83, 139, 143;
    public, 139, 155
Wille and *Willkür*, distinction between, 7–8, 24n2, 37
will, legislative part of the [*Wille*], 37, 62n42
Wood, Allen, 168n12
Wolff, Christian, 41–42, 60n17–19, 77, 143

About the Author

Alice Pinheiro Walla is Associate Professor at the philosophy department, McMaster University, Canada. Her research aims at elucidating from a Kantian perspective the nature of legal and ethical obligations, as well as the global duties arising from the territorial rights of states and the cosmopolitan rights of all persons, independently of their nationality.

www.ingramcontent.com/pod-product-compliance
Lightning Source LLC
Chambersburg PA
CBHW020744020526
44115CB00030B/916